S0-BYT-018

SEBASTIAN CASTELLIO

# DE ARTE DUBITANDI ET CONFIDENDI IGNORANDI ET SCIENDI

# STUDIES IN MEDIEVAL AND REFORMATION THOUGHT



VOLUME XXIX

**SEBASTIAN CASTELLIO**

DE ARTE DUBITANDI ET CONFIDENDI
IGNORANDI ET SCIENDI

LEIDEN
E. J. BRILL
1981

SEBASTIAN CASTELLIO

# DE ARTE DUBITANDI ET CONFIDENDI IGNORANDI ET SCIENDI

WITH INTRODUCTION AND NOTES BY

ELISABETH FEIST HIRSCH

LEIDEN
E. J. BRILL
1981

ISBN 90 04 06344 7



PRINTED IN BELGIUM

*To*

*Roland H. Bainton*

*In gratitude,*
*admiration and friendship*

# TABLE OF CONTENTS

# PREFACE

The present edition of Castellio's manuscript *De Arte Dubitandi* is reproduced from the first edition which was prepared by the present author and published by the *Accademia Reale d'Italia* in 1937. The notes are now in English and so is the introduction which is newly written. The scholarly apparatus underwent minor changes. References to the Castellio Bible are reduced to significant variations vis à vis the Vulgate. All marginal numbers are from Castellio's hand and indicate supplements that are now identified in the notes.

The manuscript of which one authentic copy exists in the Gemeente Bibliotheek of Rotterdam (no 505) starts on fol. 56 and ends with fol. 167. It is bound together with a tract on predestination against Martin Borrhaus and preceded by copies of letters written by Castellio. *De Arte Dubitandi* is divided into two books; the first counts 33, the second 44 chapters. However, in book II the numbers 23, 30, 42 and 43 occur twice so that the whole manuscript consists of 81 chapters.

The handwriting is not very difficult to read but some pages have considerably deteriorated. On the first page it is said "Coeptum ineunte 1563", the year of Castellio's death. The question may be raised, but can hardly be answered, whether Castellio considered this copy ready for publication. It is quite obvious that Castellio has worked the manuscript over several times. This is borne out by the fact that the numbers for the supplements are not continuous neither do they show any pattern but seem to be put in quite arbitrarily and at different times. Some numbers are repeated. Quite a few pages or paragraphs are crossed out. Since the supplements (except for some in book II to which we will come back) are lost it should not be claimed that we have the complete text of *De Arte Dubitandi*.

John Jacob Wetstein, the famous manuscript collector, published in his *Novum Testamentum Graecum* (1752, vol. II, pp. 856-57 and 884-89) excerpts from book I of *De Arte Dubitandi* of which, according to his own words, he owned a copy. (See p. 856). The excerpts relate to parts of chapters 12 (beginning), 13 (end), and 16 (end) and the whole chapters 14 and 15. Unfortunately, the supplements were not included in his copy. Wetstein's orthodoxy was suspect the reason why he left his native city Basel for good in 1733 and settled in Amsterdam. It is possible that several other Castellio manuscripts were in his possession. Differences between our copy and the chapters published by Wetstein are indicated in the notes.

The Bibliotheek of the Gemeente of Rotterdam possesses a manuscript-copy of the chapters of *De Arte Dubitandi* published by Wetstein together with chapter 2 of book II of *De Arte Dubitandi*, the *De Trinitate*. It has the title *Sebastionis Castellionis Tractatiunculae duae* (MS VR 537) and is based on Wetstein's dictations to his students. Differences between this version and the copy we used are also noted under "copy". (On Wetstein see B. Becker, "Sur Quelques Documents Manuscrits Concernant Castellion" in *Autour de Michel Servet et de Sébastien Castellion* ed. B. Becker Haarlem 1953 pp. 280-288).

Professor Becker has called attention to an interesting fact in connection with the *Tractatiunculae duae*. The Castellio excerpts are preceded by a manuscript written by the Englishman Thomas Chubb, *An Inquiry concerning the Inspiration of the Writers of the New Testament* (1734). (See B. Becker, "Sur Quelques Documents Manuscrits Concernant Castellion" *op. cit.* p. 285) Becker quotes a passage from Wetstein where he stated that Chubb had access to a copy of *De Arte Dubitandi* which had belonged to Faustus Socinus. (*ibid.* and n. 36) Wetstein further dictated to his students chapters XXI-XXXVI (*De Christo Benificio*) of book II of *De Arte Dubitandi.* (See Becker, *ibid.* p. 287).

The present edition of *De Arte Dubitandi* represents a marked improvement over the previous one in that certain chapters that were left out in 1937 for reasons of economy are now included. It refers to chapters VII-XXIX of book II (fols. 114r to 148r) which were published in Gouda in 1613 by Jasper Tournay together with Castellio's *Dialogi IIII.* (See F. Buisson, Sébastien Castellion, *Sa vie et son Œuvre*, vol. II Paris 1892, p. 373). In the manuscript the chapters are entitled *De Justicia*, in the Gouda edition *Tractatus de Justificatione* with a subtitle of several sentences. We have compared the Gouda text with the manuscript and have noted all variations. In some instances the Gouda edition has corrected errors in the manuscript or added a word here and there to make the sense clearer. The Gouda text, however, is not without mistakes. The greatest advantage of this publication is that it contains the supplements which are otherwise not extant. The *De Justicia* has eight supplements four of which were available from Castellio's own hand whereas the rest were supplied from another source. Regarding supplement 19 (fol. 126) it is said in the margin: "deest sed ex Sn. Hermanni libro suppletus". The person of Hermannus could not be identified. (See B. Becker, "Iets naar aanleiding van Castellio's Tractatus de Justificatione" in *Nederlands Archief voor Kerkgeschiedenis* n.s. XXXXIX 's-Gravenhage: Martinus Nijhoff 1952 p. 126) For suppls. 23, 29 and 34 it is simply stated suppletus locus. All supplements and other additions by the Gouda text are put in square brackets. All words written into the manuscript like the note to suppl. 19 show the same handwriting and must come from the same person. We refer to them in the notes. It also happens that the Gouda text omitted some words or sentences to be found in the manuscript; these omissions are indicated by asterics. The Bibliothèque Nationale of Paris has a copy of the *Tractatus* of which despite inquiries we have not yet been able to receive a xerox copy. According to Professor Becker it is complete but not altogether identical with the edition of 1613 (*ibid.* p. 128). The reader will also find in the notes references to opponents of Castellio and occasionally to authors who voiced similar opinions. Biblical references added by the editor are marked by a star.

I have checked the printed edition of *De Arte Dubitandi* of 1937 with the manuscript and found only a few minor corrections necessary. For the preparation of the 1937 edition I am indebted to the assistance I received from the late Dr. Seligsohn of Bonn and Professor Otto Morgenstern of Berlin who were both scholars of classical philology. I like to thank Mr. W. De Kreek of the Bibliotheek der Gemeente Rotterdam who has kindly made a xerox copy of the whole manuscript for me. Fom the Haverford College Library I received a xerox copy of the *Tractatus de Justificatione* for which I express my appreciation. Finally I am most grateful to the editor and publisher of the *Studies in Medieval and Reformation Thought* for including this publication in the series. Mrs. Ricarda Fröhlich has not only typed the *De Justicia* with great patience, but also checked the manuscript in cases of doubts in deciphering certain words. I like to thank her for her interest in the project. It is obvious, of course, that I am alone responsible for the result.

I dedicate my edition of *De Arte Dubitandi* to Roland H. Bainton with whom I share a deep interest in Castellio. I have still another reason for this dedication. I owe it to Roland Bainton that Yale University awarded me a Sterling Research Fellowship in 1937-38. In that year I worked closely together with him. My first acquaintance with the United States resulted in my settling permanently in the country. For personal as well as professional reasons it became a most happy experience. It included a growing friendship of my whole family with the Bainton family. For all these reasons I will always be most grateful to Roland H. Bainton.

Trenton, New Jersey

Elisabeth Feist Hirsch

# INTRODUCTION

Castellio spent his early years as a student in Lyon where he distinguished himself as a most enthusiastic humanist. It is interesting to note that Castellio like Michael Servetus, who however came to Lyon at a later date, received much stimulation for his studies from Symphorien Champier, the great admirer of Ficino and friend of Lefèvre d'Étaples.[1] Although as far as we know Servetus and Castellio never met Castellio was familiar with his work.[2] When three Lutherans were burnt at Lyon in 1540 Castellio converted to the Reform.[3] That he took such a step leaves no doubt about how deeply the event had upset him. In all likelihood it was still alive in his soul when thirteen years later Servetus suffered the same death in Geneva.

But before this happened Castellio made the acquaintance of Calvin in Strasbourg where he stayed in his house. When Calvin returned to Geneva he put Castellio in charge of the Academy as teacher of ancient languages. Here Castellio combined his interest in Antiquity with Scripture. He wrote the *Sacred Dialogues* which dramatized biblical stories in Latin and French for use by his students.[4] But his cooperation with Calvin was soon marred by differences in biblical exegesis. Castellio considered the Song of Solomon, for example, as a profane poem which offended Calvin's religious sensitivity. They had other quarrels and Castellio decided to leave Geneva for Basel. Before he had acquired a master of Arts degree and was appointed to a position at the university, Castellio did menial work to support his family. Nevertheless, he continued his scholarly activities and translated the Bible into Latin and French from 1551-55. Other writings during the 50s such as the

---

[1] The standard work for Castellio is Ferdinand Buisson, *Sébastien Castellion, Sa Vie et Son Œuvre*, 2 vls. Paris 1892.

[2] See Castellio, "De Haereticis non puniendis" 1555 written in both Latin and French in *Travaux d'Humanisme et Renaissance* no CXVIII Genève: Droz 1971. The late Professor Becker discovered the manuscript in the Remonstrants Library in Rotterdam. He prepared the Latin text for publication and M. Valkhoff the French text. Both contain informative introductions and notes. For Servetus see p. 26, n. 3.

[3] See Roland H. Bainton, *The Travail of Religious Liberty*, Philadelphia: The Westminster Press, 1951, p. 98.

[4] *Ibid.* pp. 99-104 with several examples.

*Dialogi IIII* and a translation of the *Theologia Deutsch* also into both Latin and French appeared only posthumously.[5]

After Servetus was burnt at the stake in Geneva in 1553 Castellio engaged in a long pen-battle against Calvin whom he held responsible for the Spaniard's death. From 1554-1563 Castellio wrote four pamphlets which raised the question of religious tolerance. Only the first *De Haereticis, an sint Persequendi* (1554) was published during his life-time. In this tract he used the method of quoting opinions by various religious thinkers on the subject; under several pseudonyms Castellio contributed articles to the volume.[6] In the same year that Castellio's *De Haereticis* appeared, Calvin wrote *Defensio Orthodoxae Fidei* in which he tried to justify the death of Servetus. Castellio replied with *Contra Libellum Calvini* which was printed only in 1612.[7] The debate was by no means ended. Theodore Bèze, who was to succeed Calvin in Geneva, defended the reformer against Castellio in *De Haereticis a civili Magistratu puniendis Libellus*. Castellio's answer to Bèze is *De Haereticis non puniendis* 1555.[8]

Castellio's treatises written in 1554-55 stated the case for tolerance with vigor and a deep conviction. But their highly polemical nature did not allow for any investigation in depth. It is quite possible that Castellio was aware of this shortcoming. In any event the theme kept his mind occupied with the result that Castellio wrote still another treatise dealing with religious tolerance. It is *De Arte Dubitandi* of 1563, the year of his death. Although Calvin and Bèze still serve the function as "adversaries" against whom Castellio directed his explorations, he now treats the problem of religious tolerance from a more fundamental standpoint and investigates its underlying principles.

The following pages try to introduce the reader to some basic questions Castellio raised in his last work. An introduction can hardly attempt to put the writing in a larger context considering Castellio's whole scholarly work as well as his religious background and the possible influence of the age to which he belonged. We leave such a project to a volume under preparation in which we discuss Servetus' conflict with Calvin and Castellio's reaction to it.

---

[5] For the bibliography of Castellio's writings see Ferdinand Buisson, *op. cit.*, vol. 2, Appendix.

[6] For an English translation see Roland H. Bainton, "Concerning Heretics" in *Records of Civilization*, no. XXIV, New York: Octagon books, 1965, with valuable introduction and notes. Some excerpts from *De Arte Dubitandi* are included.

[7] See F. Buisson, *op. cit.*, vol. 2, p. 365.

[8] See n. 2.

The major issue of Castellio and other opponents of Calvin was related to the interpretation of Scripture. Calvin had a strong feeling of belonging to a small circle of God's elect who had access to biblical truth. Luther and other religious thinkers were similarly convinced of their right understanding of the Bible. Castellio agreed with other observers of the religious scene in the 16th century who wondered how anybody could claim to possess *the* religious truth in view of the many different opinions in regard to doctrine. Castellio blamed the narrow approach to the biblical text for the many controversies. He criticized the custom of looking at some passage and then at another in order to settle a problem.[9] Since this method has failed a new way must be found, a cure, Castellio said, to be compared to a physician's task who could not heal a sickness with the old remedy.[10] But before he disclosed his "remedy" Castellio gave his reasons, on quite a few pages, why he considered Christianity the superior religion and Christ the best teacher.[11] He emphatically rejected the claim of some who put Moses above Christ because he had the advantage of being more ancient. Not time, Castellio stated, was the issue but truth.[12] After nobody could possibly dispute his deep appreciation of Christianity, he went into matters setting the stage for applying his yardstick to the Bible.

It was first of all important to realize that some teachings of Scripture were clear beyond doubt whereas others were obscure and open to scrutiny. To the former belonged all those that were necessary for salvation: the existence of God, that He is just and loving man, that He must be loved, that sins must be avoided etc.[13] Among the latter Castellio counted all controversial doctrines such as baptism, predestination, the Eucharist and others.[14] Furthermore, Scripture, Castellio asserted, is not free from contradictions. What Matthew says about Christ's words at the Last Supper, for example, is not identical with Luke's report.[15] Castellio ascribed this to the copyists who — as we also know from secular writers — vary in what they handed down to posterity.[16] Obviously Castellio did not propose that the Gospels were

[9] *De Arte Dubitandi*, p. 56; henceforth only the page number will be given if a quote refers to the *De Arte Dubitandi*.

[10] *ibid*.

[11] See chapters V-X.

[12] p. 28.

[13] p. 54.

[14] p. 58.

[15] p. 45.

[16] pp. 37f.

dictated by the Holy Spirit word by word rather that they were man's work. This is important because it allowed to look for the tenor in a biblical narration rather than to weigh the single expression.[17]

If one wants to detect the general meaning of a passage or doctrine one must read it with a critical eye. God has put the means for doing so at man's disposal: they are the senses and the intellect. Castellio did not rule out revelation but this is not the problem at this point. What the senses tell us is in fact one important source for knowledge. Thus we know of Christ's resurrection from the apostles who witnessed it.[18] We are further told of Christ's eagerness to have all sorts of practical experiences. He went close to a fig tree to see with his own eyes whether it bore fruit or he insisted on tasting a drink to make sure it was not too bitter.[19] Furthermore, Christ advised his disciples to try to touch Him after His resurrection in order to establish the fact that a spirit has neither flesh nor limbs.[20]

Through these examples Castellio wanted to show that the senses are limited to things present to the eyes, the taste or touch. Other things transcend sense-perception and we must suspend any judgment about them. Castellio counted among them the essence of God, the creation of the world or whether souls go to sleep with the bodies and are resurrected with them. It is the same with some cosmic phenomena. Castellio believed the stars too far away for our senses to ascertain whether they are solid bodies or not.[21]

Our senses may also be impaired or deceive us. Castellio exemplified this with the observation that large as well as small things immersed in a deep or agitated water appear to us different from what they really are. In such cases "man endowed with reason" Castellio concluded "resorts to reason and with its aid rectifies the judgment of the senses..."[22]

Reason is like a judge who investigates a doubtful case. Castellio referred to the Greeks who called "the senses and that part of the soul that comprehends and judges things criteria for passing judgment..."[23] Christ himself encouraged and accepted the judgment of even bad

[17] p. 37.
[18] p. 53.
[19] p. 63.
[20] p. *ibid.*
[21] p. 62.
[22] p. 73.
[23] p. 63.

people.[24] But reason may also be blinded in particular by a person's strong feelings about something. It was impossible, Castellio said, to discuss the Last Supper with a person who shared Luther's view because he was passionately convinced that his position was true and that no doubt was possible.[25] Like the senses reason encounters difficulties in Scripture and in some sciences such as medicine and mathematics because they are at first sight not easy to comprehend.[26]

But the worst situation arises if a reformer like Calvin makes his judgment absolute and does not allow any other person (although all men are endowed with reason) to voice doubts.[27]

Doubt was not unknown to medieval theologians but it served them as an incentive to try still harder to discover the truth embodied in Scripture. Castellio made such a strong point for doubt not primarily because of man's limited capacity for understanding but because of the obscurity that prevailed in certain respects in the Bible. His doubt had the effect of endorsing a more tolerant view in doctrinal matters. It previously appeared to me that Castellio's concept of doubt anticipated Descartes' in the next century. After having given the problem more thought, I must agree with Roland Bainton who believes that Descartes' doubt is much more radical than Castellio's.[28] Nevertheless, Castellio and Descartes may have something in common. Descartes' doubt was prompted by his desire to discover "clear and distinct ideas". Castellio's doubt enlisted the help of the senses and the intellect to come to terms with the extent and limitation of biblical truth. In addition, both Castellio and Descartes took recourse to God who willed it so that the senses and the intellect guide man to knowledge. Both thinkers had in the end the highest regard for reason.

Castellio's praise of reason in *De Arte Dubitandi* has often been quoted.[29] He called it the daughter of God who existed from eternity and will exist after the renewal of the world. He finally identified reason with Christ: "the son of the living God who in Greek is called *Logos* that is reason or word which are the same (since reason is so to speak an inner and eternal speech and word which always speaks the truth)..." It seems

---

[24] p. 63.

[25] p. 79.

[26] pp. 65 f.

[27] pp. 41, 57.

[28] See Roland H. Bainton, "New Documents on Early Protestant Rationalism", in *Church History* VII, 2 June 1938, p. 184.

[29] p. 65.

to me that the whole passage is misplaced here and reason a misnomer for what Castellio had in mind. He conjoins two disparate terms namely reason as judgment and the Spirit revealed by Christ to the world. Unfortunately this confusion persists in the last chapters of the first book. One must follow Castellio's advice to his adversaries not to cling to words but look for the tenor of the whole discourse. Moreover, when Castellio explained how reason operates he always identified it with the critical intellect. Referring to the law that forbids the Jews to work on the Sabbath Castellio asserted: "But reason judges that the Sabbath is made for man..."[30] Or when he said: "Finally this reason explores, finds and interprets truth which if it is in profane as well as in sacred writings either obscure or corrupted by time, it corrects it or doubts it until finally truth shines forth or in any event an uncertain matter is decided further".[31] It is quite significant for our problem that the chapter following the one that expressed Castellio's praise of reason contains quotations only from ancient authors: Cato, Sallust, Juvenal and Persius. At the end Castellio made the following remark: "Moreover, these [authors] did not write under divine inspiration but were led by reason; they professed this themselves since they were not accustomed to confirm and support their sayings by divine authority rather by rational arguments. One must therefore admit that the judgment of human reason is right and sane."[32] Did Castellio perhaps think of universal reason and combined it with the *Logos*? It is worth mentioning in that connection that Castellio quite often starts a sentence with "according to reason" one must conclude...

In a pamphlet against Calvin Castellio made the point that the reformer's followers value his authority higher than reason.[33] They apparently had adopted Calvin's teaching of the depraved state of all human talents after Adam's Fall and distrusted their own mind. But Castellio observed that Calvin's cynical views were not supported either by sacred writers or reason. He countered Calvin's position with the argument that the tree in paradise was not called the tree of ignorance but of knowledge. After the Fall the senses told Adam and Eve that they were naked, a fact they had not noticed nor understood before.[34]

---

[30] p. 66.

[31] p. 67.

[32] p. 68. See also Heinz Liebing, "Die Frage nach dem hermeneutischen Prinzip bei Castellio", in Autour de Michel Servet et de Sébastien Castellion, *op. cit.*, pp. 206-124.

[33] *Calumniae nebulonis cuiusdam adversus doctrinam Johannis Calvini*, 1558, p. 20.

[34] p. 69.

Moreover, God had willed it that man should use his reason and his physical abilities: "...nature gave man not bread and wine, nor clothing and houses, but grain and grapes, wool and wood and stone through which they make themselves bread, wine, clothing, houses with the help of reason and their hands".[35] Man has not only the ability to use what nature offers him to his own advantage but could also improve nature.[36] Thus Castellio's optimism stands in sharp contrast to Calvin's pessimism regarding all aspects of human capabilities. Calvin in turn strongly resented his emphasis on reason. In his answer to Castellio's *Calumniae* he employed bitter words of condemnation: "You to the contrary submit the divine mysteries to a judgment according to human perception; and you make reason which by virtue of its blindness extinguishes the whole glory of God, not only the leader and teacher but you prefer it to Scripture."[37] This is a great exaggeration the more so since Calvin must have known that there was more to Castellio's theology than the art of reasoning.

In the second book Castellio applies his yardstick of the senses and reason to the Trinity and more extensively to the Eucharist. Castellio considered the latter a spiritual communion with Christ.

Another major topic concerns faith and justification. In the debate (almost as old as Christianity) whether faith is intertwined with reason or the will Castellio aligned himself with the voluntarists. In connection with this topic Castellio investigated three major points: faith and the will, faith and knowledge, and faith as *donum Dei.* Discussing the first point he quoted as witness for his view Julius Caesar who stated: "men easily believe what they want".[38] Castellio gave the example of a loving wife and mother who finds it difficult to believe in the sinful life of her husband or children because she wants to see only their good sides."[39] The Abraham story could further advance Castellio's position. Abraham had faith in God and accepted his promise that Sarah would give him an heir although because of her age it seemed highly improbable.[40] Once Sarah had given birth to Isaac Abraham's faith yielded to knowledge. Faith, Castellio concluded, excludes knowledge but may eventually lead to it.

---

[35] p. 59.

[36] pp. 58 f.

[37] *Calumniae nebulonis...Johannis Calvini ad eadem responsio*, 1558, p. 109.

[38] p. 89.

[39] p. 90.

[40] pp. 76 f.

Abraham had faith in God whom he trusted. It is the same in everyday life. We have faith in a person Castellio said when we are confident that he speaks the truth. A child is told that his father will return soon. Did he know it, Castellio asked? Obviously not but he relied on the person's truthfulness.[41]

Since Castellio combined faith with an individual's free will, it was not a *donum Dei*. His view in the matter differed sharply from Calvin's or Luther's and Castellio took pains to make his point clear. In connection with the letter Paul wrote to the Corinthians where he enumerated the many gifts man receives from the divine being Castellio commented: "I answer that all good [things] are God's gift. But God has two modes of giving: one naturally, one miraculously. He gives naturally bread to man who cultivates the earth... But at the same time He gave bread to the Jews in their time of want miraculously..."[42] In deference to Paul, I suppose, Castellio agreed that at that time much was received by men miraculously but he added this must not always be so: People possess knowledge and practical wisdom without a miracle; it holds true for a physician who cures a sickness, a mathematician who may predict the future and a person who learns languages not without great effort on his part.[43] Those who consider faith a *donum Dei* Castellio said confuse faith with salvation. The remission of sins is indeed God's grace but it follows faith which is man's work.[44]

As one cannot command the mind *how* to think without destroying its very essence as an instrument in the search for truth, one should not make faith depend on a gift from God since it would take away a person's spontaneity. The intellect is free to judge, the will is free to espouse faith. It could easily appear to a Calvin that Castellio's concept of faith diminished its worth and effectiveness. But one can also argue for the opposite case. The chapters on faith in the second book of *De Arte Dubitandi* are unfinished. Castellio may have added some passages — now lost — that left no doubt about his high regard of what faith means to a person. A free faith need not be less powerful than a faith by the grace of God. In the dialogue *De Fide* Castellio referred to the famous biblical passage where it is said that faith can remove mountains. A free faith may be stronger than a faith as a *donum Dei*.

If faith is alive in the hearts of men and depends on the disposition of

[41] p. 52.
[42] p. 96. See I Chor 12: 8ff.
[43] p. 94.
[44] p. 96.

the will is the door not wide-open to religious anarchy? Castellio who was faced with such accusations denied that this was so. Nobody would believe Satan rather than Christ, he said, because the will far from being blind recognizes Christ's and not Satan's Word as the voice of truth. An example are the Apostles who in their souls were convinced that he was the Christ and God, his father.[45] The believer, according to Castellio accepts Christ's spirit as the source of his faith. Whereas for Calvin Christ the redeemer was central to his theology and Luther set his hope on God's grace and mercy to free man from his sins, Castellio's concern was with man's *reaction* to Christ's message. It was already noted that he did not think of man as a hopelessly sinful creature, rather he has it in his power to become a moral and just person.

The Holy Spirit pervades the whole world and all Christians have an opportunity to respond to it.[46] Such a response has another character and result than what is involved in the judgment of the mind. Reason and sense-experience are natural abilities which serve man to shape his every-day life, to engage in the sciences or to interpret biblical doctrine. Faith, on the other hand, has as its guide inspiration. The mind may be stirred up by prophecy and revelation but, Castellio asserted, faith has a more far-reaching effect: it changes a sinner into a moral person. Who was previously envious, proud, and stingy, for example, will be cured of his "sicknesses" by Christ's spirit, and will become benevolent, modest and generous.[47] Castellio argued here against the reformers who saw in Christ's mediating role man's only possible salvation. In Calvin's words: "Jesus Christ intervened, and by taking on himself the punishment prepared for every sinner by the just judgment of God, he effaced and abolished by his blood the iniquities which had caused enmity between God and men, and by that payment God was satisfied".[48] What good is it, Castellio asked, if a person is called virtuous because of another's deed for which he is given credit? As on many other occasions Castellio conjured up an analogy to elucidate his point. A leper who because of his sickness was kept away from the temple is allowed to enter the holy place after "somebody pleasing to God" has pleaded for him. Can he draw any comfort from this Castellio wondered if he is not really cured of his sickness?[49] To illustrate how the sinner is transformed into a moral

[45] p. 92.
[46] p. 112.
[47] p. 109.
[48] See François Wendel, *Calvin*, London: Collins, 1972, p. 226.
[49] p. 101.

person Castellio introduced again a concrete example referring to the plantation of a fruit-bearing tree. He described the procedure in great detail and even provided drawings showing the steps necessary to change "a wild tree" into a cultured one that brings good fruit. Like the grafting of new shoots on the wild tree promotes a healthy growth, the spirit of Christ that enters the soul brings forth fruits of virtue.[50] Rather than to see in Christ the mediator Castellio preferred to compare him to a physician who heals the soul.

The many chapters of *De Justicia* form the central piece of the second book. Castellio relied heavily on Paul in support of his view that faith in Christ was the only condition for a person to become just.[51] He deeply felt the moral deficiencies of his society and to amend them was a goal close to his heart. He therefore was less concerned with what happened to man after death than that the renewal of the soul would bring the believer his reward in this life.[52] A man of faith is a just man and receives pardon for his sins.

What degree of justice can a man achieve? Calvin thought a man makes little progress in his life and remains a sinful creature before God.[53] Castellio adopted another quite positive position. In refuting Calvin's hopeless attitude regarding any moral improvement Castellio brought into play his three "authorities": reason, experience, and Scripture. His basic argument was that the just man partakes in justice nothwithstanding the fact that he is still wanting in perfection: "Although it is an incomplete justice, it is justice," Castellio claimed, "and if justice is a good (which it certainly is) the incomplete justice is a good... If it is a good it is not corrupt. Therefore, an incomplete justice is not corrupt".[54] It is true on the other hand that no human being equals God's justice. Nevertheless, God's creation is good and according to John all men have the divine seed planted in them.[55] Scripture and reason are backed up by observation of nature, where inequalities of perfection abound. The sun Castellio pointed out is the most brilliant source of light in the universe; the moon and stars cannot match it but they are called light, nevertheless. Sweetness, another example, is unequally distributed among things in nature: honey is sweeter than the fruits

---

[50] pp. II, XXVI. See also Steven E. Ozment, *Mysticism and Dissent*, New Haven: Yale University Press, p. 200. The whole chapter VII is devoted to Castellio.

[51] passim.

[52] p. 99.

[53] See François Wendel, Calvin, *op. cit.*, p. 257.

[54] p. 125.

[55] IJn 3:9, p. 153.

but the latter share in the quality of sweetness.[56] A just man is not perfect and his actions may be defective but for that matter they are not evil. Castellio compared such shortcomings with the spoiled fruits on a tree. They do not make the whole tree bad since the good fruits outdo in number the bad ones.[57] Castellio's optimism about reason and the senses as sources of knowledge and experience is matched by his high estimation of the moral consequences resulting from a will to believe in Christ.

What did Castellio achieve with *De Arte Dubitandi*? One should perhaps dispose of some shortcomings first. The treatise seems not very well structured. There are many repetitions and some contradictions. One notices at times a certain lack of defining the concepts univocally. But the accomplishments outshine all possible defects.

The prominent places Castellio assigned to the senses and reason in his biblical exegesis had far-reaching consequences. Reason had become the judge of truth. Since all men are endowed with reason the truth regarding doctrine established by one theologian may be challenged by another. Truth was not absolute rather truth and error belong together. Castellio repeatedly pointed to the fact that even so—called common people have the ability for critical judgment. Furthermore, Castellio's concept of reason extended to all matters of human endeavor. His insight into the universal role of reason heralded a new age although he was not yet ready to enter it.

Castellio operated in the given framework of Christianity. He did not consider any other religion as accomplished as his own faith. Thus he was unable to allow other religions to contribute to religious truth. In that respect Castellio was far behind the perception of Bodin or Postel who hoped that the various faiths would find a common ground.

In the domain of faith Castellio achieved a similar result as in his biblical hermeneutics. A person's faith depends on his free will that is his free choice to believe. He *wanted* to become a Christian because Christ's teachings convinced him of His power and veracity. Castellio never mentioned the fact that any external influence, baptism or God's action, could convert a man to his faith. The believer, however, was rewarded by the infusion of Christ's spirit into his soul.

If faith was in the hands of men by inference it followed that a man may *not want* to be a Christian. For Castellio such a consequence was

---

[56] p. 122.
[57] n. 50.

unthinkable. On the other hand, although he did not wish for nor comprehend the full consequences of his position, his concepts of reason and faith laid out an avenue for future freedom of thought and the equality of all men.

The question whether Castellio was a rationalist has answered itself. The senses put restrictions on reason. Furthermore, if any rational elements are involved in the person's free will to believe, they are counterbalanced by the spirit of Christ as the deepest source of his faith.

Has Castellio's faith some relation to the mystics? He shared with them the belief that the divine spirit is infused into the soul of the believer. But the respective roads to achieve this are not identical. The mystics preached *Gelassenheit*, a mental and psychological attitude that allowed the believer to wait patiently for God to enter the soul. I did not find any evidence of an inactive will in *De Arte Dubitandi*, nor of a will ready to submit to the will of God. The reborn man of faith was imbued with the divine spirit. But Castellio was primarily concerned with the result it had on the moral conduct of the believer.[58] His overriding goal was in the last analysis for a better life on earth and to show the means to establish love and peace among men.

---

[58] p. 118.

# DE ARTE DUBITANDI ET CONFIDENDI IGNORANDI ET SCIENDI LIBER PRIMUS

ff. *56-*58

Veritatis magister Christus futurum praedixit,[1] ut postremis temporibus tot falsi Christi falsique doctores existant, ut vel electi, si fieri possit, decipiantur. Et quoniam postrema tempora iam esse cum ex aliis multis tum maxime ex tot tantisque quos vigere video erroribus et dissidiis mihi persuasum est, quibus erroribus homines etiam non mali tamen interdum sic commoventur, ut etiam de Christianae religionis veritate subdubitare incipiant, equidem saepe multumque cogitavi, ecquod usquam huic malo remedium inveniri queat. Ac si quis usquam hodie (sicut olim solebat) extaret in terris vates, qui dissidia componere et viam quaerentibus certo commonstrare erroresque divina authoritate profligare poss et, equidem nihil melius aut expeditius esset quam ad eius oraculum confugere et, quod ille divinitus respondisset, id sine ulla dubitatione aut cunctatione sequi. Sed quo confugiemus? "Signa nostra non videmus" ut habetur in psalmis; "non iam vates, non nobis adest, qui sciat, quousque duratura sint haec"[2] Denique nunc, si unquam, viget illa fames sermonis dei, hoc est oraculorum, quam olim se immissurum esse deus per Amosum vatem minatus est.[3] Igitur cum hoc perfugio destituamur, hoc superesse video, ut fiat, quod olim fecisse memoriae proditum est militiae ducem quendam, qui cum in flumen quoddam incidisset, quod omnino transeundum erat neque transeundi modum ullum videret ideoque aestuaret, edixit proposito praemio universis militibus, ut, si quis ullum transeundi consilium invenisset, id ipsi protinus indicatum veniret, quaecumque tandem vel diei vel noctis hora foret: mandavitque ianitoribus suis, ut quemvis, qui se consilium afferre diceret, quacumque hora ad se introducerent. Hac ratione consecutus est, ut quidam ex omnium numero extiterit, qui ei bonum consilium suggessit, quod ille secutus traiecit atque ita seque exercitumque servavit. Prudens sane consilium et dignum, quod in magnis difficultatibus imitemur. Nam boni consilii cupidum esse idque undique conquirere boni consilii est. Et sic consilium qui petunt, saepe inde adipiscuntur, unde minime sperassent. Verum hic

---

* [1] Mt. 24:24.

[2] Ps 74:9.

[3] Amos 8:11ff.

rursus magna nascitur difficultas, propterea quod dissimilis est in religione et caeteris negociis dandi consilii ratio. In caeteris enim negociis qui consilium dant, etiam si ipsorum consilium non approbetur, tamen propter ipsam dandi consilii benevolentiam plerumque amantur. At in religione si quid forteconsulas, quod iis, quibus consulas, non probetur, tantum aberit ut ameris, ut etiam pro haeretico habearis atque ita traductus non solum vulgo invisus fias, verum etam de vita in periculum venias. Sic nimirum solet mundus collata in se beneficia remunerari. Hinc vatum, hinc Christi, hinc apostolorum et iustissimorum quorumque neces: hinc fit, ut nonnulli exemplis territi rem sacram sibi retineant, ne, si eam canibus obiecerint, ab eis pro beneficio lacerentur. Ita fit, ut bonis aut pereuntibus aut tacentibus falsi doctores vulgo vigeant et amentur nihil curante mundo dictum illud Christi: "vae vobis, cum vobis bene dicunt omnes homines: idem enim faciebant falsis vatibus maiores eorum".[4] Haec cogitanti mihi magna sane videtur causa tacendi et mihi uni, si quid scio, sciendi.[5] Sed rursum dum Domini praeceptum considero, quo nos iubet aliis eadem omnia facere, quae nobis fieri velimus, impellit me charitas et officium et misericordia, quam tot hominum errantium capio, ad afferendum in medium, si quid habeo consilii. Quod ad periculum attinet, Dominus prospiciet, apud quem in eorum me numero esse confido, quorum "numerati sunt capilli".[6] Equidem nec periculum meum nec seminis iacturam amo et cuperem haec nec porcis dari nec canibus. Sed postquam ea est sationis conditio, ut quamvis invito agricola tamen seminis pars in viam aut inter saxa aut spinas cadat, seminandum est propter eam partem, quae cadit in bonum solum. Deus adsit et culturam nostram foecundet nosque ab inimicis nullo eorum malo tueatur.

Aggredior artem scribere, qua quis possit in mediis dissensionum fluctibus, quibus hodie Ecclesia verberatur, ita consistere itaque veritatem cognitam exploratamque habere, ut in fidei officiique sui gradu tanquam scopulus permaneat immotus. Titulum libro feci: "Ars dubitandi et confidendi, ignorandi et sciendi", propterea quod in eo potissimum docetur, de quibusnam rebus dubitandum sit aut confidendum et quid ignorare liceat quidve scire oporteat. Titulum hunc mirabitur, credo, non nemo, quasi ridiculum sit artem tradere dubitandi aut ignorandi, cum haec non arte tradi, sed natura homini inesse videantur.

---

[4] Lk 6:26.

[5] Lk 6:34 and passim.

* [6] Lk. 12:7.

Verum si totum opus perlegerit et omnia circumspecte consideraverit, comperiet profecto haec interdum et esse necessaria et homini persuaderi sine magna arte non posse. Usque adeo in eo saepe pertinaciter peccant homines, quod confidunt ubi dubitandum est, dubitant ubi confidendum, et ea ignorant quae scire debent, et scire se volunt aut putant quae et ignorant et ignorare nulla suae salutis iactura possunt. Docuit aliquando Paulus "si quis sibi sapiens videtur, eum stultum fieri oportere, ut fiat sapiens";[7] quae res (videlicet stultum fieri) si facilis esset et sine arte fieri posset, nae nos haud tam multos hodie ideremus stultos sapentes.

Illud addam, quam ego artem trado, eam esse huiusmodi, ut ea facile carere possint, qui Christo simpliciter credunt eiusque praeceptis minime curiosi obediunt. Sed quia non omnes tales sunt et cupimus etiam paulo duriores ad veritatem, si fieri potest, pertrahi (quandoquidem et Christus non solum ad faciles, verum etiam ad difficiles morbos curandos venit), dabimus operam, ut veritatem quam fieri poterit evidentissime demonstremus.

Incipiemus autem ab iis, quae cunctis gentibus manifesta sunt quaeque ne ab iis quidem, qui sacras literas vel ignorant vel repudiant, negari poterunt. Quibus deinde positis sacras literas illorum testimonio confirmabimus atque ita coniuncta religione Christiana cum natura et ratione eaque comprobata tum demum in religione Christiana toti erimus et in eius controversiis quid sequendum sit demonstrabimus, si modo permiserit deus, sine cuius ope ne cogitare quidem quicquam possumus. Ades, lector, non malevolo animo neque sinistris suspicionibus occupato: sententiam nostram tanquam in senatu dicimus, non oraculum, a quo dissentire sit nefas, effamur.[8]

## I. Deum esse eundemque et mundi rectorem et iustum esse ff. *58-*59

Principio deum esse eundemque et mundi rectorem et iustum esse dicimus et ex iis tribus principiis caetera omnia, quae in animo habemus, demonstrare cogitamus. Et quanquam haec tria tanquam artis pronunciata citra demonstrationem aut probationem assumere et, si qui haec negent, eos a iure disputandi arcere nobis licet, tamen, ut omnibus,

* [7] I Cor 3:18.
[8] In margin reference to supplement 18.

quoad eius fieri possit, satis fiat, haec quoque paucis probare conabimur. Primo mundum aut casu regi fatendum est aut providentia. Nam tertium nullum est. Casu eum regi si quis putat, is stultior est quam ut doceri posse videatur. Cum enim ne humana quidem opera, ut familias, ut ludos literarios, ut respublicas, naves, horologia et huius generis alia casu ne ad tempus quidem regi posse videamus, operis omnium summi et omnia reliqua complexi videlicet mundi gubernationem casui tribuere hominis est non multo plus rationis habentis quam habent bestiae. Proinde sic fateantur necesse est omnes homines, mundum non casu gubernari, sed providentia. Eam autem providentiam cuinam nisi deo tribuas, ne cogitare quidem possis. Nam quicquid animo concipies, in quo insit illa providentia, id ipsum erit deus nec nomen nec rem aliam invenies. Quare fatendum omnino est deum esse ab eoque mundum gubernari.

Iam si optimi operis gubernatorem optimum esse necesse est (ut certe est), fatendum est, cum mundus optimum sit opus, eius quoque gubernatorem deum esse optimum. Quod si optimus est, etiam iustus est: et si iustus est, iusticiam exercet, ubi est eius exercendae occasio. Est autem iusticiae rectoris munus bonos remunerari malosque punire. Deus ergo et bonos remuneratur et malos punit.

Sed existit hoc loco perdifficilis quaestio. Quaeritur enim, qui possit hoc probari, cum saepe et impiis hominibus bene et piis male esse videamus. Si enim iustus est deus hominumque rector, cur impios gaudere, pios plorare patitur? Ad quam ego quaestionem hoc respondeo, saepe etiam contra fieri, ut et improbis male et probis bene sit et in eo dei iustitia manifesto appareat. Nec ego hic de iis exemplis loquor, quae utrum divinitus an casu accidant dubitare possit aliquis: cuiusmodi sunt, si quis sceleratus homo perit naufragio aut a magistratu ob sua facinora in crucem tollitur aut morbo interit et huius generis alia; aut si quis homo probus ditescit et prospera valetudine est et calumniatorum insidias feliciter evadit et apud potentes et principes in gratia est et si qua sunt his similia. Quanquam enim in his saepe qui res acutius intuentur manifestam dei providentiam iusticiamque perspiciunt, tamen, quia eadem promiscue saepe probis et improbis usuveniunt, desiderari possunt exempla manifestiora et in quibus nullum fortunae esse locum etiam morosiores fateri cogantur. Itaque afferam aliquot partim ex antiquitatis monimentis, partim recentioris memoriae et nondum fortasse literis mandata.

## II

ff. *59-*59b

Primum exemplum erit Enochi,[1] quem ob pietatem suam ad deum raptum fuisse scribit Moses. Deinde Noa,[2] qui ob iusticiam suam servatus est in totius mortalium generis exitio. Lotus[3] item in Sodomae ruina missis nominatim ad ipsum servandum angelis. Abrahami[4] tantam curam gessit deus, ut Abimelecho regi mortem per visum in somnis minatus fuerit, nisi ei quam rapuerat uxorem reddidisset. Eidem Abrahamo[5] iam seni ex uxore item sene eademque sterili prolem dedit. Isaaci quoque et Iacobi pietatem haud obscure remuneratus est, sed Iacobi apertissime, dum Labani[6] in somnis minatus est, si quid illi noceret. Mosem[7] saepe adversus populi furores tutatus est. Elisaeum[8] ita defendit adversus Syros, ut missos ad eum comprehendendum Syros milites sic excaecaverit, ut Samariam, hostilem urbem, duci se siverint. Possem et alia exempla commemorare, sed nolo esse prolixior.

Vindictae quoque exempla sunt in promptu. Primum et omnibus seculis memorabilissimum est diluvium,[9] quo deus hominum impietatem ultus est. Idem de Sodomae ruina[10] dico et de plagis Aegypthiis[11] et postea de irrogatis toties divinitus poenis Israelitarum populo ob ipsius peccata et maxime de Cora, Dathame et Abiramo,[12] qui propter nefariam adversus Mosem, virum innocentissimum, coniurationem partim divino igne palam hausti, partim terrae hiatu a Mose praedicto (ne quis forte casu factum fuisse causetur) universo spectante populo absorpti sunt. Neque vero solum ex sacris, verum etiam ex profanis literis neque duntaxat antiqua, sed etiam recentioris memoriae exempla commemorare licet.

---

* [1] Gen 5:24.
* [2] Gen 6:8-22.
* [3] Gen 19.
* [4] Gen 20:3.
* [5] Gen 17:16-22.
* [6] Gen 31:24.
* [7] Ex 17:2 and passim.
* [8] II Kings 6:18ff.
* [9] Gen 7.
*[10] Gen 19:24.
*[11] Ex 11ff.
[12] Num 16.

## III. Digna suis cuique factis praemia in hac vita non reddi itaque in futura redditum iri

ff. 60-6

Haec et huius generis alia exempla, quae lectoribus multa in mentem venient, quippe cum frequenter accidant,[1] eiusmodi sunt, ut in eis dei iusticia sese manifestissime exerat.

Dicet hic aliquis: Cur ergo non semper haec fiunt? Cur saepe et insontes pereunt et sontes triumphant? Respondeo: Non, si non semper fit, ergo non fit: quin, si aliquando fit, ergo fit. Atque hoc mihi primum obtinere satis est, videlicet dei iusticiam in quibusdam esse ita manifestam, ut ne ab impudentissimis quidem negari possit. Addam et similitudinem. Est aliqua respublica, quae convocato senatu captoque consilio latronem comprehendi curat eumque in crucem tollit. Hic ego quaero, an latro ille poenas casu dederit. Minime vero, sed consilio et providentia. At in eadem republica non omnes malefici licet noti luunt poenas. Fateor: sed quid tum postea? Num tu propterea in illa republica ullam vigere iusticiam negabis? Minime gentium, sicuti neque gladios, etiam si gladiis non semper utantur. Habent enim interdum causas etiam iustas, cur vel non utantur vel nondum utantur. Est enim interdum maleficus ita potens aut gratiosus, ut ad poenam peti sine reipublicae summo periculo nequeat. Interdum expectatur alia eius puniendi occasio certis de causis: nonnunquam putat senatus ei dandam esse veniam propter ipsius praeterita in rempublicam beneficia aut in gratiam cuiuspiam principis, quem illius rei apud ipsum gratiosi supplicio irritari futurum videatur reipublicae detrimentosius quam si ei detur impunitas. Denique multae eiusmodi causae (et loquor de iustis, ut taceam iniustas) existunt, quibus motus senatus non facit, quod alioquin lex postularet. Neque tamen vere dixeris illius senatus nullam esse vel iusticiam vel providentiam. Quod si fit hoc a senatibus alioquin iustis et providis, cur a deo fieri non possit causam nullam video: ut enim non easdem aut non semper easdem habeat causas deus, quas habent respublicae, at potest alias et interdum easdem habere. Exempli gratia concedit improbo alicui res interdum secundiores et diuturniorem impunitatem, ut vel ille tandem ad sanitatem redeat vel tanto graviores ad extremum luat poenas tantoque magis ex commutatione rerum doleat. Rursumque probum aliquem patitur gravibus calamitatibus vexari, ut eius fides et constantia velut aurum in fornace exploretur idemque ad extremum remunerante deo ex illa

[1] One and a half pages of the MS are left empty. Castellio may have had the intention to insert some examples of a different kind.

vicissitudine magis gaudeat magisque deum ob tam inopinabile auxilium collaudet. Denique non magis absurdum est pios interdum a deo asperius quam impios tractari, quo deinde maiore et dei gloria et sua laetitia beentur, quam quod sapiens interdum pater charissimum sibi haeredemque futurum filium severius duriusque alit quam alienos, quo et melior evadat et haereditatem nullo impeditus scelere cernat aut quod bonus agricola vitem (quo nullam stirpem habet chariorem) putat severiusque castigat quam ullam caeterarum stirpium, quo ea fructum ferat et meliorem et copiosiorem.[2] Iam vero si deus protinus et pios praemiis et impios poenis afficeret, primum non haberent pii, ubi cum caeteras tum in primis pulcherrimam illam virtutem, patientiam, discerent et exercerent, quae extra iniurias et res adversas non magis disci potest quam ars natandi extra aquam. Deinde improborum quoque animi perversitas non pateret, quippe qui preasentis poenae formidine a facinoribus abstinerent, cum tamen animos haberent facinorum plenos ideoque reipsa non essent meliores quam si facinora ipsa opere patrassent. Quemadmodum si lupus clausus in ovili metu praesentium et ictus iamiam intentantium pastorum a iugulandis ovibus sese abstineat, cum tamen animo sit non minus lupino quam cum liber esset.

Dicet aliquis: Quid igitur fiet illis, qui in hac vita factorum suorum tum bonorum tum malorum praemia non consequuntur? Respondeo: Haec nimirum est illa quaestio, quae multos diu vexavit et ad quam responderi non potest, nisi praemia iusta dicas in alteram vitam differri. Nam si dicas etiam in hac vita id fieri, quemadmodum superioribus exemplis demonstravimus, non satisfeceris quaestioni, cum neque semper fiat et, cum fit, non satis digna sint factis praemia. Nam et multi pii ad mortem usque misere vivunt et saepe cum summo cruciatu et ignominia ex hac vita tolluntur, ut apparet ex tot vatibus et Christo eiusque discipulis et eorum imitatoribus. Et si quando in hac vita beantur, id parum est et minus etiam beantur quam multi impii. Rursumque multi impii ad mortem usque cum voluptatibus vivunt et saepe nullo cum cruciatu aut ignominia decedunt et, si quando tamen dant poenas, id quantulum est ad tot perpetrata ab eis flagitia? Quas enim dignas sceleribus suis poenas dare potuerunt in hac vita Herodes, Phalarides, Nerones, Caracallae, Heliogabali et huius generis non dicam homines, sed monstra hominum, qui saepe plus uno die poenarum commeriti sunt quam exolvere possent, si per omnem vitam summis cruciatibus afflictarentur? Quas poenas luit impius miles, qui per omnem vitam in omni

[2] In margin reference to supplement 3.

genere flagitiorum volutatus ad extremum in proelio exultans, alacris, gaudens una tormenti glande repente in auras sine ullo suo dolore (quis enim dolor sentiri potest in momento temporis?) dissipatur? Nonne multo mollius moritur quam si in lecto suo morbo extingueretur? Haec consideratio summos viros eo adduxit, ut digna factis praemia hominibus in altera vita fore statuerint. Cum enim viderent id in hac vita non fieri et tamen, nisi fierit, dei iusticiam tueri non possent, coacti sunt rei veritate sic argumentari. Dei iusticiae est suis cuique factis digna praemia solvere, atqui id in hac vita non facit; faciet ergo in futura.

## IV ff. 61b

Igitur cum deus iusticiam velit et exerceat et homo in dei potestate et arbitrio sit, hominis officium est iusticiam colere[1] et, ut colere possit, eandem cognoscere. Est autem iusticia suum cuique, hoc est quod cuique debetur, tribuere. Debetur autem et deo et homini ab homine amor et quae sunt amoris opera. Si enim quod et bonum est et homini bonum est, amari debet ab homine, deus profecto, qui et bonus est (id quod negari non potest) et homini bonus est (quando quidem, quicquid habet homo boni, a deo habet), amari debet ab homine. Et si natura comparatum est, ut, quae inter sese cognata sunt, ea ament inter sese, ut ovis ovem, columba columbam, efficitur, ut, cum omnes homines inter sese cognati fratresque sint, debeant inter sese amare nec ullum hominem ab amore suo excludere. Quod si contra faciunt, officium violant. Est igitur omnium hominum officium deum et homines alios amare et amoris opera facere atque haec est quam quaerimus iusticia. Discitur autem cognosciturque iusticia tum natura tum doctrina. Nam et natura homini rationem indidit, qua verum a falso, bonum a malo, iustum ab iniusto discernat, et doctrina, ratione duce, naturam confirmat docetque vivendum esse secundum naturam et, hoc qui faciunt, iustos, qui contra, iniustos pronunciat.

Sed nascuntur hoc loco permagnae et explicatu necessariae quaestiones duae. Quarum prima est haec:

Si secundum naturam vivendum est, quorsum opus est disciplina? Cum naturam idoneam ducem et magistram esse ipsa etiam doctrina doceat cumque bestiae sine ulla disciplina naturaliter fungantur officio,[2] ut hirundines, ut grues, ut apes, ut formicae, quae duce natura officium

---

[1] See Plato, *Republic*, bk. 1.

[2] In the margin from Castellio's hand: *catus*.

faciunt, societatem inter sese colunt, quasi ad consultandum conveniunt et quandam quasi rempublicam habent. Altera quaestio est haec:

Si secundum naturam vivendum est, cur homines natura furaces et lubidinosi et iracundi iniusti habentur, si naturam suam ducem sequentes furantur et libidini iraeque indulgent? Cur contra naturam vivere putantur, cum naturalem appetitum bestiarum ritu sequantur?

Ad harum quaestionum primam sic respondeo. Deus et natura nihil frustra faciunt.[3] Atqui si homini sine ulla rationis ope omnia naturaliter suppeterent, nihil haberet in quo se exereret vel ratio vel manus hominis atque ita utrumque esset inutiliter homini a natura datum. Cum igitur rationem et manum homini natura sapienter dedisset, voluit esse aliquid, in quo se illa exererent et exercerent, et quaedam ipsa sponte sua sina ulla hominis opera largita, in quibusdam autem operam cum homine partita ipsum sibi quasi socium adiutoremque fecit et eius rationi manibusque quaedam vel corrigenda vel meliora facienda reliquit idque tum in iis, quae ad corpus, tum in iis, quae ad animum pertinent, fecit. Hinc discrimen illud inter hominis et bestiarum res necessarias, quod homini non panem et vinum, non vestes et domos natura dedit, sed frumentum et uvas, sed lanas et ligna atque saxa, unde ille sibi panem, vinum, vestes, domos ratione manuque conficeret. Quin ne illas quidem materias omnes sine ulla hominis opera dare voluit, siquidem nec frumenta et uvae nec pecora sine hominis opera et cultura proveniunt nec mali et pyri et aliae quaedam arbores sine insitione (quae artis, non naturae est) satis bonos fructus ferunt. At pecoribus victum vestitumque natura paratum suppeditavit, antea etiam et latibula plerisque sponte sua dedit: aut si quid deerat, tantum cuique animalium industriae dedit, quantum erat ad illa sibi paranda necessaria. Igitur si in iis, quae ad hominis corpus pertinent, ita se res habet,[4] ut naturae socia et adiutrix sit hominis ratio atque manus, nec mirum nec absurdum videri debet, si idem fit in animo. Voluit igitur natura sicut in terra et stirpibus, sic in animo hominis esse aliquid, quod sit vi rationis excolendum et corrigendum. Quod si naturam illic sapientem esse constat, hic quoque sapientem esse confidendum est, quippe cum sit eadem ratio. Quare quod homini secundum naturam vivendum esse traditur, id perinde accipiendum est, ut si dicas agricolae secundum naturam esse agrum colendum, non quod nihil naturam adiuvet aut corrigat agricola, cum illud ipsum agrum colere sit naturam adiuvare aut corrigere, sed quod in omnibus naturam ipsam et

---

[3] See Aristotle, *De Caelo*, A 4,271a 33.

[4] Again in margin reference to suppl. 3.

ducem et sociam habeat. Facit enim omnia vi rationis, quae naturalis est, et, si quid forte contra naturam facit (ut dum arbores inserit, quas ipsa natura inserere non potest), id ipsum et naturali ratione dictatur et ab ipsa deinde natura promovetur et fovetur non minus quam si natura fecisset. Nam insita contra naturam arbor crescit deinde fructumque fert secundum naturam estque hic insitionis, quae artis est, et incrementi, quod naturae est, quaedam arctissima quasique coniugalis societas. Quod idem in rebus anima fieri dico itaque statuo doctrinam iusticiae esse quandam animorum quasi agriculturam. Atque haec ad primam quaestionem dicta sunto.

Ad secundam quaestionem respondeo furacitatem, ebriositatem, mendacitatem et huius generis alia esse morbos animi ideoque contra naturam, quandoquidem omnis morbus est contra naturam, etiam si quis cum eo nascatur. Itaque qui morbis illis obsequuntur, contra naturam vivunt: neque enim homini naturale est furari, mentiri, inebriari non magis quam leprosum esse. Proinde corrigenda sunt illa, non sequenda, quod etiam profitetur animorum agricultura. Sicut enim agricolae non solum illa praestant, quae recensuimus, verum etiam si quid vel in stirpibus vel in pecore morbi est, sanant, ita et iusticiae magistri utrumque animis praestare se profitentur. Quare sic statuamus, doctrinam iusticiae esse animorum quandam quasi agriculturam atque medicinam.

## V

ff. 63-

Nunc quoniam artem hanc multi et professi sunt et profitentur et, quinam sint eius authores optimi et vel ante omnes vel etiam soli sequendi, controversia est, dispiciendum nobis est, quanam ratione de eo iudicari possit, et, postquam, quinam sint optimi, deprehenderimus, in illis ipsis quid sequi oporteat considerandum. Dicet hic fortasse protinus aliquis Christianus nihil opus esse consideratione. Christianam enim doctrinam esse sine controversia omnium longe praestantissimam. Et sane de praestantia verum dicet: sed de consideratione fortasse non item. Debemus enim non temere, sed circumspecte et cum iudicio sequi quae sequimur, id quod plerique non faciunt. Maxima enim Christianorum pars in Christum non aliter credit quam Turcae in Mahometem aut quam illae ipsae nationes, quae nunc Christum profitentur, olim in Iovem aut Neptunum caeterosque peregrinos deos crediderunt. Credunt enim in Christum, quia in eius doctrina a teneris sunt educati eamque a parentibus acceperunt. Quod si in Mahometica itidem educati fuissent,

Mahometi itidem crederent. Eiusmodi fides puerorum est et hominum imperitorum, quibus si bene succedit fortunatos dixero, sapientes non dixero, quemadmodum si quis salutem suam credit urbis suae medico, quia urbis suae medicus est, non quia eum bonum esse medicum cognoverit, si succedit, bene est, sed est quod fortunae, non sapientiae suae gratias agat. Si enim malum esse medicum illum contigisset, eadem credulitate periisset aegrotus, qua sanatus est. Quare si incidimus ipsi in optimum medicum, videamus, quanam ratione optimum esse eum probari possit: ut et qui in eum iam inciderunt, magis insuper in eius fide confirmentur et, si qui forte dubitant (dubitant autem nonnulli etiam Christiani nominis homines), errore si fieri potest liberentur. Adde quod proderit haec consideratio ad externae quoque religionis homines vel pelliciendos vel saltem refellendos.

Primum illud constat, de opifice aut ex ipsius oratione aut ex opere iudicandum esse. Quod ad orationem attinet, ea saepe fallax est et existunt interdum ita diserti acutique hominis et iidem tamen minus boni opifices, ut, si ex eorum verbis iudices, praeferas eos bonis opificibus, nisi (quod paucorum est) sis admodum acutus. At ex opere de opifice iudicare quivis tuto potest. Exemplum dicam. Si contentio est de duobus fabris ferrariis, uter sit praestantior, nemo est, qui non eum protinus iudicet esse praestantiorem qui meliora ferramenta cudat non pauca (casus enim videri possit), sed pleraque, omnia. Idem dico de milite aut duce exercitus, qui hostes optime vincat. Idem de agricola, nimirum eum esse optimum qui plurimas fruges arte sua consequatur. Item de medico qui vel valetudinem optime tueatur vel morbos optime sanet. Breviter is est optimus censendus artifex, qui opera facit optima. Cum igitur hic de iusticiae doctrina quaeramus, quaenam sit omnium optima, et supra docuerimus eam esse animorum quandam quasi agriculturam atque medicinam,[1] non dubium est, quin ea censenda sit optima, quae animos reddat quam iustissimos eorumque morbos optime sanet. Hanc autem esse dico Christianam doctrinam, id quod multis equidem exemplis planum facere possum, sed ne sim prolixior pauca adducam. Scribit Lucas in Actis de Christianis haec verba: "Omnes autem credentes degebant una habebantque omnia communia et suas copias ac facultates vendebant omnibusque, prout cuique opus erat, dispertiebant ac quotidie simul assidui in fano panemque mansionatim frangentes cibum capiebant, cum laetitia animique simplicitate laudantes deum et apud cunctum populum valentes gratia".[2] Hic videmus universi populi sancti-

[1] See Sebastian Castellio, *Contra Libellum Calvini...*, esp. the chapter "Quid sit haereticus et quonam modo tractandus". See Introd. p. 2, n. 5.

[2] Acts 2:44-47.

tatem iusticiamque tantam, quanta ante tempus illud nulla in terris extiterat. Atque ut intelligas non solum mediocris, sed etiam singularis improbitatis homines hac doctrina ad frugem et iusticiam fuisse perductos, scribit idem author in eiusdem libri cap. 19 haec verba: "Eorum qui crediderant multi sua facta confessum ac declaratum veniebant. Itemque eorum, qui illicita (hoc est artes magicas) tractaverant, satis multi congestos libros in onium praesentia cremabant".[3] Hic certe non vulgaris improbitatis homines ad frugem redierunt, sed omnium pene dixerim sceleratissimi. Nam qui magicas illas artes tractant, ii ante deo renunciarunt (quo scelere haud scio an nullum ne quidem cogitari possit immanius) aut certe non procul ab eo absunt et tamen eos sanare Christiana doctrina potuit. Item Paulus ad Corinthios ita scribit: "Ne errate: nec impudici nec deastricolae nec adulteri nec molles nec pedicones nec fures nec avari nec ebriosi nec conviciatores nec rapaces divinum regnum consequentur. Et tales quidem nonnulli eratis, sed abluti estis, sed sancti, sed iusti facti per nomen Domini Iesu perque dei nostrum spiritum".[4] Hic certe de sceleratissimis hominibus loquitur, quos tamen Iesu nomen deique doctrina a sceleribus abluere potuit.[5] Item Petrus: "Igitur Christo pro vobis supplicium passo vos quoque eadem mente armamini, siquidem, qui corpore supplicium tulit, is peccare desiit, ne deinceps ad hominum cupiditates, sed ad dei voluntatem reliquum in carne tempus vivat. Satis est enim vobis praeterito vitae tempore extraneis morem gessisse versantes in libidinibus, cupiditatibus, vinolentiis, comessationibus, potationibus et nefariis deastrorum culturis. Atque id sane mirantur illi non concurrere vos ad eandem luxuriae profusionem"[6] Haec Petrus; quibus verbis ostendit usque adeo a peccatis descivisse illos et ex improbis probos evasisse, ut id mirarentur gentiles. Atque haec de vulgo Christianorum dicuntur. Nam primarios quidem hoc est apostolos quid commemorem? Quorum tanta fuit sanctimonia, quantam vel optare ne dicam sperare vix ausi fuissent vel sanctissimi philosophorum, adeo ut orbem terrae quasi quaedam luminaria (sicut eis magister Christus praeceperat) collustraverint.[7] I nunc et

---

[3] Acts 19:18-19.

[4] I Cor 6:9-11. Castellio follows his own translation of the Bible in replacing *furnicarii* with *impudici* and *idolis inservientes* with *deastricolae*. See *Biblia interprete Sebastiano Castellione*, 1551, ch. VIII, p. 466 marginal note. Ochino uses the term *deastros* coined by his friend in Dialogus XI of his *Dialogi XXX*.

[5] In margin reference to suppl. 1.

[6] I Pet 4:1-4. See previous page n. 4.

[7] In margin reference to suppl. 16.

confer opera doctrinae sapientium, quotquot unquam sub omni coelo extitisse memorantur, cum huius doctrinae operibus et videbis haec tanto illis omnibus esse maiora, quanto sol est stellis splendidior, nec aliter doctrinam sapientum[8] huius adventu evanuisse quam stellae oriente sole evanescunt. Quae cum ita esse constet, sic statuo, Christianam iusticiae doctrinam esse omnium doctrinarum longe praestantissimam.

## VI ff. 65-66b

Sed excipiet aliquis Christianos homines nec tunc usque adeo fuisse sanctos et nunc esse omnium pene sceleratissimos. Nam et Paulus suo imo tempore Galatas gravissime reprehendit et dementes[1] appellare audet, qui a spiritu exorsi in carnem desinerent. Et Corinthios[2] acerrime obiurgat, qui incestum ne quidem apud gentiles nominandum ita ferrent, ut eo propemodum gaudere viderentur: quique non solum inter sese idque sub non Christianis iudicibus litigarent, verum etiam fratres suos fraudarent.[3] Quid quod idem Paulus ab omnibus se derelictum in suo periculo conqueritur? Quid quod omnes suae[4] ipsorum utilitati studere seque in egestate desertum a suis non obscure indicat? "Recte", inquit, "fecistis quod calamitati meae opitulati estis. Scitis vos quidem, Philippenses, initio evangelii, cum ex Macedonia profectus essem, nullam ecclesiam mihi quicquam contulisse ad rationem expensorum nisi vos solos".[5] Quaeso quales erant Christiani, qui magistrum ne dicam patrem suum, hominem et coelibem nullaque familia gravem et sobrium paucissimisque contentum atque insuper suis manibus saepe victum, quaeritantem tamen egere patiebantur idque, cum essent ipsi tanto numero, quantus dici vix potest, quippe cum Paulus omnia evangelio replevisset? Quid quod alicubi suis expobrat[6] ipsos in causa esse, ut evangelium male audiat apud exteros, nimirum quia improbe viverent?

De nostri vero temporis Christianis quid multis opus est? Cum ipsimet Christiani[7] se improbos esse pene profiteantur: quid pene dixi? Cum ii

---

[8] The form *sapientum* occurs in Latin poets and once in the *Vulgate*.

[1] Gal 3:3.
[2] I Cor 5:1-3.
[3] I Cor 6:6-9.
[4] II Tim 4:16.
[5] Phil 4:14-15.
[6] Rom 2:24.
[7] See Calvin, *Petit Traicté de la Saincte Cène* 1541. Corp. Ref. ed. 1866 vol. XXXIII p. 436: "Il est necessaire que nous soyons en merveilleux trouble et torment de conscience... car il n'y a celuy de nous qui puisse trouver un seul grain de justice en soy: mais au contraire, nous sommes tous plains de péché et iniquité".

qui se non solum Christianos, verum etiam ecclesiarum reformatores esse iactant, publice et communiter et in concionibus et coram dei sancta maiestate quotidie solemniter accinente universo populo profiteantur se esse proclives ad malum et inutiles ad omne bonum suoque vitio sine ulla intermissione violare sancta praecepta dei? Quaeso quid de omnium, qui unquam fuere, populorum sceleratissimo deterius dici potest quam quod isti Christiani de se ipsis quotidie profitentur? Aut quid opus est ad eorum probanda perpetua scelera testibus, cum ipsi ea ne quidem interrogati nedum quaestioni subiecti profiteantur? Ad quae ego respondeo non doctrinae, sed hominum esse culpam, qui doctrinae non pareant, atque hic similiter accidere, ut in bonis agriculturae praeceptis, quae qui secuti sunt, copiosas fruges perceperunt, qui vero illis neglectis otio et ventri incubuerunt, iis terra pro frugibus et uvis carduos sentesque tulit. Sic illi Christiani, cum principio Christi doctrinae paruissent, sancti evaserant. Iidem postea socordiores facti degenerabant. Quod enim sancti evaserant, doctrinae erat, quae certe sanctos efficere non potuisset nisi sancta fuisset. Quod vero degenerabant, ipsorum culpa erat, qui ut mali discipuli a doctrina deficiebant. Nos autem hic non de hominum perseverantia, sed de doctrinae veritate disserimus eamque optimam esse contendimus, cum reddat optimos, sicut medicinam, quae valetudinem optime vel tenet vel recuperat, optimam esse constat, etiam si eam vel pauci sequantur vel, qui aliquando secuti sunt, deserant.

Quod vero ad nostri temporis Christianos attinet et maxime eos, quorum confessionem vel potius professionem modo attigi, nihil possum vel aptius aut verius vel quod minus eos offendere debeat respondere quam dictum illud parabolae Christi: "Serve nequam, ex ore tuo te iudicabo".[8] Cum enim ipsi se esse profiteantur proclives ad male faciendum, inutiles ad omne bonum et sine ulla intermissione violare sancta dei praecepta, si quis eis tantum mutata persona dixerit: Vos estis proclives ad male faciendum, inutiles ad omne bonum et sine ulla intermissione violatis sancta dei praecepta, non magis eis iniuriam fecerit quam ipsi sibi.[9] Nam sive nunquam sancti fuerunt: Christiani unquam fuerunt, et nos de Christianis loquimur; sive aliquando sancti fuerunt, sed degenerarunt, similes sunt "lotae suis, quae redit ad volutabrum"[10] aut "canis qui ad vomitum"[11], "arbores autumnales bis mortuae".[12]

---

[8] Lk 19:22.

[9] See n. 7 and Calvin, *Institutes*, 1936 Corp. Ref. XXIX ch. 1,28 "...omnes ignorantes Dei sumus...omnisque boni inopes. Cor vero in omne malum proclive...".

[10] II Pet 2:22.

[11] II Pet 2:22.

[12] J 12.

Nos vero verorum Christianorum veram confessionem isti plane contrariam agnoscimus eamque his verbis vere concipi posse pugnamus, videlicet: Nos sumus ad bene faciendum proclives, ad omne bonum utiles et sine ulla intermissione sanctis dei praeceptis obediemus. Et fuimus quidem aliquando improbi, "sed abluti sumus, sed sancti, sed iusti facti sumus"[13] et "dei lege delectamur deque ea dies noctesque cogitamus"[14] et in dei praeceptis currimus et lucis homines facti, repudiatis tenebrarum operibus, opera lucis facimus et corpore, anima, spiritu sancti[15] deum nostrum horum omnium bonorum datorem corpore, anima, spiritu honoramus. Haec est, haec est verorum Christianorum vera et cum sacris literis consentiens confessio, non qualis istorum est, qui Christum servatorem suum turpissime dedecorant ab eo se redemptos esse iactantes, cum se tamen servos esse profiteantur omnium peccatorum, non cogitantes Christi sententia se damnari, qui dicit: "Qui peccatum committit, is peccati servus est",[16] neque videntes (o caecitatem) eum a se dedecorari, quem putant honorari, nisi forte non dedecoraret Christum aliquis membris captus, qui ita de sanitate sua praedicaret: Ego sic sum a Christo sanatus, ut me movere loco nequeam et perpetuis cruciatibus angar. At quanto rectius ille, qui dicebat: "Unum scio, quod caecus fui et nunc video".[17] Haec ego constanter et vere nec tamen libenter dico, quia non dubito, quin eos offensura sint, qui his offendi minime debent, quippe cum ipsimet illa de se profiteantur. Sed urget me necessitas et misericordia, qua afficior erga populum, qui decipitur et caecus caecos sequitur talique vel doctrina vel confessione iam alioquin ad bene faciendum segnior magis insuper retardatur. Sed de hoc suo loco, si permittit deus, plura disseremus.

## VII ff. 66b-67b

Nunc postquam demonstravimus Christianam doctrinam esse omnium longe optimam, quippe quae optima faciat opera, hoc subiicimus, si omnium optima est, ergo ei omnium maxime credendum esse. Atque hoc, si sic sine ullis aliis argumentis assumerem, mihi abs quovis concedi deberet. Sed tamen, ut quam maxime confirmetur huius doctrinae authoritas, cur ei maxime credendum sit, alias insuper causas afferam, si

---

[13] I Cor 6:11.
[14] Ps 1:2.
[15] evidently *sancti facti.*
[16] J 8:34.
[17] J 9:25.

tamen illud prius dixero, Christianae doctrinae nomine comprehendi a me omnes in universum sacras literas, hoc est vetus et novum foedus. Cum enim Christus[1] (quem optimae doctrinae authorem esse demonstratum est) antiquum foedus approbaverit seque non ad abrogandam, sed ad implendam legem venisse testatus fuerit, nos Christi authoritate moti idem approbare debemus. Atque ego hic contra sentio quam quidam,[2] qui existimant antiqui foederis authoritatem esse maiorem quam novi et Christo hac maxime de causa esse credendum, quia de eo Moses vatesque testentur. Quanquam enim hac causa maxime moventur imperiti ideoque tum Christus ipse tum eius apostoli ipsius authoritatem antiquorum testimoniis confirmarunt, videlicet propter populi imperitiam, quem plerumque magis movet antiquitas quam veritas, tamen re vera, quanto Christus omnium maximus est, tanto omnium maxima et apud omnes esse debet et apud peritiores est eius authoritas. Quod ad antiquitatem attinet, si qui Mosi propter antiquitatem magis credunt, iidem, si Mosis tempore fuissent, Mosi minus credidissent, quippe qui tunc non esset antiquus. Enimvero rei, non tempori credendum est ac tale quicque iudicandum est, quale re vera est, neque enim veritas est casei similis, ut fiat antiquitate melior. Quaerebam aliquando ex Iudaeo, quamnam potissimum ob causam Mosi crederet. Respondebat: ob miracula, quae dei ope fecisset. Et recte meo iudicio respondebat. Et ego ei tunc idem, quod nunc dicam, dicebam. Si Mosi ob miracula credendum est, multo magis Christo credendum est, qui et plura fecerit et maiora praesertim accedente omnium longe divinissima sanctissimaque doctrina.

Igitur, ut tandem ad institutum revertatur oratio, dico Christianae doctrinae credendum esse propter eas omnes causas, quibus alicui conciliari fides solet. Sunt autem (quantum nunc animo comprehendere possum) quatuor. Primum est concordia et constantia, ut si quis nulla in re a seipso discrepat et maxime si plures id faciunt, quale est, si plures testes saepius et caute interrogati inter sese semper concordant. Alterum est hoc. Si quando in nobis ipsis assensionem testimoniumque deprehendimus eius rei, quam quis nobis dicit, ei credimus in eis etiam, quae sentimus. Ut si quis medicus aegroto ita dicit: Sentis gravitatem corporis et interdum nauseam aut ventriculi dolorem et, si quando tussis, lateris

---

[1] Mt 5:17.

[2] See B. Rothmann, *Von Verborgenheit der Schrift des Rickes Christi und von dem Dage des Herrn*, ed. E.W.H. Hochhut, Gotha, 1857, ch. 1, p. 7: "Demna di principall rechte Schrifft is Moses und die propheten. Als Christus spreckt: Se hebben Mosen und de propheten, de horen se."

compunctionem aut aliquid tale. Haec, inquam, si in seipso deprehendit aegrotus, medico in iis quoque credit, quae non sentit. Item si in animalis corpore dissecando dicit medicus: Secate pellem istam et sub ea invenietis talem nervum aut venam aut membranam aut quicquid tandem id est, si id compluribus in locis ita esse sine errore deprehendimus, eum peritum eius rei esse credimus eique in iis quoque partibus, quas non videmus, fidem adhibemus. Tertium est fidelitas, ut si quis mercator semper fidelis fuit nec unquam fidem fefellit, eum non mentiri credimus eique confidimus. Quartum est opus et experientia, ut si quem videmus fabrum serarium bene fecisse seram aut clavem, credimus et repagulum aut pessulum aut aliquid tale bene esse facturum. Item si vidimus a medico unum aut alterum morbum probe esse sanatum, confidimus ei in caeteris quoque curis, quas non vidimus. Hae sunt (meo quidem iudicio) causae, quae nos solent impellere ad fidem alicui adhibendam. Nunc quoniam cuinam doctrinae credendum sit quaeritur, dico esse Christianam propter quatuor a me modo recensitas causas, quas in ea, non in caeteris inesse dico.

## VIII

ff. 67b-68b

Ac primum quod ad concordiam et constantiam attinet, dico doctrinam hanc (id quod de alia nulla dici posse vel iniquissimi fatebuntur) ab orbis primordio ad nostram hanc aetatem perpetuo durasse firmam. constantem, immotam, sibi consentientem, eodem semper tendentem quasique catenam quandam perpetuam atque connexam posterioribus semper priorum doctrinam confirmantibus atque subsignantibus. Accedit ad eius constantiam viresque confirmandas, quod nulla unquam doctrina tot, tantos, tam potentes, tam pertinaces, tam inter sese in ea oppugnanda concordes hostes habuit: et tamen omnibus invitis non humana, sed divina dumtaxat ope semper invicta stetit. Primum enim Noa[1] in antiquo illo mundo huius doctrinae praeco non paucos quosdam aut debiles ipse copiis pollens, sed in universum, quicquid hominum usquam sub coelo erat, ipse solus nullisque humanis viribus fultus habuit adversarios solusque per tot annos in aedificanda illa arca constantissime cum hac doctrina perseveravit et cum eadem in arca quasi sepultus cum eadem, finito tandem diluvio, ex arca egrediens quasi ex morte in vitam resurrexit eiusque doctrinae semina posteris ad perpetuitatem tradidit.

---

* [1] Gen 6:9-22.

Secuti postea Abrahamus, Isaacus, Iacobus eorumque nepotes eandem doctrinam tenuerunt et in Aegypti ferrea illa servitutis fornace tamen ab ea nunquam defecerunt.[2] Quid Mosem[3] commemorem, qui ante oppugnatus quam natus solo dei praesidio et providentia victis insidiis,[4] victis magis,[5] victo rege,[6] victis Aegypti copiis, victo denique calcatoque mari doctrinam hanc partim per manus a maioribus, partim recens a deo acceptam literisque mandatam posteritati commendavit, quae deinde tot calamitatibus et bellis oppugnata per tot secula ad Christi usque tempora invicta duravit? Quid de Christo eiusque legatis referam? Quibus armis nixi doctrinam hanc antea una in natione habitantem et caeteris omnibus invisam propagarunt? Homunciones pauperculi, indocti, nullius authoritatis aut splendoris, inermes, nullis denique humanis praesidiis muniti, invitis et summa ope repugnantibus divitibus, doctis, potentibus, principibus, sapientibus, quicumque usquam terrarum erant, denique invito universo orbe terrarum ipsi nullo usquam loco coniuncti, sed diversis regionibus toto orbe dissipati doctrinam hanc ita severunt et propagarunt, ut ad hunc diem per mille quingentos amplius annos victrix et intemerata permanserit. Accedit ad eius virium commendationem, quod non solum ab externis, verum etiam a suis et oppugnata fuit et adhuc quotidie oppugnatur, dum eam ore profitentes factis hoc est impietate vitae negant et sectarum opinionumque diversitate ac repugnantia quantum in ipsis est labefactant. Nam per Christianorum scelera, dissidia, persecutiones, bella plus quam civilia idque ob diversas in eadem doctrina opiniones suscepta non stat, quo minus doctrina Christiana funditus ex hominum memoria deleatur. Et tamen permanet et ita permanet, ut ipsi impii, qui eam ore profitentes factis negant, mori malint et quodvis belli periculum adire quam committere, ut ea priventur. Haec est nimirum vis veritatis, ut ipsa per se nullius ope adiuta, quin potius omnium summis viribus oppugnata victrix perrumpat. Hanc ob causam magister ille veritatis Iesus sola veritate et pugnavit ipse et suos pugnare docuit. Et quandiu discipuli magistrum secuti sunt, hoc est nuda veritate pugnarunt, victores extiterunt. Iidem, si quando, omissis illis spiritualibus armis, humana praesidia adhibuerunt, ecclesiae spirituale divinumque imperium humana tyrannide turpificarunt et aethereum illum veritatis splendorem crassis errorum nebulis obscurarunt.

---

* [2] Deut 4:20.
* [3] Ex 2:1-9.
* [4] Ex 2:12-15.
* [5] Ex 7:8ff.
* [6] Ex 14:5ff.

## IX

ff. 68b-69b

Quod ad secundum attinet, illud certum est, nullam unquam doctrinam fuisse, quae sic totum hominem penitus rimaretur et ipsum sibi tanquam in luce ostenderet ut doctrina Christiana. Itaque quemadmodum qui humana corpora dissecant et cum dissectione sua libros conferunt eorum, qui ea de re conscripserunt, ii facile iudicant, quinam optime conscripserint, ita qui in animorum et maxime suorum natura rimanda et exploranda ac quasi membratim dissecanda versantur eamque explorationem cum sacris literis conferunt, ii facile perspiciunt ei spiritui, quo dictante[1] conscriptae fuere sacrae literae, ita perspectam fuisse naturam hominis, ut eius cognitio nusquam aliunde sit petenda. Hoc si quis scire cupit, experiatur et seipsum in eis serio exploret operamque det, ut eis obsequatur, et dicet: Ita est, habebitque ex eis, quae sentiet et experietur, iustam causam eis quoque credendi, quae sunt extra sensus et experientiam.

Idem dico de tertio, videlicet fidelitate. Dixit Noa[2] sui temporis hominibus venturum diluvium, et venit. Dixit Abrahamo deus[3] itemque Angeli[4] Loto perituram esse Sodomam, et periit. Dixit eidem Abrahamo[5] deus eius posteros peregrinae genti servituros esse quatuor secula, deinde illinc in Chananaeam venturos, et evenit. Iacobus[6] moriens natis suis futura praedixit, et evenerunt. Praedixit Iosephus[7] Pharaonis pistori et pocillatori, quae ipsis eventura forent, et eius praedictionem eventus comprobavit. Idem Pharaoni septem hubertatis et totidem famis annos vere praenunciavit. Denique ut omnes tum veteris tum novi foederis literas perpendas, comperies [ea], quae in eis divinitus hominibus patefacta traduntur, ea semper vera extitisse et nominatim in novo foedere, quae tum de Iudaeis tum de Christianis praesignificata fuerunt, videlicet Ierosolymam[8] eversum et pedibus conculcatum iri et evangelium[9] toto orbe predicandum; item quae Paulus[10] praedixit, intraturos esse lupos graves qui non parcerent gregi futurumque ut homines deficerent a fide

---

* 1 *Dictantae* MS.
* 2 Gen 7.
* 3 Gen 18.
* 4 Gen 19.
* 5 Gen 15:13.
6 Gen. 49.
* 7 Gen 40:9ff.
8 Lk 21:24.
9 Mt 26:13.
*10 Acts 20:29.

et veritate et ultimis temporibus tales fore, quales nunc videmus esse: breviter quaecumque ibi praedicta fuerant, ea sic evenisse palam est, ut de caeteris quoque, quae adhuc vel futura vel tecta sunt, si quis dubitare potest, dignus sit, qui veritati non nisi sero credat. Neque enim verisimile est eum, qui ab orbe condito ad hunc usque diem nunquam mendax deprehensus est, nunc demum mentiri incipere, et qui semper vera dixit in eis quae nos novimus, idem mentiatur in iis quae ignoramus? Quod si quis interea pertinax incredulusque manet et quamvis de praeteritis convictus, tamen futuris non credit, suo malo non credit accidetque ei, quod ante diluvianis aut Sodomitanis caeterisve, qui non nisi sero et frustra crediderunt. Nam si quis tum demum credit diluvio futuro, cum iam incipit diluvium, frustra tum demum de arca, in qua evadat, fabricanda incipiet cogitare.

## X

ff. 69b-

Quod ad quartum attinet, videlicet effecta et experientiam, hic allegabo miracula, quae cum ad logis tum ad evangelii confirmationem edita fuere, tot et tanta tamque prodigiosa, ut nulli tam vel duri vel pertinaces homines fuerint, quin obstupuerint![1] Ipsimet Iudaei (quo hominum genere nullum unquam sub omni coelo pertinacius aut veritati minus credens extitit) Christi miraculis attoniti sunt et, cum ea negare non possent, quippe quae luce palam in omnium praesentia fierent, fatebantur equidem ab eo miracula fieri, sed in nomine Beelzebub, principis daemoniorum. Quin et multis post saeculis quidam Iudaeorum magistri, quos Rabbinos appellare solent, patres illos suos imitati, quia Christi miracula ne ipsi quidem, quamvis tanto post tempore, negare audebant, scripserunt ea edita fuisse vi nescio cuius nominis, quod Schem Hamphoras appellant, sicuti narrari perhibent a Rabino [sic] quodam Purcheto,[2] quae narratio, quamvis ridiculis alioquin fabulis impudentibusque[3] mendaciis scateat, hoc saltem habet boni, quod testatur a Christo aedita fuisse summa miracula, quod testimonium hac quidem in parte locuple-

---

[1] In margin reference to suppl. 6.

[2] Professor Julius Guttmann of the Academy of Judaism in Berlin until 1934 has kindly helped me to identify Porchetus de Salvaticis. He was a Dominican of Barcelona who published the *Victoria contra Judaeos* in 1303 (new ed. 1520). Porchetus treats of Christ's miracles according to the Jew to which Castellio refers. He relied on an earlier publication by Ramón Martín, *Pugio Fidei*. On the latter see Karl A. Kottman, *Law and Apocalypse: The Moral Thought of Luis de Léon* (1527 ?-91) The Hague: Martinus Nijhoff, 1972, pp. 20-22, p. 22 note 5 and passim.

[3] MS: *impudentibuque*.

tissimum et fide dignissimum haberi debet, quippe pro Christo dictum ab ipsius hostibus capitalissimis. Qua autem vi edita fuisse tradant, non curo. Nam mali cum sint, bene loqui nesciunt: illud satis est, quod aedita fuisse confitentur. Loquor autem de corporeis et aspectabilibus miraculis et quae ab omnibus miracula vocantur, quibus duo addam, quorum iam superius est obiter facta mentio. Primum est, quod apostoli homines tales, quales modo demonstravimus, evangelii doctrinam omni ambitioni et avaritiae et voluptati (quae tria quasi numina totus orbis colit) contrariam per totum orbem invito et repugnante ac tanquam pro aris et focis (et vere pro aris et focis, nimirum pro tribus illis quae modo dixi mundi numinibus) pugnante toto orbe tamen ita publicarunt orbique persuaserunt idque nullis prorsum humanis praesidiis armati, ut eam ad hunc usque diem nulla seculorum series, nulla hominum bella, insidiae, conatus, scelera potuerint abolere. Hoc ego miraculum quibus verbis exaggerem? Praedicat et ad miraculum usque extollit Ciceronis eloquentiam Plinius, quod Romanis ea persuadere potuerit, quae ipsorum voluptati et utilitati et honori adversarentur. Plinii verba sunt haec ex libro 7 cap. 30. "Te dicente (inquit conversa ad Ciceronem oratione) legem agrariam, hoc est alimenta sua abdicaverunt tribus: te suadente Roscio theatralis authori legis ignoverunt notatasque se discrimine sedis aequo animo tulerunt".[4] Haec Plinius de Ciceronis eloquentia, quam sane non sine causa praedicat. Neque enim illa praestari sine singulari vi dicendi potuerunt. Sed si comparentur cum iis, quae praestiterunt apostoli, frigebit Cicero et nullus fuisse videbitur. Hic enim omnibus ad dicendum praesidiis munitus, summa authoritate vir, multa fingens, multa simulans et dissimulans et auditorum animis interdum (id quod ipse de se alicubi iactat) tenebras offundens, oratione meditata, ornata, fucata Romanis persuadere potuit non equidem, ut voluptatum aut quaestus aut honoris amori in perpetuum vale dicerent (id enim ne quidem a semetipso Cicero unquam impetravit), sed ut in praesentia durante adhuc illo orationis calore aliquod decernerent, in quo ipsi sibi aliquid detrahere viderentur. At apostoli nullis ad dicendum praesidiis muniti, nulla authoritate, homunculi omnia sine ulla simulatione aut arte ex tempore dicentes oratione inculta, inornata, non meditata et, ut in quodam Psalmo[5] vocatur, puerili atque lactenti, gentibus persuaserunt, ut, quae semper habuerant charissima et pro quibus labores omnes

---

[4] Pliny, *Natural History*, Loeb Classical Library, Cambridge: Harvard University, 1942, vol. II, p. 582.

[5] Ps 8:3.

pertulerant, pericula subierant, bella gesserant, ea in perpetuum ita desererent, ut etiam nunc post tot secula, post tot tantasque rerum et regnorum mutationes, deserta iaceant. Nam Ioves, Neptuni, Mercurii et huius generis gentiles dii, quos totus orbis (excepta una gente Hebraeorum) sacris ceremoniisque colebat, in adventu apostolorum ita obsolescere coeperunt et eorum non solum cultis aboleri, verum etiam celebrata tantopere creditaque oracula obmutescere, ut nunc ne quidem apud eas nationes, quae temporis spacio depravatae a Christi doctrina defecerunt, illorum usquam vestigia appareant, sed solum Iovam Hebraeorum deum (id quod olim praedixerat vates Esaias[6]) omnes nationes agnoscant. Fuit nimirum illa divina vis orationis et vere ignearum linguarum authore et in illis loquente sancto spiritu, quarum linguarum ardori nihil potuit resistere. Accedebant et illa, quae diximus miracula, quae eiusmodi erant, ut divina vi illa fieri omnes fateri cogerentur. Nam sine miraculis profecto illa facta non fuerunt. Aut si quis miracula abfuisse contendet, is miraculum fateri cogetur omnium vel maximum, nisi forte miraculum non fuit illa, quae diximus, mundo sine miraculis persuadere et ita regnorum gentiumque religiones evertere, ut nova forma inducta alius quodammodo mundus esse videatur.

Alterum miraculum est (de quo et ante diximus et suo loco deinceps, si volet deus, accuratius disseremus) animorum mutatio, quae doctrinam hanc et tunc consequebatur et hodie etiam nunc consequitur in iis, qui vere in Christum credunt, sed quae mutatio non itidem ut externa illa miracula ostendi potest. Ut enim quid sit amor solus amans novit, ita quid sit haec animorum mutatio et, ut in sacris literis[7] appellari solet, novus homo novaque creatura solis iis notum est, in quibus inest, nec verbis ullis sic exprimi potest, ut ab eo, qui non gustaverit, sentiatur. Sed illud ad testimonium satis est, quod ii quoque, in quibus ea non inest, tamen eam in aliis inesse ex ipsorum operibus possunt animadvertere. Igitur, ut rem concludam, postquam doctrina Christiana constans et sui semper similis est et ea dicit, quae suae cuiusque conscientiae testimonio comprobentur, et fidelis ab omnique fraude aliena est et operum magnitudine et admirabilitate caeteras omnes doctrinas tantum superat, quanto nocte dies clarior est, sic statuo, huic doctrinae certo et sine ulla dubitatione esse credendum.

---

* [6] Is 55:5.

* [7] Eph 4:24, II Cor 5:17 and passim.

## XI

ff. 71b-73

Sed hic existunt tria...,[1] quorum unum est quod in sacris literis insunt quaedam, quae absurda et dei maiestatem parum decentia esse videantur. Cuiusmodi est, quod de Mose[2] narratur, intrasse eum in cavum saxi et a deo fuisse manu coopertum atque ita demum praeteriisse deum et a Mose a tergo, non a fronte fuisse visum. Item quod praecepit deus[3] Israelitis, ut sibi bestias immolarent carnemque torrerent, ut eius nidor ad illius nares[4] suavis perveniret, quasi ipse nidore carnis pasceretur. Idem dico de tabernaculo, templo, vestibus et ceremoniis, quae deus sic praecepit, quasi is humano more delectaretur et, ut paucis absolvam, de omnibus, in quibus inesse videtur aliquid absurditatis.

Alterum est, quod videntur alicubi sacrae literae ipsae secum pugnare, tum in historiis tum in sententiis.

Ex quo deinde nascitur tertium, quod earum interpretes ipsi quoque tum verbis tum scriptis ita non solum diversa, verum etiam saepe pugnantia docent et tamen omnia sacrarum literarum authoritate tuentur, ut saepe quid sequendum sit dubitent homines nec mali nec imperiti.

Ad quorum primum sic respondeo. Fieri videmus tum natura tum arte quaedam, quae si per se consideres, foeda ineptaque videbuntur. Eorundem finem si perpendas, iudicabis et optime fieri et sapientissime, nisi eris et naturae et arti inimicissimus. Nam primum ipsa natura quomodo gignit et alit hominem? Concipitur homo in utero foeminae inter stercoris et lotii conceptacula collocato. Ibi alitur augescitque spacio circiter novem mensium sanguine menstruo, hoc est re haud scio an omnium, quae sunt, sub omni coelo immundissima, nasciturum deinde antecedit liquor quidam haud sane mundissimus, in quo foetus ipse in utero mersus iacuit. Prodit tandem per obscoenissimam foeminae partem involutus infans membrana quadam sordida (secundas appellant) ipse lividus et totus obsitus immundicie. Haec est generatio, haec origo, hi natales hominis, in quibus nihil nisi meras sordes foeditatemque videas, ut, si nihil aliud consideres, naturam impuram stultamque esse iudices. At si finem inspicias, quid sit homo, quam nobile et divinum cuique rei destinatum animal, tum vero iudices nihil illa naturae stultitia cogitari posse sapientius, quae ex tantis sordibus tantam mundiciem tam mirifice

---

[1] Castellio has cancelled the sentence *quae nonnullus offendunt et ut de sacris literis subdubitent faciunt*. In margin reference to suppl. 19.

* [2] Ex 33:18-23.

* [3] Ex 29:17-18.

[4] We replaced *aures* in the MS with *nares* since the former makes no sense here.

sciat elicere. Quid deinde natus homo, quomodo alitur? Primum demissus in ventriculum cibus sic acescit et corrumpitur, ut, si eum deinde forte ex ventriculo eiectum (id quod fit vomitu) videas, nauseam pariat. Quinimo, si quis uno in catino misceat, quicquid uno cibatu cibi potionisque sumere solemus, videlicet lactucam, nasturcium, acetum, oleum, ova, intritam, panem, vinum, lac, carnem tum elixam tum tostam, orizam, sinapi, omphacium,[5] omasum, ficus, uvas, pira, mala, butirum, caseum et huius generis alia, vix gustare sustineamus idque immundum iudicemus. Et tamen his omnibus infercitur ventriculus ac postquam acuerunt eis natura corpus alit atque auget. Quinetiam postquam probe concoctus est in ventriculo cibus et ex eo suxit ipse ventriculus, quantum opus fuit, aperitur hiatque sua sponte inferiore meatu et in intestina exoneratur ac protinus, qui fuerat in ore, cibus in ventriculo chylus, ut vocant, in intestinis est stercus. Quod stercus deinde ab innumeris venulis ad corporis alimoniam exugitur. Hae sunt naturae ut videntur sordes, in quibus incredibilem sapientiam sapientissimi quique deprehendunt. Quid illud? Quod eodem ore et mundissimos[6] cibos mandit homo et non mundissimum sputum expuit? Iisdem naribus et odores suavissimos olfacit et sordidam pituitam eiicit? Iisdem virilibus et hominem gignit et lotium emittit, iisdem manibus et obscoena corporis absterget et mundissima opera tractat nec ab ullo horum abhorret? Quid, quod cibis vescitur, qui alioquin videri possint immundissimi: ranis, erinaceis, limacibus, testudinibus, suilla et quidem rostro suis. Et haec omnia convertit ad utilitatem suam. Nonne in his omnibus cernitur naturae sapientissima quaedam stultitia mundissimaque spurcities? Quid de arte dicam? Nonne fimo et eo immundissimo agrum stercorat agricola et hac arte laetissimas fruges consequitur? Nonne terram sulcando deformat et hac arte formosissimam segetem elicit? Nonne vineam putando ac circumcidendo feraciorem efficit? Quid medicus? Nonne medicinis corpus perturbat doloresque ciet, ut sanet dolores? Nonne aegroti sanguinem elicit, ut sanguinem reddat puriorem? Quid multis? Dies me deficiet, si huius generis omnia pergam enumerare. Quod si talia et natura et hominis ars sapienter facit eiusque sapientiam ex fine percipientes suspicimus et praedicamus, debemus in dei quoque doctrinae operibus eodem uti iudicio neque offendi, si qua sunt, quae speciem habeant vel absurditatis vel insipientiae. Nam multa sunt, quae prima fronte stulti-

---

[5] MS: *omphacinum*.

[6] MS: *mundicissimos*.

tiam prae se ferunt. Eadem in recessu immensam tegunt sapientiam, iis notam, qui res non obiter aut leviter, sed penitus acriterque considerant.

## XII ff. 73, 73b

Quod ad secundum attinet, videlicet discordiam aut etiam repugnantiam quae videtur esse sacrarum literarum, sciendum est eam discordiam aut verborum esse aut rerum. Ac de verbis primum dicemus. Verborum discordia aut librariorum est aut authorum. Librariorum discordiam ostendunt varia exemplaria, in quibus idem locus aliter atque aliter legitur, sicut multi compluribus in locis annotarunt. Sed ea discordia offendere nos non debet: primum, quia authorum non est, sed librariorum, quorum culpam praestare authores nec possunt nec debent, deinde, quia plerumque eiusmodi discordia unius aut alterius verbi est, in quo nihil laeditur sententia, aut, si quid forte laeditur, aliunde corrigi potest, quandoquidem authorum sententiae non semper ex singulis verbis superstitiosius observandis, sed plerumque ex orationis tenore aut similium locorum observatione aut mentis ratiocinatione sunt investigandae, sicuti suo loco, si deus permiserit, dicemus. Ac tales librariorum discordiae etiam in profanis authoribus inveniuntur, ut in Platone, in Aristotele, in Homero, in Cicerone, in Virgilio et caeteris. Quamvis enim summo in precio semper fuerint apud gentiles hi authores summaque cum diligentia describi soliti, tamen caveri non potuit, quin multa scripturae menda et discrepantiae annorum longitudine obrepserint. Nec tamen ea res studiosos deterret nec facit, ut, qui libri Ciceronis habentur, ii aut non boni aut non Ciceronis esse ducantur. Sicut enim detorti aliquot aut etiam decussi arboris[1] ramuli agricolam non offendunt nec arborem vitiant, quippe quae ramorum infinita multitudine sic abundet, ut tantulam iacturam alibi sine ullo detrimento resarciat, ita, si in authore pauculis in locis simile quidpiam usu venit, id nec bonum lectorem offendit nec authorem vitiat. Manet enim ipsa stirps et, ut ita loquar, corpus authoris, ex cuius perpetuo tenore[2] dictorumque hubertate percipi possunt sine ullo detrimento fructus pleni.

## XIII ff. 73b, 74

Sed existunt hoc loco scrupuli duo, quorum prior est quorundam, qui putant non esse verisimile passurum unquam fuisse deum, ut vel unum

---

[1] *Arboris* not in Wetstein (henceforth quoted Wet).

[2] The concept of *tenor* plays an important part in the history of music from the 13th to the 16th century inclusive of Luther. See Grove, *Dictionary of Music*.

verbum in sacris literis corrumperetur. Itaque ne syllabam quidem in eis unquam vitiatam fuisse aut periisse existimant. Alter est eorum qui metuunt, ne, si hoc concessum fuerit, labascat sacrarum literarum authoritas, ut, si de pauculis quibusdam verbis dubitetur, toti[1] etiam authores in dubium vocentur. Ad quorum primum ego respondeo nusquam promisisse deum sese ita librariorum manus esse recturum, ut in sacris literis describendis nunquam errent, quin ne illud quidem promisit cauturum se, ne ulli sacri libri pereant. Itaque peto, ut isti dicti sui verisimilitudinem probent. Nam et errasse et hodie etiamnum errare librarios videmus et librorum sacrorum aliquot (quos certe maiori curae deo fuisse quam paucula quaedam verba credendum est) videmus temporum iniuria intercidisse. Quod si dicent deo curae esse sacras literas, quippe quarum ipse sit author, respondebo eidem deo etiam maiori curae esse suos natos hoc est suum populum, cuius causa dictaverit sacras literas. Quod si tamen suum populum aliquando non equidem perire (id enim semper cavit), sed certe sic mutilari passus est, ut ex multitudine, quae esset arena numerosior, tantum reliquiae superessent, mirum videri non debet, si in sacris literis mutilationem aliquam fieri permisit. Quod si hoc et fieri potuisse ratio ostendit et factum esse experientia docet, causam non video, cur hoc cuiquam scrupulum iniicere debeat.

Ad secundum scrupulum hoc respondeo: non esse scriptorum authoritatem in paucis quibusdam verbis, quae vitiari detrahive potuerunt, sed in perpetuo orationis tenore,[2] qui mansit incorruptus, positam. Itaque quemadmodum Cicero apud sui studiosos nihilo minoris est authoritatis propter paucula quaedam mutilata aut depravata quam esset, si id non accidisset, ita debet et sacrarum literarum authoritati nihil detrahi, si quid in eis tale quale ostendimus contigit.

Quod ad eum verborum discrepantiam attinet, quae authorum est, non librariorum, ne ea quidem cuiquam debet esse scrupulosa. Sicut enim in testimoniis, sic et in authoribus nihil refert, quibus verbis quaeque res efferatur, dum modo vere et uti est efferatur. Debent, enim ut authores rebus, sic et authoribus verba servire, non imperare.

---

[1] MS: *totis*. it remained in the text from a sentence Castellio later cancelled: *totis etiam authoribus dubitare necesse est.*

[2] See previous chapter n. 2.

## XIV

ff. 74b-75b

Sed in rerum discrepantia maior existit difficultas et de qua alioquin tacere quam loqui mallem ad vitandam vel infirmiorum offensionem vel iniquiorum invidiam, quae in hoc argumento vix aut[1] ne vix quidem videtur posse vitari. Verum quia sine huius explicatione instituto meo satisfacere et latentem in rebus ad conscientiarum[2] tranquillitatem necessariis veritatem in lucem[3] eruere non possum, audendum est. Interea ab infirmioribus peto, ut rem septies perpendant, antequam iudicent. Multa enim prima fronte, quia nova sunt, displicent, quae postea diligentius considerata placent et probantur. Igitur primum omnium illud sciendum est, in sacris literis quatuor esse orationis genera[4] de quibus quia loquitur obiter Paulus, eius verba ex priore ad Corinthios epistola hic subiiciam: "Alioquin, fratres", inquit, "si ego vos alienis linguis allocutum veniam, quid vobis prodero, nisi insit in oratione mea patefactio aut cognitio aut vaticinatio aut doctrina".[5] Patefactionem appellat, si quid homini divinitus patefactum est. Vaticinatio est alioquin eadem cum patefactione, nisi quod coniuncta est cum mentis agitatione atque permotione. Cognitionem interpretor eam, quae ex visis aut auditis efflorescit.[6] Doctrinam appellari a Paulo arbitror eam, quam homini literae et ratio conferunt.[7]

Certe etiam, si illa nec Paulus nec quisquam alius dixisset, res ipsa per se vera est, videlicet haec orationis quatuor esse genera sacrorum authorum.[8] Sic enim scripserunt, ut alioquin[9] loqui inter sese de rebus divinis soliti erant. Neque enim alia mens aut scientia aut spiritus erat scribentium quam loquentium, nec aliud sunt illorum scripta quam

---

[1] Wet: *ac*.

[2] Copy: *Conscientiae*. See *Preface* p. 3.

[3] *In lucem* not in Wet.

[4] The theory distinguishing four levels of interpreting the Bible played an important part in scolastic theology.

5 I Cor 14:6.

[6] This recalls Hugo of St. Victor, *De Sacramentis* I, 10, 3, 1980: "Cognitionem autem hic intelligimus scientiam rerum non illam quae ex praesentia ipsarum comprehenditur, sed quae ex auditu solo percipitur et ex verborum significatione manifestatur.

[7] In the MS are the following sentences which Castellio later cancelled: "*Ut est Pauli eius ad Galatas de legis operibus et fide et justificatione disputatio, in qua sacrarum literarum authoritate rationibusque nititur. Hanc illic esse mentem Pauli nemo, opinor, negabit. Aut si quis tamen negabit, afferat sane, per me licet veriorem; interea mihi concedat, etiamsi* Paulus illa non dixisset..." Wet keeps the sentence Hanc-negabit in the text. This was not Castellio's intention which is indicated by what follows. Copy has the sentence too.

[8] Wet: *scriptorum*.

[9] Wet: *alioqui*.

ipsorum cum absentibus aut[10] posteris colloquia. Id quod planum facere facile est. Nam patefactionis exemplum est in Paulo, qui se evangelium non ab ullo[11] homine, sed Iesu Christo patefaciente didicisse dicit ad Galatas.[12] Vaticinationis in Agabo,[13] sed ea quidem, quatenus mentis habet agitationem, ad institutum nostrum non pertinet. Siquidem illa mentis agitatio et ut vocatur vatum bacchatio non literarum, sed actionis et gestus est, qui in scriptis cerni non possunt. Cognitionis exemplum est in Lucae et Iohannis historiis, qui narrant hic, quae ipse vidit et nonnulla ex parte gessit, ille, quae ex viris fide dignis cognovit. Doctrinae exemplum est in Pauli ad Galatas[14] disputatione de legis operibus et fidei iustificatione, in qua sacrarum literarum authoritate rationibusque nititur.[15] Quae cum ita sint, nobis ita versandum est in sacris authoribus, ut haec tria, videlicet patefactionem et[16] cognitionem et doctrinam, non confundamus, sed quae patefactione tradita sunt, ea pro oraculis, quae cognitione, pro testimoniis, quae doctrina, pro hominum sententiis habeamus. Ita fiet, ut tantum cuique rei, quantum ipsius natura postulat, tribuentes eas perturbationes evitemus, quae ex huiusce distinctionis ignoratione nascentes non nisi eadem cognita et admissa tolli possunt. Igitur, si quae occurrent in sacris literis vel discrepantiae vel repugnantiae,[17] diligenter considerandum erit, utrum eae sint in oraculis an in testimoniis an in hominum sententiis.[18] Nam si erunt in oraculis oportebit circumstantias omnes et locorum et temporum et personarum et occasionum atque causarum sedulo perpendere, ut in ea, quae videbitur[19] discordia, concordiam inveniamus. Quod si ne sic quidem invenerimus, tribuendum id erit ignorantiae nostrae et credendum aliquid ibi esse nobis ignotum, quod si perciperemus, summam ibi concordiam esse videremus. Nam spiritus veritatis, qui oraculorum illorum[20] author est, non pugnat ipse secum nec in eum vel oblivio vel

---

[10] Copy: *ac*.

[11] Copy: *ab alio ullo homine*.

[12] Gal 1:1.

[13] Acts 21:11.

[14] Gal 2:16.

[15] Wet: *utitur*.

[16] *et* not in Wet.

[17] See Erasmus, *Methodus* (Introduction to the New Testament, 1516), esp. p. 4a.

[18] See Matthias Flacius, *Novum Testamentum, Jesu Christi, Filii Dei ex versione Erasmi*, glossary 640: "authorem scripti nosse multum prodest. Inde enim scio, an fuerit singulare organon Dei quod errare plane non potuerit, cuiusmodi fuerunt Apostoli et Prophetae...".

[19] Wet: *videbatur*.

[20] Wet: *istorum*.

error vel ignorantia ulla cadit.[21] Sin erunt in testimoniis, non oportebit nos minus esse superstitiosos[22] neque singula verba curiosius observare atque inter sese componere, sed ea concordia, quae est in summa rei, contentos esse. Nam si duorum aut trium testimonio credi leges tum profanae tum sacrae[23] recte iubent, cum tamen eiusmodi testimonia raro (praesertim si de re sunt paulo vel prolixiore vel implicatiore) in singulis verbis concordent, etiam si testes sint alioquin[24] viri probi et veraces, debemus in sacrorum authorum testimoniis illam legum[25] vel prudentiam vel aequitatem sine morositate imitari. Alioquin nostra morositate nihil aliud consequemur quam quod aut nulli authores sive sacri sive profani nobis satisfacient aut eas minutias conciliare conantes, quae conciliari nequeunt, ineptos nos ne dicam ridiculos praebebimus.

Ac quod dixi de testimoniis, idem dico de hominum sententiis, videlicet tantum eis tribuendum esse, quantum sanctorum hominum dictis tribui debet vel quantum ipsimet sibi tribuunt, non tamen, ut eodem cum oraculis loco habeantur,[26] cum ne ipsi quidem hoc a nobis postulent.

## XV

ff. 76-77b

Non dubito quin hoc loco nonnulli offendantur. Clamabunt esse blasphemiam. Sacras enim literas esse divino afflatu conscriptas neque hominum, sed dei arbitrio aeditas, quarum si vel unum verbum in dubium vocetur periculum sit, ne cadat earum authoritas.[1] A quibus ego postulo,[2] ne ante de dictis meis iudicent quam ea rite ac diligenter perpenderint. Ego sacris literis non minus tribuo quam quisquam alius et secundum earum doctrinam et vivo hactenus et, ut spero, ad finem usque vivam. Ac deum precor, ut me potius[3] ex hac vita tollat quam ut a tam sancta ac divina doctrina vivum deflectere patiatur. Sed quorundam superstitioni hominum alioquin, ut ego existimo, non improborum

---

[21] Copy: *Vel oblivio vel ignorantia vel ullus error.* In margin reference to suppl. 2.

[22] Copy: *Scrupolosos.*

[23] Deut 19:15.

[24] Wet: *alioqui.*

[25] Wet: *legem.*

[26] Wet: *habeamus*

[1] See Calvin, *Institutes*, Corp. Ref. XXIX, p. 631: "verbum suum mandari scripto et consignari voluit... addere vero ac minuere nefas illis est... and p. 637: "Vetuit autem, ne quid verbo suo adderet, ne quid ex eo detraheret".

[2] Copy: *postulabo.*

[3] Wet: *potius me.*

obviam eundum puto, qui, dum sic singula verba, ubi nihil necesse est,[4] mordicus urgent, perturbant imprudentes[5] ecclesiam opinionum dissensionibus, quae qua alia via componi possint, nondum videre quivi. Et tentatae sunt idque et[6] iamdiu et a multis multae viae. Ego vero sententiam meam et rationibus et ipsarum de quibus agimus sacrarum literarum authoritate planam, ut spero, faciam, deinde, si quid est in ea incommodi, conferam cum dissentientis sententiae incommodis, quae si maiora esse evicero, postulabo, ut ea sententia, quae et vera est et minus habet incommodi, non repudietur. Quod si impetravero, viam, ut spero, habebimus ad dirimendas graves et perniciosas controversias.

Ac primum quod ad rationem attinet, illud mihi negabit nemo, solere legatos, quae a principe mandata acceperunt, ea ut principis mandata exponere, quae in dubium vocari[7] non liceat. Quae vero ipsi sua sponte dicunt, ea ipsos (si boni fidique sunt legati) non principi, sed sibi ascribere nec eandem his quam illis authoritatem poscere. Deinde illud constare debet, Christum ea hominibus conferre solitum bona, non quae iam a natura haberent ipsi, sed quibus carerent. Quod si, quod iam habebant a natura bonum, etiam si id non esset undiquaque[8] perfectum, tamen quia eius usus eis commode constabat, id ipse nec novum conferebat nec melius aut perfectius reddebat. Itaque si quando claudum sanabat, tantum clauditatem sanabat. Linguam quidem aut aures aut oculos aut os claudi nec sanabat (quippe iam sana) nec corrigebat aut perfectiora reddebat, quippe quibus iam alioquin commode uti poterant, quod idem et de caeteris dictum volo. Quod si in corpore id faciebat, idem in animo quoque eum facere ut mihi concedatur postulo, cum sit in animo eadem et causa et ratio, quae in corpore. Ipsemet pronunciavit sanos[9] non egere medico, sed aegrotos.[10] Id quod de animorum morbis dixit, in quibus idem quod in corporum morbis factitabat. Quare sic statuamus, Christum homini ea conferre, quibus homo caret. Quae vero alioquin iam habet homo, non item. Igitur ut haec duo, videlicet quae tum de legatis tum de morborum sanationibus dixi, ad institutum nostrum accommodentur, haec dico. Erant Apostoli (ut ab his potissimum exemplum petamus) Christi legati, a quo quae mandata acceperant, ea ut Christi mandata atque oracula bene et fideliter (quippe sancti

[4] Copy: *erat.*
[5] Wet: *imprudenter.*
[6] *et* not in Wet.
[7] Wet: *vocare.*
[8] Wet: *undequaque.*
[9] Wet: *sani.*
[10] Mk 2:17.

iustique viri) vel iis, qui ipsos praesentes audiebant, verbis vel absentibus et porro nobis scriptis exposuerunt ac de iis dubitare non licet. Sin aliquid non a Christo mandatum, sed ipsi sua sponte dicebant, id non Christo aut spiritui sancto, sed sibi ascribebant.

Iam cum Christus eorum opera usus fuerit, non dubium est, quin eos instruxerit rebus ad id munus necessariis, sed sic instruxerit, ut, si quid iam alioquin habebant, id non dederit. Exempli gratia erat eis ad loquendum opus lingua: eam nemini eorum dedit, quippe qui[11] iam haberent. Erat opus auribus ad auditorum verba audienda: ne[12] eas quidem dedit. Erat et pedibus opus ad iter: neque eos dedit. Denique nihil eis dedit, quod iam haberent. At peregrinarum linguarum scientiam, qua et opus erat ad docendos populos et ipsi carebant, dedit, et miraculorum potestatem contulit et eis ad percipienda oracula mentem aperuit; denique omnia illis ad munus illud[13] necessaria, quibus alioquin carebant, contulit. Iam cum et memoriae et intellectus vim a natura haberent, si qua[14] erant vel memoriae vel intellectus ope scribenda, Christus eis ad illa scribenda memoriam aut intellectum non dabat, non magis profecto quam oculos aut manus aut chartam aut atramentum, quippe cum omnia illa iam haberent, sed ipsi sua memoria suoque ingenio illa scribebant. Quod si cuius eorum erat vel memoria vel ingenium infirmius, ei poterat in scribendo idem accidere, quod in loquendo et quod caeteris bonis viris interdum accidit, videlicet ut ei dictum aliquod excideret infirmioris vel memoriae vel iudicii. Scripsisse autem eos non omnia patefaciente spiritu sancto, sed quaedam ope memoriae, alia ingenii, patet ex ipsorum[15] scriptis. Nam quod ad memoriam attinet, didicerunt Evangelistae evangelium non patefactione, ut Paulus, sed vel quia ipsi adfuerunt, ut Matthaeus et Iohannes, vel ex iis, qui adfuerant, cognoverunt, ut Marcus et Lucas, id quod ipsimet testantur. Si quidem et Iohannes in Evangelio testatur se visa testari et[16] idem in primae epistolae suae initio tradit se, quod et oculis viderit et auribus audiverit et manibus palpaverit, id testari.[17] Ex quo apparet eum dicere testimonium, ad quod dicendum nihil ei, sicuti Paulo, opus erat patefactione.[18] Lucas quoque testatur se ex aliis audita scribere,[19] id

[11] Wet: *quam.*
[12] Wet, copy: *nec.*
[13] Wet: *istud.*
[14] Copy: *quae.*
[15] Wet: *eorum.*
[16] *et* not in Wet.
[17] Jn 19:35.
[18] I Jn 1.
[19] Lk 1:1-2.

quod profecto non dixisset si evangelium sicuti Paulus patefactione cognovisset. Quod idem et de caeteris duobus, videlicet Matthaeo et Marco, censendum est.

Item quod ad ingenium attinet, scribit disertis verbis[20] Paulus in priore ad Corinthios epistola: "Coniugibus praecipio non ego, sed dominus"[21] etc. et mox: "Caeteris ego dico, non dominus".[22] Et paulo post: "De virginibus autem Domini praeceptum non habeo, sed consilium do, ut qui is sim, cui Domini clementia fidentem esse datum sit".[23] Hic certe palam ostendit non omnia se ex Domini praecepto scribere, sed in nonnullis suam sententiam dicere.

## XVI

ff. 77b

Nunc dicenda sunt quae contra adduci possunt incommoda. Dicet enim aliquis periculum esse, ne hac ratione detrahatur authoritas sacris literis neve eis minus fidei[1] adhibeatur. Ad quod ego respondeo etiam, si ita esset, non iccirco non esse vera quae dixi, aut, si quis falsa putat, refellat. Quod si vera sunt, ut certe sunt, eis locus dari debet praesertim propter ea, quae suo loco dicentur. Nunc non ita est meo quidem iudicio. Non enim sita est sacrorum scriptorum authoritas in paucis quibusdam locis scrupulosius ad calculos revocandis, sed in ipsius doctrinae tenore[2] atque corpore, quemadmodum supra demonstravimus.[3] Itaque quemadmodum legati authoritas sarta tecta manet, etiamsi dicas eum interdum quaedam dicere non iussu principis, ita et sacrorum scriptorum authoritas nihil diminuitur, si de eis idem dicas, quod de seipso dicere Paulum paulo ante demonstravimus.[4] Et vero cur illis plus tribuamus[5] quam ipsimet sibi, nullam causam video. Quin id sine vitio fieri non posse puto. Ipse Paulus, quantum sibi et caeteris tribuendum sit, non obscure docet, dum ad Corinthios ita loquitur: "Sic de nobis existiment homines, ut de Christi ministris et divinorum arcanorum dispensatoribus".[6] Hoc qui

---

[20] Wet: *diserte* in place of *disertis verbis*.
[21] I Cor 7:10.
[22] I Cor 7:12.
[23] I Cor 7:25.

[1] Wet: *fides*.
[2] See ch. XII, n. 2.
[3] See ch. XV.
[4] See above ch. XV.
[5] Copy: *tribueremus*.
[6] I Cor 4:1.

tribuit illis, satis tribuit, etiam si illorum singula verba non sic ubique[7] ad vivum resecet. Equidem quid aliis accidat, nescio: ego hac sententia tanto magis in illorum[8] authoritate acquiesco atque confirmor, dum eos video ita rei et hominum saluti fuisse intentos, ut verborum non usque adeo magnam habuerint rationem, quae res illorum testimonia tanto ostendit esse veriora. Qui enim sibi sunt veritatis conscii, ii de verbis minus laborant. Qui vero mentiuntur, ii summam adhibere solent diligentiam, ut orationis arteficio et consensu mendacium occultent.

Sed dicet rursus aliquis: At Petrus docet "non hominis voluntate editum unquam fuisse oraculum, sed sancti spiritus instinctu[9] locutos fuisse vates".[10] Item Paulus "omne scriptum esse divinitus inspiratum".[11] Ad quod ego respondeo de oraculis illa dici, sicut ipsimet testantur, sed non ideo tolli illam, quam supra ex ipsomet Paulo citavi, distinctionem oraculorum et testimoniorum et humanarum sententiarum. Atque haec sunt quae incommoda adversus nostram sententiam videntur adduci posse.

Nunc quae in adversaria sententia sint[12] incommoda, videamus. Primum illud est, quod, qui sic verba consectantur et omnia ad unguem componere conantur, illud ipsum, quod conantur, assequi non possunt atque ita in illud ipsum, quod vitant, malum incurrunt: videlicet ut suspectam reddant scriptorum authoritatem aut, si assequuntur, ita assequuntur,[13] ut, an ita sit, valde dubitari queat. Ac prioris exemplum esto in verbis Coenae Domini, ubi Matthaeus Christum sic facit loquentem: "Hic est sanguis meus novi foederis pro multis effundendus ad veniam peccatorum".[14] Marcus[15] item eodem modo, nisi quod pauciora scribit. At Lucas sic: "Hoc poculum est novum foedus, quod fit per meum sanguinem, quod est pro vobis effundendum".[16] Atqui Christus illa verba et semel et uno modo pronunciavit. Quod si pronunciavit ut habentur in Matthaeo, non pronunciavit ut habentur in Luca. Et tamen, si uterque illa verba scripsit dictante spiritu sancto et dictavit spiritus sanctus non solum sententiam, sed etiam ipsamet verba Christi (sicuti

[7] Wet: *ubique non sic.*
[8] Wet: *eorum.*
[9] Wet: *impulso.*
[10] II Pet 1:21.
[11] II Tim 3:16.
[12] Copy: *sunt.*
[13] Copy: *ita assequantur.*
*[14] Mt 26:28.
*[15] Mk 14:24.
[16] Lk 22:20.

certe potuit et, si potuit, debuit, quandoquidem id praestabat), oportet illorum scripta inter sese nullo verbo discrepare. Quod cum non sit, fatendum est, velimus nolimus, quocumque nos vertamus, illa verba non sic, ut isti[17] volunt, posse componi. Alterius[18] exemplum est in narratione de Petri negatione Christi. Nam ter negaturum esse Christum ipse Christus praedixit et ter[19] negasse singuli Evangelistae quatuor narrant.[20] Ex quo mihi valde fit verisimile eum non plus quam ter negasse. Nam si saepius negasset, omnino ex quatuor evangelistis unus aliquis commemorasset neque tam constanter omnes in eo numero[21] consentirent. Atqui Andreas Osiander, homo diligens et doctus, in Harmonia[22] sua, dum narrationem hanc componere nititur, Christum facit octies a Petro negatum. Quod quam verisimile sit, viderint alii: mihi quidem id nemo facile persuaserit.

Alterum in ea opinione incommodum est, quod, qui falsam aliquam sententiam tuentur (id quod a multis fieri in tot dissensionibus omnes confitebuntur), si forte locum aliquem in sacris authoribus nacti sunt, cuius verba ipsorum sententiae patrocinari videantur,[23] eum mordicus retinent et, quia sic author locutus est, sic omnino esse pertinacissime contendunt nec ullam moderatam interpretationem admittunt. Quod si alios locos illi contrarios adducas, nihil agas. Exempla de multis afferam unum aut alterum. Scripsit Paulus ad Romanos haec verba: "Rebeccae ex uno Isaaco, parente nostro, uterum ferenti foetibus nondum natis nec ullo bono malove functis, ut dei per electionem decretum non ex operibus, sed ex vocante ratum esset, Rebeccae, inquam, dictum est: Maior serviet minori quemadmodum scriptum est: Iacobum amavi, Esaum vero odio habui".[24] Haec Pauli verba nonnulli ad calculum revocantes statuunt quosdam deo invisos esse antequam natos. Quod si dicas verba illa "Iacobum amavi, Esaum vero odio habui"[25] nec Rebeccae nec foetibus[26] nondum natis fuisse dicta, sed a Malachia multis post seculis scripta, sicuti manifestissimum est, nihil proficias. Pauli enim verba urgentes suam sententiam mordicus tuentur hoc unum

---

[17] Copy: *illi.*
[18] Wet: *alterum.*
[19] Copy: *se.*
*[20] Mk 14:66.
[21] Wet: *in uno numero.*
[22] *Harmoniae evangelicae*, libri IV, authore Andrea Osiandro, Basel 1561, p. 128.
[23] Copy: *videntur.*
[24] Rom 9:10-13.
*[25] Mal 1:2ff.
[26] Wet: *fratribus.*

spectantes:[27] Paulus sic[28] allegavit; ergo ita[29] est, quamvis repugnante historia, repugnantibus tot annis, repugnante omni ratione. Alterum exemplum est in eodem loco. Scripsit ibi Paulus[30] ea de Pharaonis induratione, ut statuere videatur Pharaonem et porro caeteros reiectaneos mera dei nullo ipsorum peccato impulsi voluntate indurari et ad poenam fuisse nominatim conditos. Hic qui in ea sunt sententia, urgent verba Pauli: sic Paulus dixit, ergo sic est. Quod si et argumenta et ipsiusmet Pauli alios locos et aliorum authorum quam voles plurimos contra afferas, nihilo plus agas quam si des operam, ut cum ratione insanias.

Haec sunt incommoda quae affert illa sententia, magna sane et digna, quibus obviam, si fieri potest, eatur. Quare sic statuamus in sacris literis non eodem loco habenda esse hominum vel testimonia vel sententias,[31] quo dei oracula.

## XVII

ff. 79-80b

Hactenus sacrarum literarum authoritatem constituimus et eas veraces esse et, quo pacto veraces sint, ostendimus et in eo quidem faciles, ut spero, et assentientes habituri sumus auditores, excepta fortassis illa, quam ex Paulo adduximus, distinctione oraculorum et testimoniorum et sententiarum,[1] in qua fieri poterit, ut aliqui praebeant se difficiliores. Ita enim comparatum est, ut, quae hactenus hominibus incognita fuerunt, ea principio aegre admittantur, quamvis sint verissima, Nam assueti homines veteri vino, quemadmodum docet Christus, novum non protinus probant magisque vetere delectantur.[2] Sed audendum aliquid est, modo verum, si iuvare homines volumus. Alioquin si eamdem cum iis, qui nihil hominibus profuerunt, rationem perpetuo sequemur, hominibus non magis quam illi proderimus. Fit enim hic, quod in morbis: ut, si maiorum remedia frustra fuere, alia tentanda sint aut de sanatione desperandum. Fecit hoc nostro tempore medicorum industria, qui, cum maiores morbum Neapolitanum sanare nequivissent, nova remedia idque alia super alio excogitarunt, donec tandem eius sanandi rationem invenerunt. Vidit hoc Isocrates quoque, qui in Euagora[3] eos reprehendens, qui

[27] *Pauli-spectantes* not in copy.
[28] Wet: *ita*.
[29] Copy: *sic*.
[30] Rom 9:17-19.
[31] MS: *sentias*.

[1] Copy: *humanarum sententiarum*.
* [2] Lk 5:39.
[3] vol. III, pp. 4-5. Loeb Class. Library, Cambridge: Harvard University Press, 1928.

consueta mala insuetis bonis anteponunt, dicit hanc sententiam. Videmus tum artium tum caeterorum omnium incrementa fieri non per eos, qui usitatis contenti sunt, sed per eos, qui, si quid perperam comparatum est, corrigere ac mutare audent.

Restat nunc totius operis nostri pars longe et difficillima et plurimorum invidiae obnoxia, videlicet ut, postquam sacras literas optimas esse iusticiae magistras demonstravimus, in iis ipsis, quidnam sequendum sit, ostendamus. Cum enim, qui se sacrarum literarum doctores et populorum magistros profitentur, tot et tam diversis, saepe etiam pugnantibus opinionibus et sectis inter sese tam acriter vel, ut verius dicam, capitaliter et inexpiabiliter dissideant, difficile est ex tantis opinionum quasi fluctibus veritatem in tranquillum eruere et, ubi erueris, non eos, a quibus dissideas (a multis autem dissidendum omnino est), graviter offendere. Quippe ita comparatum est et ii sunt hodie mores hominum, ut opinionum dissensionem comitetur plerumque animorum quoque offensio paucique sint ea aequitate praediti, ut eos ament, qui non cum ipsis sentiunt, quod tamen fieri iubet Christiana charitas. Et sane si meae vel utilitati vel tranquillitati consulere vellem, tacerem et quasi ex tranquillo conscientiae meae portu reliquos in opinionum tempestatibus fluctuantes ac periclitantes vel dispicerem vel nullam opem ferens tantum eorum miseriam deplorarem. Sed quia me charitas alteri opem ferre, sicut alterum mihi ferre velim, iubet, faciendum est et vel cum periculo meo periclitantibus pro virili subveniendum.

Possem autem hoc in loco compendium invenire ac, quemadmodum superius Christianam doctrinam optimam esse iusticiae magistram ex eo demonstravi, quod homines reddat iustissimos, ita hic Christianarum sectarum eam esse optimam pronunciare, cui qui adhaerent eiusque disciplinae pareant, reddantur caeteris hominibus meliores. Et sane cum venerit Christus, ut Diaboli opera, hoc est peccata aboleret, quin ea doctrina, quae melius quam caeterae peccata abolet,[4] sit non solum bona, sed etiam caeteris in eo certe melior, negari non potest. Ut enim nec Satan Satanam eiicit nec mala medicina morbum sanat, ita nec mala doctrina malos mores pellit. Sed quoniam hoc sic generaliter et inexplicate dictum plerisque non satisfaceret et laborant interdum etiam bene morati homines erroribus, a quibus abesse Christianos expedit et optandum ac, si fieri potest, efficiendum est, res est altius repetenda ac dilucidius copiosiusque enucleanda.

---

* [4] I Jn 3:8.

## XVIII

ff. 80b, 81b, 82

Primum sciendum est quaedam esse, de quibus sit dubitandum, alia, quae sint citra ullam dubitationem credenda. Item quaedam esse, non dicam quae sint ignoranda, sed quae ignorari liceat et nonnumquam necesse sit, alia, quae sciri et possint et debeant. Quaenam autem ea omnia sint, declarandum est, si prius tamen dictum meum planum fecero propter quosdam, qui id fortassis negabunt. Est enim genus quoddam hominum, qui nihil dubitari, nihil nesciri volunt, omnia audacter affirmant et, si ab eis dissentias, sine ulla dubitatione damnant neque solum ipsi nihil dubitant, sed ne quidem ab aliis dubitari patiuntur et, si dubites, non dubitant Academicum[1] appellare, qui nihil certi, nihil explorati haberi posse putes. Ego vero certi et explorati plus etiam habeo quam ipsi velint. Nam, ut caetera taceam, eos in omnia affirmando et caeteros non suae opinionis homines tam audacter damnando temerarios esse certum exploratumque habeo idque, ut ipsimet quoque, quod nunc ignorant, certum exploratumque habeant, effecturum me deo volente credo, si modo eo adduci se, sicuti debent, patientur, ut deposito amore sui rem ipsam aequis animis audiant atque considerent.

Docet Salomo in Ecclesiaste suum cuiusque rei tempus esse. "Est nascendi tempus", inquit, "est et moriendi. Est serendi tempus, est et sata evellendi",[2] et caetera, quae ibi habentur. Eadem ego ratione dico: Est dubitandi tempus, est et credendi; est ignorandi tempus, est et sciendi. Sed de sciendo quidem aut credendo non est, quod pluribus disseram, cum in eo nemo, opinor, sit mihi contradicturus. At dubitandum interdum aut ignorandum aliquid, quod dixi, id vero propter contradicentes est demonstrandum, id quod et ratione faciam et authoritate. Ac dubitandi quidem ratio est haec. Incerta pro certis habere deque eis nihil dubitare et temerarium est et plenum periculi, id quod nemo negabit. Atqui incerta et adhuc incomperta quaedam sunt in religione; ergo de eis non dubitare temerarium est plenumque periculi. Esse autem incerta quaedam, quid opus est, ut planum faciam? Cum id aperte ostendant innumeri libri et disputationes contentionesque quotidianae et perpetuae summorum doctissimorumque virorum. Neque enim profecto de rebus certis exploratisque contendunt, nisi plane mente capti sunt. Quare sic statuo, de rebus incertis esse dubitandum. Authoritatem autem adducam ipsius dei, qui de lepra in Levitico praecipit, ut, si cuius in

[1] See Cicero, *De Oratore*, pp. 307, 317, 355. Loeb Class. Library, Cambridge: Harvard University, 1928.

[2] Eccles. 3:2.

corpore leprae morbus apparuerit, is ad sacerdotem adducatur et, si manifesta lepra erit, immundus pronuncietur. Sin adhuc incertum erit, an lepra sit, includatur in septem dies et, si ne tum quidem certo scietur, includatur in totidem alteros, donec tandem re probe explorata aut immundus aut mundus certo pronuncietur.[3] Hic certe de lepra tantisper dubitari iubet, donec lepram esse certo constet, id quod ab eo in una re praeceptum in omnibus eiusdem generis hoc est incertis rebus locum habere debet.

De ignorando quoque hoc dico: Ignorare nobis ea licet, quae homini non sunt ad salutem necessaria, quae multa esse nemo sapiens negabit. Atque hic citabo Christum, qui sciscitantibus post ipsius resurrectionem Apostolis, num illa tempestate Israelitis regnum instauraturus esset, respondit his verbis: "Non est vestrum tempestates aut tempora novisse, quae pater in sua potestate posuit. Sed vim accipietis spiritus sancti, qui vos invadet mihique testes eritis et Ierosolymae et in tota Iudaea ac Samaria, denique ad ultimas terras".[4] Haec Christus; quibus verbis ostendit ne Apostolorum quidem, nedum caeterorum esse omnia scire, sed suo potissimum officio incumbere. Quapropter sic statuo, esse quaedam, quae ignorari liceat.

Quod autem interdum dubitandum esse doceo, id non sine magna causa facio. Video enim non minus malorum ex non dubitando, ubi dubitari debet, existere quam ex non credendo, ubi credi debet. Exempla sunt in promptu. Saulus,[5] cum apud eum a calumniatoribus accusaretur David, quod ipsius vitae insidiaretur regnumque affectaret, non dubitabat, quin illi vera dicerent eamque ob causam Davidem insontem petebat ad necem. Idem David[6] Sibae, Mephibosethi famulo, herum suum item calumnianti, quod regnum affectaret, non dubitavit credere eique heri, hominis innocentissimi, facultates propterea dare. Id quod non fecisset, si de illius fide dubitasset. Iosua[7] necnon Israelitarum principes Gabaonitis temere crediderunt non consulto deo, id quod non fecissent, si dubitassent. Ipsi Israelitae tot vates et sanctos viros, denique dei filium et eius apostolos nunquam interfecissent, si dubitassent. Et Israelitarum, non Christi imitatores sive Christiani sive gentiles tot sanctorum Martyrum millia per tot iam secula nunquam interfecissent, si dubitassent. Et hodie, cum in Christianis ecclesiis sanctissimi quique passim interficiun-

[3] Lev. 13.
[4] Acts 1:7f.
[5] I Sam 26.
[6] II Sam 16.
[7] Josh 9.

tur, si Christiani de facto suo dubitarent, nunquam tot tam nefanda homicidia (quorum paulo post eos poenitere necesse erit) perpetrarent.

## XIX

ff. 82-84

Nunc quaenam sunt dubia, de quibus dubitari debeat, quaenam certa, quae credi debeant, quaenam item ignorari liceat et quaenam sciri et possint et debeant, deinceps disserendum est. Dubia[1] sunt ea, quae in coniecturis posita sunt, hoc est quae habent probabilitatem, qualia sunt quae nec sensibus nec intellectu percipi possunt nec ab authoribus fide dignis tradita aut certe non aperte tradita sunt et tamen nec sensibus nec intellectui nec fide dignis authoribus repugnant, cuiusmodi est in Evangelio Iohannis haec quaestio, utrum Iohannes non sit moriturus, quia Christus de eo dixerit Petro: "Si eum volo manere, donec veniam, quid ad te?".[2] Certa autem sunt ea, quae ab authoribus fide dignis aperte ac perspicue tradita sunt nec sensibus nec intellectui nec veris authoribus repugnant. Cuiusmodi est haec Pauli sententia: "Ne errate: nec impudici nec deastricolae nec avari etc. divinum regnum consequentur".[3] Ignorare autem ea licet, quae nec a deo praecepta nec homini ad deum cognoscendum officiumve suum discendum aut faciendum iusticiaque fungendum sunt necessaria. Cuiusmodi est haec quaestio: Utrum Maria, postquam Iesum virgo peperit, alios filios ex Iosepho ediderit. Sciri possunt ea, quae sub sensus corporis animive cadunt, ut, quod Christus Lazarum in vitam suscitavit, id sciverunt, qui aderant Iudaei, quippe quod oculis viderint.[4] Item quod aquam in vinum convertit, id sciverunt, qui ipsi et aquam aut hauserant aut hauriri viderant et vinum deinde gustarunt.[5] Sciri autem debent ea, quae vel ad dei cognitionem vel ad hominis officium sunt necessaria, cuiusmodi sunt dei opera et quae in hominem vel contulit vel confert beneficia et quae vicissim ab eodem exigit officia.

Et quoniam credendi et sciendi facta mentio est, demonstrandum est, quid credere quidve scire sit et quomodo inter sese differant; quibus cognitis eadem opera patebit, quid sint altera duo hisce contraria, videlicet dubitare et nescire. Ut autem haec demonstranda sint, quae alioquin sunt indoctis notissima, facit quorundam doctorum (ut ingenue

Fidem non esse noticiam

---

[1] On Castellio's concept of doubt see Introduction p. 7.
[2] Jn 21:13.
[3] I Cor 6:9-10.
* [4] Jn 11.
* [5] Jn 4:46.

verum dicam) ignorantia, qui clarissimam lucem tenebris obscurarunt, ne dicam extinxerunt. Fidem enim tradiderunt esse notitiam sive scientiam,[6] in quo plane sese ostenderunt minus sapere quam illiterati homines, quam foeminae, quam denique pueri sapiunt. Omnes enim quid sit credere quidve fides (quod idem est) ita intelligunt, ut nihil magis. Itaque eam inter loquendum a scientia discernunt, ut nihil prorsus habeat difficultatis aut ambiguitatis oratio. Nam vel pueri ita loquuntur, dum novi aliquid nunciatur: Quid narrat ille? Rediisse patrem. Credisne rediisse? Credo. Scisne certo? Nescio. Cur ergo credis? Quia semper veracem eum cognovi, qui narrat. Est igitur credere dictis seu veris seu falsis fidem habere. Saepe enim non minus creditur falsis quam veris, id quod de sciendo dici non potest, quippe falsa quae sunt, sciri non possunt, at credi possunt. Denique fides Christiana virtus est, id quod nemo inficiabitur. At scientia quomodo virtus sit, non video nec eam in sacris literis ut virtutem laudari comperio, nisi forte scientiae verbum alicubi pro affectu ponatur, de qua hic non agimus. Et, ut paucis absolvam, ubi scientia incipit, ibi fides desinit, ut, qui ante dixit "Credo", idem iam dicat "Scio".[7] Sic et homines vulgo et authores tum profani tum sacri loquuntur.[8] Quod si quis negat, alleget contraria. Nam quod Thomam credidisse dicit Iesus, quia ipsum vidisset et ideo iam resurrexisse crederet,[9] id non proprie, sed figurate dixit, quasi ita loqueretur: "Quia me resurrexisse, Thoma, vidisti, credidisti". Enim vero istud non est credere (quis enim isto pacto non credat?), sed scire, quae scientia, quia virtus non est, nihil homini confert ad beatitatem. Nam et sepulchri custodes Iudaei me non iam resurrexisse, ut tu, sed, quod plus est, resurgere viderunt idque non ut credentes, sed ut scientes ac testes nunciarunt. Sed non scire beatum est, quippe quod non sit fides neque ex auditu ut fides, sed ex aspectu existat[10] et in homines etiam sceleratissimos et ab omni virtute alienissimos cadat. Quis enim non credat, quod videt! Sed credere, cum non videas aut scias possisque non credere (quippe quod multi non credant, credituri profecto, si fides esset

---

[6] Comp. Calvin, *Institutes*, ed. 1559, C.R. XXX, p. 402: "Iam ergo habemus, fidem esse divinae erga nos voluntatis notitiam ex eius verbo praeceptam".

[7] This is a reference to the *credo ut intelligam* of St. Anselm.

[8] For Castellio the terms *scientia* and *cognitio* have the same meaning. In the following chpts., Castellio elaborates on this problem and establishes the difference between knowledge through the senses, through reason and faith.

[9] Castellio refers to the acts of Thomas 320:29 *See also Jn 20:24-29.

[10] Calvin, *Calumniae nebulonis*, p. 112, refers to Castellio: "Unde porro tibi fides? Si respondeas ex auditu: verum hoc quidem est, sed non absque speciali Spiritus revelatione". See Introduction, n. 37.

scientia. Nam intellectus non posset non assentiri), hoc vero non omnium est et beatum est. Hanc esse verborum Iesu sententiam potest cum ex aliis tum ex eo potissimum planum fieri, quod apostoli testes vocantur resurrectionis Christi. Testis enim is dicitur non qui ex fide, sed qui ex scientia loquitur. Hoc est non qui dicit, quae credit, sed quae scit. Si enim, qui credit, testis esse posset, nos quoque testes esse possemus resurrectionis Christi, quippe quam credamus. Sed non ita est. Testes enim ii demum fuere, qui eum vel resurgere vel resurrexisse viderunt. Ante quidem quam id vidissent, credentes dici potuerunt, si aliis, qui viderant, crediderunt. Sicut contra incredulitatem exprobrat Iesus quibusdam, "quod eis, qui se resurrexisse viderant, non credidissent".[11] Sed postquam viderunt, non iam crediderunt, sed sciverunt et caeteris non auriti, sed oculati testes fuere. Indicat hoc Petrus in Actis super Matthiae surrogatione. "Oportet unum" inquit "eorum virorum, qui nobiscum toto eo tempore versati sunt, quo nobiscum consuetudinem habuit dominus Iesus usque a Iohannis baptismate ad eum diem, quo nobis subductus est, eius resurrectionis testem una nobiscum fieri".[12] Indicant idem et leges tum divinae tum humanae, quae testes non nisi eos et vocant et admittunt, qui ipsi sciunt, non qui credunt. Credunt enim iudices testibus. At testes non credunt, sed sciunt. Alioquin si, qui credunt, testes esse possent perinde ac si scirent, possent eius rei, quam unus tantum vidit, vel mille esse testes, hoc est quotquot ei narranti crederent, possent denique ipsi iudices testimonium dicere, si testanti crederent, quod falsum est. Quare sic statuimus, fidem non esse scientiam, sed a scientia sic differre uti docuimus esseque Christianam fidem omnibus dei dictis credere. Sunt autem dei dicta aut narrationes aut praedicationes aut praecepta aut promissiones aut minae; his omnibus qui non credit, is fidens non est, etiam si aliquibus credat, quemadmodum, qui omnibus dei praeceptis non obedit, is obediens non est, etiam si aliquibus obediat.[13] Sed de fide suo loco nominatim plura deo volente dicemus.

---

[11] Mk. 16:14.

[12] Acts 1:21ff. In his transl. of the Bible Castellio originally used *lotio* for *baptisma*: but because of the criticism he changed back to the Biblical term. See his *Defensio suarum translationum Bibliorum...*, Basel, 1562, p. 12.

[13] See W. Musculus, *Loci communes sacrae theologiae*, Basel, 1573, p. 176: "Sunt autem in Scripturis quae fidem veritatis peculiariter requirunt ista: Narrationes, praedicationes, doctrinae, prophetiae, promissiones et minae. Habentur praeterea in scripturis praecepta et prohibitiones quae postulant obedientiam".

## XX

ff. 84-8

Nunc de scientia dicendum est, quam definire nihil opus esse iudico, quippe quae et ex iis, quae modo diximus, satis pateat et res sit alioquin ita per sese perspicua, ut quaevis definitio eam magis obscuratura quam illustratura videatur. Diximus superius[1] ea sciri debere, quae vel ad dei cognitionem vel ad hominis officium sunt necessaria, cuius dicti membrum prius non sic accipi velim, quasi homini necesse sit omnia dei opera, ex quibus ipse sicut opifex ex opificio cognoscatur, ad unguem callere. Id enim neque fieri potest neque necessarium est. Satis est, si in universum ex eius aspectabilibus et sub sensus vel corporis vel animi cadentibus operibus cognoscitur eius inaspectabilis divinitas. Quemadmodum, ut architectum pro dignitate admireris, non necesse est, ut singulas eius aedificii particulas perfecte teneas, modo in universum eius excellentiam cognoscas. Ne secundi quidem membri ea notio est, ut omni homini omnis hominis officium scire sit necesse. Fit enim hic idem, quod solet in rebuspublicis, ubi praeter commune omnium civium officium in singularibus tantum cuique civi cognoscendum praecipitur, quantum ipsius postulat officium; caetera si novit, bene est, sin ignorat, nihil obest. Sic in republica Christiana praeter commune Christianorum omnium officium in singularibus tantum cuique cognoscendum est, quantum singulorum postulat officium. Ut enim sartoribus agriculturae, ita et coelibibus coniugii leges cognoscere non est necesse. Tamen si cognoscunt, bene est. Quare de scientia hoc dico, hominis officium esse deum eiusque praecepta, hoc est officium suum cognoscere. Haec si novit et officium suum facit, beatus est, etiam si alioquin plurima ignoret. Haec autem scire facile est. Nam et mundus (quod dei opus est) nulli homini in universum ignotus esse potest et charitatis praecepta, a quibus et legis et vatum et Christi doctrina pendet et in quam unam desinit, ita sunt perspicua, ita naturalia et homini cognata, ut etiam impii homines et qui eis obtemperare nolunt, tamen ea, velint nolint, sciant et, si eis dicantur, non possint non assentiri, cuius rei, ut caetera omittam, hoc argumentum est evidentissimum, quod, si vel sceleratissimo homini dicas et deum esse amandum[2] et alteri non faciendum quod tibi nolis fieri, fatebitur. Sunt enim haec dei quasi digito inscripta cordibus omnium nec magis deleri possunt quam caeterae communes hominum notiones. Quare hoc iam confidenter audeo dicere, quae sunt homini cognitu necessaria, ea esse cognitu perfacilia. Haec est via salutis, in qua discenda parum temporis,

---

[1] See above, p. 62.

* [2] Tob 4:15.

in eadem perambulanda totum aevum consumendum est. Hanc viam Christus docuit, hac via servati sunt publicani et meretrices, qui ex una aut altera Christi concione (in qua plerumque de officiis disserebat) Christiani facti officium faciebant plurimarum certe quaestionum, quibus hodie dissipatur ac laceratur ecclesia, ita ignari, ut ne nomina quidem unquam audiverint. Quin et hodie nulli sunt meliores Christiani quam qui de quaestionum subtilitatibus minime laborantes in officio secundum Christi praecepta occupantur. Et ipse Christus iudex in ultimo die omissis quaestionibus secundum officia feret sententiam. Esurivi, sitivi et me pavistis aut non pavistis.[3] Hic erit finis disputandi. Haec omnium controversiarum compositio, ad quam beati qui sese parant. Atque hic cuperem finem facere scribendi et lectores recta ad pietatis praecepta, quae in sacris literis aperta habentur, mittere et, ut in eis exequendis sese exercerent,[4] adhortari. Et sane, si qui sic sunt animati, vadant et quaestionibus omissis officio incumbant, ad metam perventuri, dum caeteri, dum caeteri in carceribus haerentes de meta disputant. Sed quoniam medicinam morbi faciunt necessariam et sunt, quos Christianorum inter sese de Christiana doctrina discordiae solicitant atque angunt, iis pro virili medendum est. Deum precor, ut, qui medicinam dedit, idem medicinae det vires ad sanandum.

## XXI ff. 85-86

Deinceps quaenam in hisce quaestionibus certo sciri possint, aggredior dicere, ut, qui veritatis sunt amantes, ii liquido cognita perspectaque veritate deinceps in eo, quod ab homine potissimum deus exigit, hoc est in praestando officio toti possint occupari.

Igitur illud in primis admoneo, quamdiu sic mordicus haerebunt homines literis, ut hactenus haeserunt, nihilo plus esse consecuturos quam hactenus consecuti sunt, videlicet ut mutuo rodentes tandem mutuo consumant. Nam ita sunt sacrae literae, ut plerique omnes suas opiniones earum authoritate tueantur et quidem probabilia argumenta nonnunquam etiam aperta verba (si verba spectes) suae sententiae suffragantia utrique habeant, cum tamen ipsi inter sese tota via dissideant. Exempla de multis pauca afferam. Sunt qui negant ullam ob causam fas esse iurare. Habent aperta verba Christi, omnino non esse iurandum,[1] sed, si est, simpliciter esse affirmandum, sin contra, negan-

---

[3] Mt 25:35.

[4] MS: *exercererent.*

* [1] Mt 5:34ff.

dum. Si quid aliter fit, id a Malo esse, hoc est a Diabolo. Alii iurare fas esse contendunt et ii habent aperta verba Mosis,[2] apud quem deus Israelitis praecipit, ut per suum nomen iurent. Habent et exempla etiam Christi[3] et apostolorum. Nam et Christus obtestanti sive, ut vocant, adiuranti pontifici, ut diceret, num esset dei filius, fassus est, id quod fuit iurare. Quemadmodum, si te magistratus adiuret, utrum illud feceris, et tu respondeas: "Ita", sit iusiurandum. Et Paulus[4] in epistolis suis aliquoties conscientiae suae testem invocat deum, id quod profecto iurare est. Nam iurare est deum aut aliquid ut deum religiose testificari. Aliud exemplum. Sunt qui dicant hominem fide iustificari atque etiam servari non operibus, et hi aperta verba habent. Nam Paulus[5] diserte dicit fide hominem iustificari, non legis operibus. Et alicubi sic loquitur: "fide servati estis".[6] Alii addunt opera et ii non carent ne ipsi quidem sacrarum literarum locis. Nam et de Phinee in Psalmis[7] diserte scriptum extat ad eius preces prohibitam fuisse cladem. Idque ei iusticiae datum fuisse in omnem seculorum perennitatem. Et Abrahamo[8] deus ob ipsius opus, qui ne a filio quidem manus abstinuisset, felicitatem idque cum iureiurando promisit. Idemque promissum postea eiusdem filio Isaaco eandem ob causam confirmavit, quoniam, inquit, "mihi dicto audiens fuit Abrahamus meaque instituta, praecepta, decreta legesque confirmavit".[9] Denique, ut in pauca conferam, pleraeque omnes opiniones sacrarum literarum authoritate defenduntur et, qui eas mordicus retinent, ii ab opinionibus suis divelli nequeunt. Neque vero illud ad rem conponendam satis est, quod quidam tradunt, videlicet literas per literas, hoc est alios locos per alios esse interpretandos. Quamquam enim id commodum est, tamen aliquid desideratur. Nam idem sectae omnes faciunt nec tamen invenitur concordia. Qui enim locum aliquem male citat, idem et alios locos ad illum interpretandum facile invenit, quos aeque male citet. Proinde nisi alia ineatur ratio, nullam hic adhuc video rationem concordiae. Acciditque hic, quod in podagra, quam medici sanare nequeunt. Nisi enim alias quam superiores adhibeant medicinas, non dubium est, quin eam non magis quam superiores sanare queant.

---

* [2] Deut 6:13 and passim.
* [3] Mt 26:63ff and passim.
* [4] Rom 1:9 and passim.
* [5] Rom 4:5.
* [6] Eph. 2:8.

[7] Ps 106:30-31.

[8] Gen 22:16ff.

[9] Gen 26:5 In his Bible. Castellio says *conservavit* in place of *confirmavit*. The term *decreta* in the above text replaces *ceremonias* of the Vulgate.

Neque enim mutavit podagra naturam neque magis hodie huic medicinae cedet quam haeri. Quod idem dico de controversiis theologis. Si usitatis modis componi hactenus tot seculis non potuerunt, ne deinceps quidem iisdem adhibendis modis unquam componentur. Quare aut de compositione conscientiarumque tranquillitate desperandum est aut alia ineunda est ratio. Desperare charitas vetat, quae sperat omnia; est igitur alia ineunda ratio.

## XXII

ff. 86b-88

Primum omnium monendus est lector, cum de scientia agimus, non agere nos de sacrarum literarum authoritate, in quam fides intuetur, sed de mente sive sensu, cuius est scientia. Constat enim inter omnes Christianas sectas (quarum causa nos hic laboramus) de authoritate, neque an veraces sint sacrae literae, sed quomodo sint intelligendae, quaestio est. Nam veraces esse fatentur omnes, sed de earum mente digladiantur. Esse autem obscuras vel hae ipsae, de quibus agimus, controversiae planum faciunt. Neque enim profecto tam caeca sunt tot doctorum hominum ingenia omnia, ut per tot iam secula tam acriter de rebus apertis dissentiant, praesertim cum in quibusdam apertis rebus consentire eos videamus. Quin accidit hic, quod Babyloniis sapientibus accidisse memorat Daniel.[1] videlicet non potuisse eos legere scriptum illud a manu quadam in pariete in aula regis Baltasaris[2] exaratum, nimirum propter obscuritatem. Nam nisi obscurum fuisset scriptum illud, profecto tot eruditi homines legere potuissent. Quod idem dico de divinis literis; nisi essent obscurae, profecto tot eruditi homines eas iampridem ita enucleassent, ut de earum mente ambigi desiisset. Et vero, quotquot in eas scribunt, hoc ipso obscuras esse profitentur. Cum enim sua scripta vocent commentaria aut expositiones aut declarationes aut interpraetationes aut enarrationes, satis hoc ipso ostendunt se lucem afferre velle, non luci certe, sed tenebris, nisi forte plane delirant perinde ac si quis meridie accensa lucerna sereno coelo sub dio tibi solem velit ostendere. Neque vero, obscuras dum esse dico sacras literas, sic obscuras dico, ut in eis nihil sit apertum. Sunt enim et quidem plurima aperta et in primis ea, quae ad hominis officium et porro salutem pertinent, ne quis forte omissi officii culpam reiiciat in praeceptorum obscuritatem. Sed obscura certe sunt ea, de quibus vulgo solent esse

---

[1] Dan 5:7ff.

[2] MS: *Balsasar* as in Castellio's transl. of the Bible.

controversiae, id quod exemplo probare in promptu est. Quis deus sit, quin idem bonus iustusque sit, quin amari colique debeat, quin fugienda sint peccata sequendaeque virtutes et huius generis alia, nemo ambigit. Cur? Nimirum quia aperta sunt haec omnia. At de baptismo, de coena Domini, de iustificatione, de praedestinatione et caeteris multis dissensiones sunt capitales. Cur? Nimirum quia haec obscure nobis in divinis literis sunt tradita. Si enim aeque aperta forent atque illa sunt, non magis profecto de his ambigeretur quam de illis, et si tam aperte dixisse Christum narrarent sacrae literae: "Ne baptizate pueros" quam aperte dixit "Nolite inebriari vino",[3] non magis puerorum baptismum tueretur quisquam quam ebrietatem. Aut si tam aperte dixisset: "Baptizentur pueri" quam aperte dixit: "Hoc facite in mei commemorationem",[4] tam pueros suos baptizarent Anabaptistae quam Coenam celebrant. Quare sacras literas obscuras esse fatendum omnino est, at, si obscurae sunt, etiam dei voluntate obscuras esse quippe eiusdem voluntate scriptas. Et vero qui deo volente aperte scripsit scortatores[5] (ut hoc exemplum afferam) non esse dei regnum adepturos, idem, si deus voluissset, aperte scripsisset, quae obscure innuat illis verbis: "Sceleris mysterium iam agitur. Superest tantum, ut, qui nunc tenet, e medio tollatur. Tum demum existet ille scelerosus".[6] Denique qui obscure scripsit: "Ut ovis ad caedem actus est utque agnus ante suum tonsorem obmutescens",[7] idem aperte scribere potuisset: "Erit in Iudaea praetore Pontio Pilato Romano quidam Bethlehemae natus nomine Iesus Mariae filius, qui in crucem insons agetur tanquam ovis mactabitur". Possem huius generis mille exempla[8] adducere, ex quibus omnino fatendum est voluisse deum, ut inesset in sacris literis obscuritas. Quod si quaeritur, cur voluerit, et ego id me nescire respondero, nihil absurdi respondero satisque illud ad praesens institutum fuerit, quod voluisse demonstravi. Si enim, quod obscuras esse voluit, id nihil habere absurdi credendum est, postquam ipse nihil vult absurdi, ita, si eiusdem obscuritatis causam nobis ignotam esse vellet, ne in eo quidem quicquam esset absurdi. Sed tamen, postquam ut in victu et vestitu, sic et in scientia voluit interdum suis aliquid etiam ex abundanti largiri neque ea sola, quae necessaria sunt, suppeditare, dicemus et huiusce rei causam ex abundanti. Cur volucribus

---

* [3] Eph 5:18.

* [4] I Cor 11:24.

* [5] I Cor 6:9.

[6] II Thess 2:7f.

[7] Js 53:7 and Acts 8:32.

[8] See previous note.

pabulum non dedit in suo cuique nido? Sicut arboribus alimentum in suo cuique solo? Quia volucribus alas dederat ad volandum et pabulum sibi passim conquirendum. Noluit igitur alas, opus suae sapientiae, esse otiosas. Cur mergis caeterisque piscatricibus avibus non exposuit in terra pabulum sicuti passeribus? Quia eis dederat et industriam et instrumenta piscandi. Cur aurum caeteraque metalla ad hominis usum creata non passim per vias tanquam silices exposuit, sed in imis montium visceribus insono labore eruenda abstrusit? Quia homini ingenium manusque dederat ad illa quaerenda atque effodienda. Cur eundem hominem nudum, non uti bestias lana aut pilis adversum frigora et ardores munitum condidit? Nimirum eandem ob causam, ut esset in quo se divina illa hominis industria exereret. Denique, ut omnia rimeris, invenies noluisse deum, ut sapientiae suae opera essent otiosa. Quod si hoc in naturae operibus perspicuum est et sapienter id fieri omnes non a natura degeneres fatentur, dicamus et in sacris literis et doctrina eandem esse rationem atque causam, nimirum voluisse deum, ut ea esset obscura, quo haberet humana industria, ubi se exereret et hunc animi quasi panem cum sudore non minus quam corporis pabulum sibi compararet. Itaque, si quis de difficultate veritatis inveniendae conqueritur, dico eum non minus inique facere quam si vel aves de difficultate conquirendi undique pabuli vel ipse homo eruendi auri victusve sibi comparandi conqueratur.

## XXIII

ff. 88-89b

Igitur postquam sacras literas in rebus controversis obscuras esse et saepe in utramvis partem probabiliter trahi constat, quo fit ut ex nudis earum verbis pleraeque controversiae dirimi hactenus tot seculis nequiverint, quaerendum aliquid est, in quo sit ita aperta veritas quodque ita sit apud omnes in confesso, ut in alteram partem nulla vi, nulla probabilitate flecti possit. Quo deinde invento dispiciendum erit in controversiis, utra pars et sacrarum literarum verbis se tueatur et insuper cum hac aperta inflexilique veritate conveniat, atque ita secundum eam pronunciandum. Neque enim dubium est, quin, quae utroque nitetur, ea sit firmior quam quae altero. Est autem id, de quo loquor, sensus et intellectus. Cum enim haec sint instrumenta iudicandi, dubitari non potest, quin eis sit permittendum iudicium. Sed in primis animadvertendum est duo esse genera controversiarum, unum videlicet quod sub sensus et intellectum cadat, alterum quod supra sensus supraque intellectum sit. Ac de posteriore quidem suo loco disseretur. Nunc de priore hoc dico, quaecumque controversiae sub sensus et intellectum cadunt, de iis omnino esse sensu intellectuque iudicandum.

Sed hoc loco reclamant et tumultuantur quidam:[1] dicunt Christum usum fuisse parabolis, ne a vulgo hominum intelligeretur. Animalem hominem, authore Paulo,[2] non esse rerum divinarum capacem itaque stultescendum et hominem proprio sensu exinaniendum, quicumque in caelesti schola Christi proficere cupiat. Denique lucem intelligentiae ubique sibi vendicare deum infinitisque sacrarum literarum testimoniis sensum communem ita caecitatis damnari, ut non nisi a caelis lux petatur ac suae perspicaciae renunciare oporteat, quisquis deo sapere cupit. Adducunt exempla. Quod evangelii doctrinam gentibus promulgari noluit deus usque ad adventum Christi, id a Paulo mysterium[3] appellari, quod ab omni aevo fuerit abditum atque adeo coelestibus ipsis angelis incognitum. Citant et prophetae[4] locum, qui de dei providentia loquens dicat magna esse eius opera et profundas cogitationes. Citant et Pauli exclamationem illam: "O homo, tu quis es?"[5] Item: "O altitudo et profunditas etc.".[6] Hic obstupescendum esse, quia, ubi ad incomprehensibile dei iudicium venietur, obstupescant omnes sensus. Alii[7] etiam docent fidei Christianae propium officium esse credere incredibilia tantum propter hoc argumentum: Nullum verbum dei est impossibile deo. Hoc est verbum dei: "Hoc est corpus meum, hic est sanguis meus".[8] Ergo hoc verbum non est impossibile deo et per consequens credendum est propter solam authoritatem loquentis dei nulla alia ratione requisita, etiam si et oculi et aures et nares et gustatus et tactus et ratio, universa denique rerum natura reluctetur. Praecipuum hunc honorem praestari deo eiusque filio, ut credamus verbo eius, quantumvis incredibili contra omnem sensum nostrum aliorumque hominum.

---

[1] See Mk 4:12.

* [2] I Cor 2:14.

* [3] Col 1:26.

* [4] Dan 2:22.

* [5] Rom 9:20.

* [6] Rom 11:23.

[7] See M. Luther, *Predigten* ed. Gogarten, Jena 1927. esp. p.. 432. Also *Die Bekenntnisschriften der evangelisch-lutherischen Kirche* ed. Deutscher evangelischer Kirchenausschuss, 1930 vol. II p. 986: "Haec cum ita se habeant profecto aeterni, veracissimi atque omnipotentis filii Dei, Domini, creatoris, et redemptoris nostri Jesu Christi verba non figurate, metaphorice, tropice dicta aut prolata in aliam sententiam detorquenda sunt, ut nostrae humanae rationi verisimilia fiant... Neque committendum est, ut ullae obiectionis aut hominum contradictiones, quae ab humanae rationis acumine promanant, utcumque humanae rationi blandiantur, nos ab expresso illo Christi testamento, abducant."

* [8] Mk 14:22ff.

Haec sunt et alia in hanc sententiam, quae a quibusdam magna cum diligentia et scripta fuerunt et dici solent accommodate sane ad fallendum. Postquam enim semel hominibus persuaserunt, ut clausis oculis, hoc est remotis reiectisque tum corporis tum animi sensibus, credant verbis, quamvis omnes sensus verba refellant, nihil deinde tam absurdum, tam impossibile, tam falsum est, quod non persuadeant. Quid enim non credas ei, qui tibi persuasit id, quod album vides, non esse album? Quod auribus audis, non esse sonitum; quod ore gustas, non esse, quod gustas? Quod manibus attrectas, non esse, quod attrectas? Quod animo percipis, non esse, quod percipis? Et postea miramur tot errorum monstra viguisse hactenus in iis populis, quibus haec fuere persuasa? Aut hodie tam pertinaces vigere inter theologos contentiones? Cum enim verbis ipsis mordicus adhaereant et verba saepe verbis repugnent, si sensuum iudicium removeris, quanam re iudicabis? Aut quo pacto alter utrum vel refelles vel defendes, cum uterque verba (quibus te sine sensibus et intellectu credendum censes) alleget et sequatur? Contendet aliquis comedendam esse ipsam Christi carnem, si salvus esse velis, et habebit aperta verba Christi: "Si quis non comederit carnem filii hominis etc.".[9] Alius negabit Christi carnem quicquam homini prodesse ad salutem et citabit ipse quoque aperta verba Christi: "Caro non prodest quicquam".[10] Hic tu mihi quid facies? Si enim verbis haerendum est, sunt ab utroque et utriusque vera erit sententia, cum tamen pugnent. Sin res spectanda est, id non nisi sensuum aut intellectus iudicio fieri poterit; quos si illi repudiabunt, nihilo plus sensibus et intellectu proficias quam si homini, qui pertinaciter claudat oculos, persuadere coneris, ut scriptum aliquod legat et cognoscat aut ut, cuius sit iste pannus coloris, iudicet. Ita perpetuum et irreconciliabile manebit dissidium. Enimvero non ferendus est tantus et tam perniciosus error et, postquam isti eum magno studio et diligentia et innexerunt et defendunt, est idem magno studio et diligentia et removendus et oppugnandus. Ac quod in quibusdam erroribus hactenus factum video, ut multi eos magno conatu nec parvo successu aggressi fuerint, idem hic quoque faciendum iudico et caeteros, qui idem vident (quos esse iam passim nonnullos video), ut eidem operi incumbant, moneo atque hortor. Ego interea pro virili certabo et monstrum hoc, si non conficiam, at, ut spero, certe non leviter vulnerabo.

---

* [9] Jn 6:53.
*[10] Jn 6:63.

## XXIV

ff. 89b

Ante omnia sciendum est fallaciam in eo esse, quod, si admittenda neges ea, quae sunt contra sensus, id isti sic accipiunt, quasi admittendum neges quicquam, quod sit supra sensus, quasi vero supra sensus et contra sensus esse sit idem, cum plurimum inter sese differant. Itaque, ut tollatur haec fallacia, distinguenda sunt haec. Supra sensus[1] esse tum in humanis tum in divinis rebus dicimus primum ea, quae sensibus percipi nequeunt, ut quid sit deus et an mundum creaverit et quoto quidque die creaverit, an hominum animae una cum corporibus obdormiant cum iisdem resurrecturae. Deinde ea, quae sensibus percipi possent illa quidem, si adessent, sed quia nec adsunt nec adesse in hac vita (in qua eae de quibus agimus controversiae versantur) queunt, eodem quo illa loco habentur, ut an sidera corpora sint solida, an in centro terrae sit aliquid vacuum, utrum in coelo an in terra habitaturi sint pii post resurrectionem. Et talia quidem multa esse fatemur, quae non sint ad sensuum iudicium revocanda, sed aut credenda, si aperte, aut dubitanda, si ambigue, aut ignoranda, si ne ambigue quidem extant in sacris authoribus. Contra sensus autem dici dicimus ea, quae, cum sub sensus cadant, tamen ita traduntur, ut sensibus repugnent, hoc est sint sensibus contraria, ut si quis ignem dicat esse frigidum, cum tactus iudicet calidum, aut nivem nigram, cum oculi iudicent albam, aut absinthium dulce, cum palatum iudicet amarum. Talia si qua in opinionibus traduntur, ea nos constanter falsa ac repudianda esse contendimus et clamamus et, ut spero, ostendemus ac tum naturae tum authorum tam divinorum quam profanorum atque adeo istorum ipsorum, qui haec tam fastidiose damnant ac repudiant, testimoniis planum faciemus.

Ac primum quod ad naturam attinet, ne quidem cogitari potest ullum aliud instrumentum ulla de re iudicandi homini a natura datum quam sensus et intellectus, adeo, ut, si haec homini sustuleris, omne omni de re iudicium sustuleris.

Quod ad authores profanos, naturae discipulos, attinet, usque adeo

---

[1] See Hugo of St. Victor, *De Sacramentis* I, 3, ch. 30, col. 231, in DPL vol. 176, 1880: "Alia enim sunt ex ratione, alia secundum rationem, alia supra rationem: et praeter haec quae sunt contra rationem. Ex ratione sunt necessaria, secundum rationem sunt probabilia, supra rationem mirabilia, contra rationem incredibilia. Et duo quidem extrema omnino fidem non capiunt. Quae enim sunt ex ratione, omnino nota sunt et credi non possunt, quoniam sciuntur. Quae vero contra rationem sunt nulla similiter ratione credi possunt, quoniam non suscipiunt ullam rationem, nec acquiescit his ratio aliquando. Ergo quae secundum rationem sunt et quae sunt supra rationem tantummodo suscipiunt fidem. Et in primo quidem genere fides ratione adiuvatur, quoniam secundum rationem sunt quae creduntur". Although Castellio uses scholastic terms, the result is quite different.

idem tradunt, ut negent quicquam sine sensibus posse disci et, si quis sensus neget, eum non iam verbis, sed verberibus docendum esse tradant. Itaque sensus et animi partem illam rerum intelligentem atque iudicem vocarunt a iudicando Graeci criteria, quasi tu dicas Iudicatoria.

De sacris quoque authoribus idem dico atque, ut caeteros, de quibus nulla forsan erit controversia, taceam, ad Christum, de quo narrant authores, veniam. An putamus Christum aliter de coloribus aut saporibus iudicasse quam nos? Cum diceret suis: "Aspicite agros, ut iam albeant ad messem",[2] an putamus ei segetum colorem alium fuisse visum quam album aut flavum? Qui ad album proxime accedens albus generaliori vocabulo appellatur. Quid cum ad ficum accessit, ut videret, an in ea fructus esset, nonne ex aspectu iudicavit?[3] Quid "cum gustatum acetum felle mixtum bibere recusavit",[4] nonne gustatu amarum esse sentiens repudiavit? Nam ut demus eum etiam sine sensibus illa pro sua divinitate scivisse, qua etiam hominum cogitationes videre solebat, at ibi certe ex sensibus eum iudicasse fatendum est et quidem sic iudicasse, ut hominum quivis iudicat. Nec solum ipse sensibus iudicabat, sed etiam alios iudicare iubebat. "Ite" (inquit Iohannis discipulis) "renunciatum Iohanni, quae videritis ac audiveritis: caeci cernunt, claudi gradiuntur" etc..[5] Quid quod, cum resurrexisset, ut resurrectionem suam probaret discipulis, iussit se tangi? "Spiritus" (inquit) "carnem et ossa non habet, sicuti me videtis habere".[6] Hic certe illorum et oculos et manus testes iudicesque facit suae resurrectionis: et merito, cum iidem oculi testes fuissent eius et vitae et mortis. De intellectu quoque idem dico. "Simon, inquit, habebat quidam debitores duos, quorum unus multum, alter parum debebat. Ii cum solvendo non essent, utrique condonavit; uter eum plus amare debet? Utri plus condonavit, inquit ille. Recte, inquit Christus, iudicas".[7] Hic certe illius intellectum iudicem facit et approbat.[8] Neque vero est, quod quisquam haec tantum de renatis dici contendat, de improbis neget. Nam et improborum iudicium approbat Christus. Siquidem improbos alloquitur in illa parabola, ubi dicit: "Quid faciet vineae dominus illis agricolis?" Respondent illi: "Malos male perdet"[9] et recte respondent et ex eorum recto iudicio praedicit Christus

* [2] Jn 4:35.
* [3] Mt 21:19.
* [4] Mt 27:34.
[5] Lk 7:22.
* [6] Lk 24:39.
* [7] Lk 7:41.
[8] In margin reference to suppl. 17.
* [9] Mt 21:40.

similia ipsis usuventura, quia similia faciant. Denique, dum omnia considero, nusquam comperio quicquam a Christo vel factum vel dictum fuisse, quod esset vel sensibus vel intellectui contrarium, et merito. Cum enim sensus et intellectus sint opera patris et Christus non ad patris, sed ad Satanae opera abolenda venerit, non mirum est, si hominum sensus et intellectum non sustulit. Ille vero tantum abest, ut illa ab habentibus sustulerit, ut potius ab illis (sicut omnes faciunt doctores) initium duxerit docendi, quinetiam, sicubi illa vitiata erant, ut in caecis, in surdis, in furiosis, correxerit nec unquam quenquam docuerit nisi sensibus et intellectu praeditum. Et sane quis ei vel tunc credidisset vel nunc crederet, si vel sensibus et intellectu carentes tanquam praeditos allocutus fuisset vel ea dixisset, quibus vel sensus vel intellectus repugnaret? Ut si lapidem panem appellasset aut nivem calidam aut ignem frigidum aut avaritiam invidiamve laudabilem aut discipulum magistro superiorem dixisset?

## XXV

ff. 91-9

Veniam nunc ad eos ipsos,[1] qui nos clausis oculis quaedam credere volunt, quibus sensus repugnant, et ab ipsis primum omnium quaeram, utrum id ipsum ipsi clausis oculis, hoc est nullo iudicio atque intellectu aut ratione, dicant an potius cum iudicio. Nam si sine iudicio dicunt, merito dictum eorum repudiamus. Sin cum iudicio atque ratione, inepte faciunt, qui suo ipsi iudicio nobis persuadere conentur, ut nostrum deponamus, nimirum ut ipsi deinde nos quasi oculis orbatos ipsi scilicet oculati in quaslibet absurditatum fossas praecipitent.

Deinde quaero, cur non solum in eo, quod dixi, sed etiam in multis aliis idem faciunt, hoc est ratione utantur contra aperta dei verba? Nam apertum est illud Christi, quosdam esse, qui se ipsos propter dei regnum castraverint.[2] Et tamen isti Origenem damnant, qui se ipsum castrasse perhibetur.[3] Putant enim eum errore deceptum perperam accepisse verba Christi. Apertum est et illud verbum Christi: "Nolite vobis vocare patrem aut magistrum in terris. Nam unus pater magisterque vester est in

---

[1] See Calvin, *Institutes*, ed. 1536, C.R. 29-30, col. 48: ... "haec fidei natura est, aures arrigere, oculos claudere, hoc est promissioni attendere".

* [2] Mt 19:12.

[3] See Melanchthon, *Annotationes et conciones in evangelii Matthaei*, IV, C.R. 14, col. 598: "Hic autem jubet oculum erui et praecidi manum. Hic discatis recte intelligere sermonem. Non vult, ut corporaliter effodias oculum vel praecidas manum, sicut olim stulti aliqui castraverunt se, ut Origines".

caelis".[4] Et tamen isti patres et magistros sibi in terris vocare non dubitant et Christi verba illa aliter quam sonant interpretari. Apertum est et illud: "Si quis tibi dexteram percusserit, obverte ei sinistram et omni petenti dato etc.".[5] Et tamen isti nec illa faciunt et Anabaptistas, quia illa verba sic accipiant, graviter accusant atque damnant. Quod idem et de Christi verbis illis[6] dico, quibus omnino iurare vetat. Denique sexcentos citare locos possum, in quibus ipsimet contra verba pro sententia sentiunt et disputant. Cur? Nimirum quia alii loci reperiuntur illis, quod ad verba attinet, contrarii. Sed cur illos locos tam apertos torquent et accommodant suae sententiae? Cur non potius sententiam suam torquent et accommodant illis locis? Exempli gratia: Dixit Christus non esse resistendum malo.[7] Cur ergo isti magistratum contra Anabaptistas approbant, qui resistat malo? Cur non potius eos locos, in quibus approbatur magistratus, torquent et interpretantur secundum aperta verba Christi, qui vetet iniuriae resistere? Hic non video, quid aliud respondere possint, et sane nihil aliud (quod sciam) respondent in suis vel scriptis vel sermonibus quam quod iudicet ratio sententiam verbis illis repugnantem esse sequendam, ne quid absurdi admittatur. Recte. Ergo si rationis iudicium et in illis et in aliis, quibus ipsis libet, locis sequendum et verbis anteponendum censent et in eo rationem verbis recte anteponunt, nimirum quia de rebus agatur, quae sub rationis iudicium cadant, patiantur idem a nobis in aliis quoque locis fieri, si quos sub rationis aut sensuum iudicium cadere ostenderimus, neve nobis ratione praeditis denegent, quod sibi ratione praeditis arrogant. Nam ratio[8] est ipsa, ut ita loquar, dei filia, quae et ante literas et ceremonias omnes atque adeo ante orbem conditum fuit et post literas et ceremonias omnes atque adeo post mutatum novatumque hunc mundi statum semper futura est neque magis quam ipsemet deus aboleri potest. Ratio, inquam, est aeternus quidam sermo dei longe tum literis tum ceremoniis et antiquior et certior, secundum quam deus suos et ante ceremonias et literas docuit et post easdem ita docebit, ut sint vere divinitus docti. Secundum hanc et Abel et Henochus et Noha et Abrahamus caeterique multi ante Mosis literas pie vixerunt et iisdem antiquitatis multi et hactenus et deinceps victuri sunt. Denique secundum hanc ipse Iesus Christus, viventis dei filius, qui Graeco sermone *Logos* dicitur, hoc est

Loci verbus pugnantes.

Ratio

---

* 4 Mt 23:9.

* 5 Mt 5:39ff.

* 6 Mt 5:34.

* 7 Mt 5:39. In his Bible Castellio replaces *malo* with *iniuriae*.

* 8 Prov. 8:22f.

ratio aut sermo, quod idem est (nam ratio est quasi quaedam interior et aeterna semperque loquens veritatis oratio atque sermo) et vixit ipse et alios docuit et literas ceremoniasque, quibus plus quam rationi tribuebant Iudaei, refutavit. Nam et die Sabbathi saepe operatus est et Iudaeos idem sine crimine facere ostendit, qui etiam die Sabbathi pecora ex fossis attollerent et adaquarent, et quidem, cur fieri liceret, ratione, non literis ostendit. Nam legis literae citra ullam exceptionem ullum opus die Sabbathi fieri vetabant. Sed ratio iudicabat "non hominem propter Sabbbathum, sed Sabbathum propter hominem esse conditum".[9] Itaque hac ratione Christus literas refellit. Neque non in eo, quod Davidis factum allegat, qui contra legis praeceptum de panibus illis apposititiis comederit, rationem sequitur, non literas. Quamvis enim illud Davidis factum literis mandatum extaret, non tamen id, quia scriptum extaret, ideo allegabat Christus (nam et alia quaedam Davidis facta literis erant prodita, quae in exemplum trahere utpote vitiosa non licebat), sed quia rationi consentaneum esset, videlicet quod illud de panibus apposititiis[10] praeceptum propter hominem, non homo propter praeceptum factus esset ideoque ratio iuberet, ut illud praeceptum, si res postularet, homini, non homo praecepto cederet.[11] Idem dico de eo, quod dicit illi Samaritanae foeminae, fore et iam esse veros cultores, qui deum non Ierosolymis neque in monte illo, sed in spiritu et veritate colerent.[12] Nam illud dictum nullis literis, sed tantum hac ratione confirmat. Deus est spiritus et tales, hoc est spirituales, postulat cultores, qua quidem una ratione, quicquid est ceremoniarum, prosternit et homines a literis ad rationem adducit. Haec ratio illa est, quae unum quemque in die iudicii vel accusabit, si male, vel excusabit, si bene fecerit, sicut scripsit Paulus ad Romanos: "Cum exterarum nationum homines" inquit "legem non habentes natura legitima faciant, ii legem non habentes ipsi sibi lex sunt qui quidem ostendant legis opus in suis animis inscriptum, id quod testabitur eorum conscientia et utrorumque cogitationes eos vel accusabunt vel defendent, quo die iudicabit dominus arcana hominum ex Evangelio meo per Iesum Christum".[13] Loquitur enim hic Paulus de sua cuiusque conscientia, quae est quaedam naturalis scientia cognitioque sui cuiusque vel recte vel prave facti a ratione proficiscens. Nam quid rectum quidve pravum sit docet ratio, unde nascitur conscientia, quae ideo nec in

---

*[9] Mk 2:26.
*[10] Mk 2:26.
[11] MS: caederet.
*[12] Jn 4:21ff. In margin reference to suppl. 5.
[13] Rom 2:14ff.

bestiis nec in pueris aut mente captis ulla est, quia ratione carent. Denique haec ratio illa est veritatis indagatrix, inventrix, interpres, quae, si quid in literis tum profanis tum sacris vel obscurum vel tempore vitiatum est, aut corrigit aut in dubium tantisper vocat, donec tandem vel veritas elucescat vel saltem de re incerta amplius pronuncietur.

## XXVI

ff. 93b-94

Quid quod in profanis authoribus multa eadem extant, quae in sacris literis? Vel illud Catonis illius, cuius disticha de moribus circumferuntur:

Si deus est animus nobis, ut carmina dicunt,
Hic tibi praecipue sit pura mente colendus.[1]

Hic certe eandem adduxit rationem, qua Christus Samaritanam illam, ut supra diximus,[2] docebat. Quid illud Sallustii: "Discordia maximae res dilabuntur?".[3] Nonne convenit cum illo dicto Christi: "Omne regnum dissidiis laborans desolatur?".[4] Quid illud Iuvenalis:

Si consilium vis,
Permittes ipsis expendere numinibus, quid
Conveniat nobis rebusque sit utile nostris.
Nam pro iucundis aptissima quaeque dabunt di.
Carior est illis homo quam sibi.[5]

Haec certe conveniunt cum illo "fiat voluntas tua".[6] Item cum illo: "Non quod ego volo, sed quod tu vis fiat".[7]

Item cum illo: "Nescimus quid petendum sit".[8]

Item illud eiusdem:

Loripedem rectus derideat, Aethiopem albus,
Quis tulerit Gracchos de seditione querentes? etc..[9]

quadrat cum illo Christi: "Qui fit, ut festucam videas in oculo fratris tui, trabem in tuo non videas?".[10]

Et mox:

---

[1] See Dicta Catonis I,1 ed. Naples, 1897, p. 39.
[2] See previous ch. n. 12.
[3] See Sallust, *Jugurtha*, ed. Heidelberg: Klostermann, Winter 1971, p. 56.
* [4] Mt 12:25 and passim.
[5] Juvenal 10, ed. G.G. Ramsay, Loeb Class. Library, 1942, *loc. cit.*, pp. 218-19.
[6] Mt 6:10.
* [7] Mk 14:36.
* [8] Rom 8:26.
[9] Juvenal 2,23 pp. 18-19. See n. 5.
*[10] Mt 7:3.

Dat veniam corvis, vexat censura columbas.[11] cum illo: "Qui culicem percolant, camelum autem deglutiunt";[12] et paulo post:

dedit hanc contagio labem
Et dabit in plures sicut grex totus in agris
Unius scabie cadit et porrigine porci,
Uvaque conspecta livorem ducit ab uva.[13]

cum illo: "Mores bonos colloquia corrumpunt mala".[14] Item "paululum fermentum totam massam fermentat".[15]

Item illud Persii:

Dicite, pontifices, in sacro quid facit aurum?
Nempe hoc, quod Veneri donatae a virgine pupae.
Quin damus id superis, de magna quod dare lance
Non possit magni Messalae lippa propago:
Compositum ius fasque animi sanctosque recessus
Mentis et incoctum generos pectus honesto[16]

convenit et cum eo, quod modo citavimus ex Ioh. 4[17] et cum iis, quae sacrae literae tradunt de spiritualibus sacrificiis. Sed quid opus pluribus? Sciunt, qui in profanis authoribus versati sunt, innumeras in eis esse sententias, quae cum sacris prorsus conveniant.[18] Atqui non scripserunt illi divinitus sed rationis ductu, sicut ipsimet ostendunt, qui sua dicta non deorum authoritate, sed rationis argumentis tueri et confirmare soleant. Quare hoc fatendum est rationis in homine iudicium esse rectum atque sanum.[19]

## XXVII ff. 94-

Restat, ut ea, quae contra dici solent, perpendamus. Dicunt hominis sensus et iudicium fuisse Adami peccato vitiatum, quo vitio corrupto eius

---

[11] Juvenal 2,63 pp. 22-23. See n. 5.
[12] Mt 23:24.
[13] Juvenal, pp. 22-25. See n. 5.
*[14] I Cor 15:33.
*[15] Gal 5:9.
[16] Persius, pp. 340-41. See n.5.
[17] Jn 4:21. See note 5.
[18] In margin reference to suppl. 7.
[19] See Calvin, *Institutes* C.R. XXX,II,9: "Et Paulus omnem dubitationem tollit, corruptionem docens non in una tantum parte subsidere, sed nihil a mortifera labe purum esse, aut sincerum. Nam de vitiosa natura disputans, non tantum inordinatos, qui apparent, appetituum motus damnat, sed praecipue contendit mentem caecitati et cor pravitati addictum esse".

semine eam labem propagatam esse ad posteros idque cum aliis tum illis in primis locis confirmare conantur, quos supra commemoravimus. Quibus et alii possunt adiungi.[1] Animalis homo non percipit, quae dei sunt. Quin ea pro stultitia habet. "Sapientia huius mundi stultitia est apud deum".[2] Quod apud homines praeclarum habetur, id deo est abominandum. Si quis sapiens vult evadere, is stultus fiat. Sapientes se professi stultos praestiterunt. Christum praedicamus Graecis stultitiam.[3] "Ne quis vos philosophia fallaciaque vana depraedetur".[4] Item quod Christus suis mentem aperuit ad intelligendas sacras literas, quod profecto nihil opus fuisset, si eas humano ingenio percipere potuissent. Hi et huius generis alii loci videntur pugnare cum iis, quae diximus, quo fit, ut egeat res consideratione non prava. Igitur gemina hic surgit quaestio. Primum enim quaeritur, an hominis sensus et intellectus fuerit Adami peccato vitiatus. Deinde, quaenam sit illorum, quos citavimus, locorum mens. Ac quod ad primum attinet, vereor, ne magis sit publicus et vetustate confirmatus error quam veritas. Primum enim nulla vel authoritate vel ratione dictum est. Sed tantum in medium a quopiam temere prolatum arripuit et tamquam oraculum retinuit caeca caecosque sequens posteritas. Dicunt enim, quis sacrorum authorum id tradiderit? Nullus. Quae ratio doceat? Nulla. Quin imo et experientia et historia contra docet. Nam quod ad experientiam attinet, videmus humani et corporis et animi sensus integros sanosque esse, sicuti hactenus copiose ostendimus. Historia vero, hoc est Mosis, tradit hominis oculos gustato fructu arboris scientiae fuisse apertos ac vidisse, quam ante non videbant nuditatem.[5] Et merito. Nam et arbor certe non ficte neque falso vocata est arbor scientiae. Itaque mirari satis non possum, quid istis in mentem venerit, ut ex arbore scientiae fecerint arborem ignorantiae. Iam vero utri sensus vitiati fuerunt? Corporisve an animi? Corporis dici non potest. Nam et oculis viderunt se esse nudos et auribus audivere vocem dei. Atqui si vitiati fuissent sensus, nec vidissent nec audivissent, aut certe male vidissent et audivissent. Quod tamen non est. Ne animi quidem sensus vitiati fuere. Quod enim se nudos esse viderunt, animi fuit per oculos videntis et iudicantis. Nam etiam ante peccatum videbant oculis alter alterum, sed non videbant nuditatem. Hoc est: non animadverte-

---

[1] See ch. XXIII.

[2] See I Cor 3:18ff.

* [3] I Cor 1:23. In his Bible Castellio replaces *gentibus* of the Vulgate with *Graecis*.

* [4] Col 2:8.

* [5] Gen 3:7.

bant, quod certe (videlicet animadvertere) animi, non corporis est. Videbant igitur alter alterum, sicut vel ovis ovem vel puer puerum, nescientes, quid esset nuditas, non magis quam puer aut ovis. Sed gustato pomo id animadverterunt et sciverunt. Itaque quonam pacto fuerint eorum vitiati sensus, videre nequeo. Quin et hodie similia fieri videmus. Nam et pueri, antequam peccarunt, non vident se esse nudos nec ante peccatum incipit in eis illa nuditatis animadversio atque pudor, et mente capti et bestiae, quia ratione carent, nunquam id vident. Et in futura vita impii (quorum certe sensus aut intellectus non erit renascentia Christique spiritu renovatus, quippe quo carebunt) tantum aberit, ut intellectu careant, ut hoc ipso maxime torqueantur, quod se peccasse veritatemque repudiasse intelligent, scient sibique conscient. Quare sic statuimus, hominis sensum et intellectum non fuisse Adami peccato vitiatum.

## XXVIII

ff. 95-

Superest, ut ad eos qui contra allegari solent locos respondeamus. Referemus autem omnes illos locos in classes duas. Aut enim de rebus dicuntur, quae sensuum intellectusque captum superant, aut de rebus, quae non superant. Si superant, hic non agimus de illis et fatemur eas humano ingenio idque non solum ab impiis, sed ne quidem a piis posse comprehendi. Itaque eas illi demum sciunt, quibus patefecit deus; caeteri sive boni sive mali ignorant. Sin non superant, dicimus eas ad sensuum rationisque iudicium esse referendas. Sed sciendum est existere interdum quaedam, quae iudicium hoc impediant, quae quidem sint vel in homine vel extra hominem. Atque ut primum de corporis sensibus agamus, in homine impedimenta sunt duo, videlicet voluntas aut morbus. Voluntas est, dum non vult homo sensus applicare ad rem aliquam, ut si picturam intueri et considerare aut cantilenam attendere aut cibum aliquem gustare non vult, fit ut de eo iudicare nequeat, non quia non insit alioquin in eo facultas iudicandi, sed quia non vult. Morbus est, dum ipsi sensus vitiati sunt, ut si caecus aut caecutiens aut surdus aut surdaster est; tunc enim acute iudicare aut bene iudicare, etiam si velit, non potest. Vitiati sunt autem aut iam ab utero matris, ut si quis caecus natus est, aut postea, ut si quis caecus factus est. Fit autem hoc posterius multis modis, sed nos duos tantum commemorabimus, qui animo postea accommodandi sunt et ad institutum nostrum pertinent. Aut enim ab ipso homine aut a deo vitiati sunt sensus hominis idque utrumque ipsius hominis culpa factum est. Ab homine vitiati sunt, si quis sua ebriositate aut immodica librorum lectione caecus aut caecutiens factus est, quales

Impedime sensuum corporis i

nonnullos videre licet. A deo autem, si quem deus ipsius peccato offensus caecavit, ut de Elyma[1] mago memoriae proditum est.

Impedimenta sensuum animi in homine.

Iam in animo idem fieri dico. Aut enim voluntate aut morbo impeditur rationis iudicium. Voluntate, dum non vult homo ratione rem aliquam perpendere, sed ab ea animi avertit oculos, ut dum litigator aliquis adversarii sui causam considerare non vult; ita enim fit, ut de ea iudicare nequeat, non quia non habeat alioquin iudicandi, si velit, facultatem, sed quia non vult. Ut autem nolit, in causa est avaritia aut ambitio aut voluptatis amor. Ac tales fuisse videntur illi Iudaei, qui dicebant a Christo eiici in nomine Beelzebulis daemonia.[2] Cum enim laborarent illis quae modo dixi vitiis, quibus vitiis Christus adversaretur, nolebant aequis animis negocium perpendere. Alioquin tam erat profecto in eis facultas vere ratiocinandi quam in Nicodemo, qui sic ratiocinabatur: "Magister, scimus te venisse doctorem a deo. Nam ista tam miranda facere, quae tu facis, nemo possit, nisi adsit ei deus".[3] Aut quam in illo, qui caecus natus fuerat: "Scimus" inquit "improbos a deo non audiri, sed, si quis pius est et eius voluntati paret, hunc audit. Nunquam fando auditum est quenquam aperuisse oculos caeci nati. Nisi esset is a deo, nihil posset facere".[4] Tales et illi fuisse videntur, qui Stephanum lapidantes "sublato ingenti clamore aures suas obthurabant"[5] videlicet, ne divina et invicta Stephani dicta audirent atque ita eorum vi victi vera esse iudicarent. Cum enim essent ratione praediti et Stephanus maxime rationi consentanea diceret, fieri non poterat, quin ea, si aequis animis perpenderent, perspicerent, quemadmodum fieri non potest, ut homo non caecus, si colores aequis oculis intueatur, eos non perspiciat. Ac tales, qui sunt et in ea veri aversatione voluntaria diu perseverant, ii interdum in morbum incurrunt, de quo iam dicemus, ut, quoniam videre noluerunt, ipso tandem visu priventur, ut videre ne quidem possint, etiam si velint, quemadmodum servus ille piger, de quo narrat Christus in illa parabola: quia domini sui pecuniam, quam habebat, foenerari cum posset noluit, ea privatus est, ut postea, etiam si vellet, non posset.[6] Et haec de rationis impedimento, quod in hominis voluntate situm est.

---

* [1] Acts 13:11.
* [2] Lk 11:15.
[3] Jn 3:2.
[4] Jn 9:31ff.
[5] Acts 7:56.
* [6] Mt 25:26ff.

## XXIX

ff. 96b 100, 1 Rationis

Morbo autem vitiata est ratio, dum animus ita affectus est, ut, quemadmodum caecus videre nequit, ita nec ille veritatem cognoscere. Accidit autem hoc aut iam inde ab utero matris, ut sunt qui mente capti nascuntur et per omnem vitam nullum habent rationis usum. Nam hi ratiocinari aut iudicare non magis possunt quam bestiae et porro ne quidem doceri aut peccare. Itaque tales homines nunquam vel docuit vel reprehendit Christus. Frustra enim vel reprehendas vel doceas eum, qui nec doctrinam nec reprehensionem sentire possit, quemadmodum surdum frustra alloquare aut caeco frustra colores ostendas. Aut accidit id non ab utero, sed postea idque duobus item modis, cuius utriusque ipse in culpa sit. Aut enim id malum ipse sibi homo conflavit, dum consuetudine bonum aversandi ita contraxit habitum, ut iam de veritate tanquam caecus iudicare nesciat. Aut deus ipse eius sceleribus offensus eius animi iudicium sicut Elymae[1] oculos excaecavit, hoc est ei, quod aliquando dederat, animi iudicium ademit. Et tales fuisse videntur illi Iudaei, quorum corda a deo excaecata fuisse traditum est in evangelio.[2] Sive autem iam ab utero sive postea hominis culpa vel ab ipso homine vel a deo vitiata est eius ratio, nullum horum ab Adami peccato ortum est. Nam nec in ipso Adamo fuit ullum horum trium ideoque ad posteros ab eo propagari non potuere et, si ab eo orirentur, inessent omnibus, quemadmodum mors, quae ab illius peccato originem habet, in omnes pervasit et quemadmodum pariendi dolores ab Evae culpa proficiscentes sunt omnium mulierum communes. Iam vero, qui sic sunt vel a se ipsis vel a deo caecati, de iis nos docendis in hoc libro non laboramus, ne surdo (ut est in proverbio) fabulam canamus.[3] Sanari enim tales aut non possunt aut non nisi magno dei miraculo possunt. Ne ii quidem, qui veritatem aversantur, quandiu aversantur, doceri possunt, non magis quam illi. Frustra enim ei canas, qui aures suas obthurat. Et verum est illud proverbium *nullum esse surdiorem quam qui audire non vult*. Superest ut de iis loquamur, qui horum malorum nullo laborant, sive probi sunt sive improbi. Sunt enim quidam ita improbi, ut tamen veritatem non aversentur nec iam volentes aut scientes repudient. Et hi quidem de veritate iudicare possunt. Ac tales erant illi publicani et meretrices, qui Christum audientes recte de eo iudicabant et Scribas ac Pharisaeos in regno dei antecedebant.[4] Hactenus de iis sensuum impedimentis, quae

---

* [1] Acts 13:8.
* [2] Mk 8:17.
[3] Comp. for instance Cicero, *Atticus*, Loeb Class. Library, *loc. cit.*, vol. 1, p. 304.
* [4] Mt 21:31.

sunt in homine, dicendum. Iam dicendum est de iis, quae sunt extra hominem. Sunt autem huius modi. Si nivem per rubrum vitrum intueare, rubra videbitur. Aut si sol per rubra specularia albam mappam collustret, rubra videbitur. Si unum numum per quaedam perspicilla, quae sunt ita formata, ut quasi ex pluribus perspicillis composita sint, intueare, complures numos tibi videre videbere et quidem ita, ut, quis sit verus, dignoscere et manu certo contingere nequeas. Sunt et quaedam perspicilla, quae faciunt, ut res vel maiores vel minores esse videantur, alia, quae ex sinistris dextera, ex superioribus inferiora reddant, alia non item. Nonnulla, quae faciem longiorem aut obliquiorem aut deformiorem reddant. Item, quae procul spectantur, minora videntur aut rotunda, etiam si sunt quadrata. Mons procul spectanti parvus et caeruleus apparet et, quae moventur quamvis celerrime, tamen procul spectanti stare videntur ut sidera. Rectus baculus dimidio in aquam merso fractus videtur. Aqua limpida, si profundissima est, interdum viridis speciem exhibet. Sol per vapores interdum sanguineus videtur. Denique mille sunt casus externi, qui oculorum iudicium quamvis nullo vitio laborantium ita vitiant, ut male iudicent. Alii sunt, qui efficiunt, ut iudicare nequeant. Si saxum in aqua agitata aut admodum profunda intueare, non possis discernere, quid sit, neque item de rebus nimium minutis, ut sunt membra pulicum. Atque idem de caeteris quoque dico sensibus. Haec impedimenta si quando accidunt, homo ratione praeditus ad rationem confugit et eius ope sensuum iudicium reprehendit et aliud credit quam sensus iudicant. Itaque, si iudicant oculi nivem per rubrum vitrum spectatam esse rubram, non credit eis, sed rationi experientiaeque praeteritae, quae albam esse docet, idemque facit in caeteris impedimentis. Hinc fit, ut pueri et bestiae, quia ratione carent, semper credant sensibus nec possis eis persuadere non esse ea in speculis, quae videntur esse. Quod ad ea attinet, de quibus iudicare sensus nequeunt, de iis dubitare hominem natura docet atque ita dicere: video equidem aliquid, sed utrum lapis sit an quid aliud, nescio. Et haec de impedimentis sensuum corporis quae sunt extra hominem.

Impedimenta sensuum corporis extra hominem.

## XXX

ff. 100b, 101, 97b

Impedimenta sensuum animi extra ipsum animum.

Iam in animo idem fieri sciendum est idque diversis modis, quos equidem singulos explicare non possim. Sed exempla quaedam afferam, ex quibus res perspici queat. Interdum res est quasi remotior, ut dum artem aliquam discere aggredimur, ut medicinam, ut mathematicas, eas protinus percipere non possumus, etiam si insit in animis nostris eas percipiendi facultas. Nonnunquam non est res illa quidem remotior, sed est subtilior, ut dum quaeritur, quae causa sit, ut adustione terra reddatur fertilior, aut quae causa sit aestuum oceani, aut quae causa sit visus aut auditus caeterorumve sensuum. Quandoque res est neque remotior neque subtilior, sed confusa atque mixta, ut dum disputatur, utrum fide an operibus iustus fiat homo. Hic enim quia utrumque et ratio et sacrae literae tradunt, iudicare difficilius est. Nonnunquam obscurius res traditur, ut fit in vatum oraculis, quo fit, ut de eis iudicare tamquam in obscura luce de coloribus sit difficile. Haec et eius generis alia animi iudicio officiunt, quamvis nullo alioquin vitio laborantis. Hactenus de sensuum tum corporis tum animi impedimentis, quae si vel in homine sunt vel extra hominem, iudicium impediunt. His igitur sublatis dicimus hominem de iis rebus iudicare posse, quae sub sensus rationemve cadunt. Atque ex iis, quae diximus, satis alioquin generaliter responsum est ad ea quae contra dici vel solent vel possunt, quippe quae omnia in harum classium aliquam referenda sunt. Sed tamen ne quid desideretur, ad singulos locos paucis respondebimus, non equidem ad omnes, ne nimis prolixi simus, sed ad ita multos, ut de caeteris idem ratiocinari sit facile.

## XXXI ff. 97b

### Responsa ad ea, quae in cap. XXIII contra dicta fuerunt

Dicunt Christum usum fuisse parabolis, ne a vulgo hominum intelligeretur. Respondeo hunc locum pro me facere. Si enim ideo parabolis utebatur, ne a vulgo intelligeretur, indicium est vulgus potuisse intelligere, si ei parabolas sicuti discipulis suis explicasset. Atque hoc ex ipsius Christi verbis perspicuum est. Sic enim apud Matthaeum interrogantibus discipulis cur vulgum per similitudines alloqueretur, respondet: "Quoniam vobis regni coelestis arcana nosse datum est, at illis non datum est. Qui enim habet, huic dabitur isque abundabit: qui vero non habet, huic etiam, quod habet, auferetur. Propterea per similitudines eos alloquor, quoniam videntes non vident et audientes non audiunt nec intelligunt",[1] in eisque comprobatur illud Esaiae oraculum, quod sic habet: "Audietis quidem, sed non intelligetis, et ita videbitis, ut non perspiciatis. Obtorpuit enim animus huius populi et auribus obtusi audiunt et claudunt oculos, ne et oculis videant et auribus audiant et animo intellegant redeantque ad frugem atque ita ego eis medear".[2] Ex his Christi verbis

---

[1] Mt. 13:11ff.
[2] Is 6:9ff.

apparet illos potuisse intelligere, si ipse aperte locutus fuisset. Alioquin si quamvis aperte loquentem intelligere non potuissent et tamen ipse eis, ne intellegerent, tecte locutus fuisset, non minus inepte fecisset quam si quis taceat, ne praesentes surdi audiant, aut lucem tectam ferens seorsum videntibus ostendat, ne, si palam ostendat, eam videant caeci quidam praesentes, a quibus eam videri ipse nolit. Et sane in eius illa parabolarum explicatione, quid sit, quod non et vulgus hominum intelligere potuisset, non video, cum ea hodie etiam ex Evangelistarum scriptis (quibus certe minus aperte quam tunc viva voce illa explicari credibile est) a vulgo hominum facilime intelligantur. Sunt enim parabolae alioquin per sese obscurae et quae plerumque rationis acumine percipi non possint, nisi loquentis mentem (quae ex tectis illis verbis saepe non magis quam pisum per siliquam perspici potest) teneas, sed earundem explanatio est intellectu facilima idque fit non solum in divinis, verum etiam in humanis literis, ubi multae parabolae, proverbia, aenigmata sunt, quae sine explicatione saepe nullo ingenio possunt percipi. Ipsi quidem Christi discipuli, quamvis a Christo et mundati et aliquandiu iam edocti, tamen parabolas non intelligebant, at earundem explanationem facile. Itaque post explanationem quaerenti Christo, an illa omnia intelligerent, respondent: "Etiam, domine".[3] Quod idem et vulgus respondere potuisset, si illi sicut discipulis datum fuisset, hoc est si Christus illi sicuti discipulis explanasset. Sic enim accipienda sunt illa verba Christi: "vobis regni coelestis arcana nosse datum est"[4] sicut ex universa Matthaei narratione videre est. Quod si quis nunc quaerat, cur ergo nollet, ut vulgus hominum illa intelligeret, quamquam haec quaestio non est huius loci propria, quippe in quo non de causis rerum, sed de hominis intellectu agamus, tamen obiter respondebo primum illud non in universum sic accipiendum esse, quasi Christus nunquam[5] aperte voluerit hominum vulgus alloqui. Nam et in eiusdem Mat. cap. 5 et 6 et 7 et aliis multis in locis vulgus hominum aperte et sine parabolis alloquitur et ipsarum parabolarum explicationes suas ad huc usque diem literis mandatas extare voluit venturas in aures certe multorum illis, quibus eas tunc explicare noluit, similium et forsan etiam deteriorum. Itaque quod de uno vel tempore vel coetu dictum est, id de quovis allegari non potest. Cur autem illis tunc ea explicare noluerit, causam ipsemet reddit, dum dicit: "Qui non habet, huic auferetur".[6] Quoniam enim, cum oculos

---

[3] Mt 13:51.

* [4] Mt 13:11.

[5] MS: *unquam*.

* [6] Mt 13:12.

haberent, eos, ne viderent, claudebant sicut ipsemet mox dicit, ipse vicissim eis quam aversabantur lucem subducebat. Atque hoc ipsum est, quod supra declaravi[7] citato servo illo pigro, qui, quia pecuniam domini cum haberet foenerari noluit, ea privatus est. Sic non solum deus, sed et homines facere solent, qui si quem vident ab aliqua re bona, quam ipsi afferant, abhorrere (cuiusmodi sunt merces, cibi, vina), offensi illa bonae rei aversatione eam solent subducere[8] idque ita, ut interdum postea ne rogati quidem afferant. Aequum est enim, ut, qui bonum aspernatus est, is a bono vicissim contemnatur et, qui sapientiae admonitionem (ut scribit Solomo) repudiavit, is vicissim a sapientia repudietur.[9]

Allegant illud Pauli: "Animalis homo non percipit ea, quae dei sunt".[10] Respondeo hoc nihil ad rationis iudicium pertinere. Loquitur enim de rebus divinis, quae non ratione, sed divina partefactione cognoscuntur. Quod idem dico et de illo mysterio, quod evangelii doctrinam deus usque ad adventum Christi gentibus publicari noluit [deus]. Illud enim ne apostoli quidem quamvis renati sciebant, donec eis divinitus patefactum est, sicut apparet in Petri visione illa,[11] qua linteum vidit de coelo demitti omni animalium genere refertum, de quibus mactare et vesci iussus est. Et in universum idem dico de caeteris huiusce modi locis.

Quod ad eos attinet, qui exemplo Abrahami, qui credidit in spem contra spem, volunt a nobis ea credi, quibus etiam omnes sensus repugnant quaeque maxime sunt incredibilia, mihi videntur ipsi propemodum carere sensu, qui non sentiant illud ipsum, quod pro se citant, exemplum ipsis maxime adversari. Quid enim quaeso credidit Abrahamus, quod vel contra sensus vel incredibile nedum impossibile esset? Credidit se fore patrem multarum gentium, cum tamen et ipse iam senex et uxor sterilis et insuper iam vieta foret.[12] Quid tum postea? Quid habet ea res, quod sit sensibus contrarium? Nihil. Quid quod rationi? Ne hoc quidem. Ratio enim iudicat deum, qui mundum creavit, posse etiam ex sterili foemina fertilem facere. Atque hanc rationem secutus Abrahamus credidit "exploratum habens" (ut ibidem Paulus docet), "deum, quae promisisset, praestare etiam posse".[13] Quin et dictum illud dei "Estne

---

[7] In margin reference to ch. XXVIII.

[8] MS: *subdecere*.

* [9] Prov 1.

*[10] I Cor 2:14. In his Bible Castellio renders the sentence: "Animalis autem homo non capit quae sunt divini spiritus".

[11] Acts 10:11ff.

[12] Rom 9:7ff and Gen 15:2ff.

*[13] Rom 4:21.

res ulla, quam Iova non possit?"[14] quod isti citant, ut ostendant credenda esse, quae sunt impossibilia, maxime ipsos refellit. Illud enim a deo dictum est propter Sarae incredulitatem, quae promittente deo concepturam riserat,[15] quasi fieri non posset, ut sterilis senexque foemina conciperet. Cuius opinionis falsitatem deus hoc argumento refellit. Deus, qui omnia potest, istud quoque potest efficere. Quod enim homini impossibile est, id deo possibile est idque maxime iudicat ratio. Cum enim a deo alia non minus mira fieri videat, illud quoque fieri posse iudicat. Atque idem dico de eo, quod, cum Abrahamo promissum fuisset eius progeniem ab Isaaco denominatum iri, tamen eum nondum patrem factum iussus immolare paruit. Cogitabat enim "deum" (ut scribit author ad Hebraeos) vel "ex mortuis suscitare eum posse"[16] atque ita promissum praestare. Itaque nihil video, quod contra rationem crediderit. Hac eadem ratione argumentatur et Paulus apud regem Agrippam. "Itane vero", inquit "incredibile apud vos iudicatur mortuos a deo suscitari?".[17] Haec, inquam, contra rationem non sunt. Nihil enim videt ratio, quod sit his contrarium. Contra rationem essent, si credidisset Abrahamus Isaacum sine prole immolatum iri neque in vitam revocandum et tamen ex eo, quamvis nec esset nec futurus esset, nasciturum esse populum. Haec enim fieri non possunt. Et quia fieri non posse sciebat Abrahamus, credidit id quod fieri poterat, videlicet deum, si ipsius iussu occisus esset Isaacus, in vitam esse eum suscitaturum, ut in eo promissum praestaret. Itaque longe aliud est credere rem impossibilem et credere rem miraculosam. *Miracula multa credunt pii, sed impossibile nihil. Supra sensus item multa credunt, sed contra sensus nihil.* Quare sic statuimus, quae contra sensus contraque rationem sunt (ubi quidem nullum intervenit impedimentum), ea non esse admittenda. Quae vero sensibus rationique probantur, iis esse assentiendum.

## XXXII

ff. 99b, 101-103

Igitur quoniam de iudicando agitur et iudicari non nisi sublatis impedimentis potest et impedimenta partim in homine sunt, partim extra hominem, de iis hic agamus. Quae impedimenta sunt extra hominem, de iis tollendis nullum homini consilium damus. Frustra enim consulas ei, qui eius rei, quam consulas, potestatem non habeat. Sicuti medicus

[14] Gen 18:14.
*[15] Gen 18:13.
[16] Heb 11:19.
[17] Acts 26:8.

aegroto frustra consilium det de aeris intemperie tollenda, cum ea in aegroti potestate non sit. Quae vero sunt in homine, eorum sunt duo genera, sicuti supra iam demonstravimus. Aut enim sunt ipsius arbitrii aut non sunt. Si non sunt (quale est, quod supra docuimus de iis, qui vel a seipsis vel a deo caecati sunt),[1] ne iis quidem consilium damus de iudicando. Frustra enim vel surdo ut audiat vel caeco ut videat consilium des. Eos igitur alloquimur, in quibus aut non sunt impedimenta aut, si sunt, tolli ab eis possunt. Ac si non sunt, bene est: tanto erit eis iudicare expeditius. Sin sunt, tollenda sunt atque ita sublatis illis tum demum iudicandum. Alloquimur igitur hominem laborantem illum quidem morbis animi, sed neque deploratis neque sibi charis, atque huic sic praecipimus.

Ante omnia tibi tollenda sunt impedimenta, quae sunt in animo tuo,[2] hoc est carnales affectiones. Nam quandiu eae in te vigebunt, non poteris non perperam iudicare. Neque tamen hoc dico, quovis vitio cuiusvis rei iudicium corrumpi. Sic enim iudico, posse interdum avarum hominem de ebriositate aut luxuria recte iudicare vicissimque ebriosum aut luxuriosum de avaritia caeterisque vitiis quibus ipse non laboret. Sed quid proderit de una aliqua re bene iudicare, si in alia decipiaris? Quid avaro proderit de ebriositate rite iudicare, si avaritia caecus et porro poena dignus erit? Quid prodest volucri nec rostro nec collo nec alis capi, si pede tenetur? Numquid minus tenetur quam si toto corpore teneretur? Quid prodest homini morbos omnes vitare uno excepto, quo extinguitur? Aut omnia praeter unum, propter quod capite plectitur? Quare ut de rebus omnibus rite iudices, renunciandum est omnibus animi perturbationibus. *Sunt enim huiusmodi perturbationes tanquam dona quaedam, quae iudices caecant*, quam etiam ob causam deus in lege iudicibus interdicit, ne dona accipiant, quippe quae etiam perspicaces caecent et iustorum orationem pervertant.[3] Sic sunt carnales affectiones. Exempla sunt in promptu. Avaritia pecuniam tibi promittit aut donat eoque dono ita tibi praestringit oculos, ut de avaritia vere iudicare nequeas. Ambitio honores, luxuria voluptates, simultas et odium vindictam aut mortem inimici, breviter singula vitia iucundum aliquid carni promittunt et hoc quasi dono caecant hominem. Neque vero est, quod ita cogites, posse te quamvis istis vitiis servientem tamen recte iudicare. Cum enim ipse deus omnia sciens dixerit donis etiam perspicaces caeceri, visne te plus illo

---

[1] See above ch. XXVIII.

[2] In the margin from the hand of Castellio: *prins du chap. prius* (?). See ch. XXXI.

* [3] Ex 23:8.

sapere? Si iudex dono aliunde accepto caecatur, an dubitas quin tuae carnis illecebris caecari possis? Memento, quid homini omnium mortalium sapientissimo Solomoni acciderit, qui venereis voluptatibus usque adeo non dicam caecatus, sed plane dementatus est, ut etiam deastros coluerit.[4] Memento, quid scripserit antiquorum quidam: "Impedit ira animum, ne possis cernere verum",[5] quid item vulgo authores, dum aliquem avaritia aut libidine aliave quapiam animi perturbatione caecum aut dementem vocitant. Denique hoc tibi persuadeto, quemadmodum per coloratum vitrum colores intuens de eis vere iudicare non possis, ita pravarum cupiditatum obiectu impediri animum, quo minus vera a falsis vere discernat. Nec solum id fit in iudicando de iis vitiis, quibus ipse laborat et delectatur animus, eamque ob causam, quae contra illa vitia dicuntur, aversatur, quippe quae ipsius voluptati officiant, verum etiam in iis opinionibus, in quibus quid sentias nihil interest voluptatis. Exempli gratia si quis Lutheri opinioni de Coena Domini sit addictior, is adduci vix poterit, ut adversantem opinionem aequo animo perpendat, nedum ut sequatur, quod idem dico de caeteris opinionibus, usque adeo perturbationibus impeditur animi iudicium. Quamobrem statuo tibi fugiendas esse omnes animi perturbationes et in primis pertinaciam. Pertinaciae mala. Nam hoc vitium non unius, sed omnium rerum iudicium impedit estque pertinax homo perinde ac si quis oculos suos claudat aut aures obthuret atque ita seipsum non unum sonitum audire aut colorem videre, sed omnes prohibeat. Sic pertinax, homo, ubi semel quidpiam affirmavit, nihil iam quod contra sit videre aut audire sustinet adeoque mordicus opinioni suae adhaeret, ut, si deus ipse omnesque eius sancti atque angeli contra dicant, malit deumque sanctosque angelosque omnes condemnare quam opinionem suam recantare. Quocirca vitium hoc tanquam mortem ipsam fugito et, ut effugias, veritatem amato eamque omnibus in rebus, parvis iuxta ac magnis, ludicris ae seriis agnoscere ac confiteri, simulatque eam animadverteris, assuescito. Neve te errorem tuum fateri pudeat aut, si pudet, pudorem ferto et teipsum ad honorandam hoc est confitendam Dominam veritatem aut certe ad non resistendum cogito. Alioquin periisti nec te hominum quisquam ac ne deus quidem unquam sanabit, quin tibi idem usuveniet, quod Ierosolymae, quam, cum Christus saepius sanare voluisset, ipsa recusavit, quae pertinacia quantum illi malorum conflaverit et tunc praedictum a Christo fuit et nunc palam est. Praestat brevem pudorem apud homines in praesentia devorare quam

---

* [4] I Kings 11.

* [5] *Dicta Catonis*. See ch. XXVI n. 1.

paulo post in sempiternum probrum et apud deum et apud universos homines incurrere. Pudere nos deberet veritatem non confiteri et pudet confiteri: an non hoc argumentum est eam nobis non esse charam nosque admodum esse corruptos? Quis natorum est, quem matrem agnoscere pudeat? Quod si est veritas nostra mater, cur eam agnoscere verecundamur? Aut si ob peccatum nostrum filii sumus falsitatis, cur non valedicimus falsae isti obscoenaeque matri et ad veram illam pulchramque matrem veritatem nos recipimus? Vae qui malum bono, luci tenebras, vero falsum praeferunt. Quare ama verum oderisque falsum. Alioquin nihil tibi nisi mors et exitium expectandum est. Dices: sed quis istud praestare poterit? Respondeo: qui credet in Christum, cui data est tum in coelo tum in terra omnis potestas et in quem qui credunt, iis quoque ea datur potestas ut filii dei fiant, qui quidem non ex sanguine nec ex voluntate carnis nec ex voluntate viri, sed ex deo nati sunt.

Dices: sed ad ista praestanda opus est spacio. Quid interea faciet homo superantibus interdum animi perturbationibus necdum victoria potitus? Respondeo: si perturbationes illas agnoscit et odit, licet eis nondum prorsus imperet, non tamen iccirco non recte de eis iudicabit, id quod exemplo sic demonstrabo. Est aliquis, cuius gustatus ita est morbo corruptus, ut et panis non sapiat, ut si palati sui iudicium, sicuti pueri et dementes solent, sequatur, pronunciet panem non esse bonum. At si rationem sequitur ducem, quamvis repugnante gustatu bonum esse censebit. Sic accidit et in animi affectionibus. Est aliquis ita peccato infectus, ut eius carni castitas et modestia non placeat. Idem si veritati credet, carnis iudicio renunciabit et virtutem bonam esse iudicabit et ratione ac spiritu vitium oderit virtutemque amabit atque ita peccato carne serviens virtuti spiritu serviet. Huius hominis iudicium hac in parte corruptum non est. Atque haec de renunciando carnis affectionibus. Et quoniam haec res est maximi momenti et rursus homo tardus est ad ea discenda, quae sunt ipsi ad salutem necessaria, adeo,[6] ut sit interdum tanquam asinus quidam stimulandus eique veluti puero cibus praemansus in os inserendus, placet explicare quidnam sit carnis affectio, deinde eius exempla afferre, ex quibus manifeste videas, quemadmodum ea excaecet hominem.

---

[6] In margin from another hand "contradictio to fol. 85 verso". One could see a contradiction to what Castellio says on fol. 84 verso: "Quare hoc iam confidenter audeo dicere, quae sunt homini cognitu necessaria, ea esse cognitu perfacilia. Haec est via salutis, in qua discenda parum temporis, in eadem perambulanda totum aevum consumendum est". See ch. XX, pp. 54 f.

## XXXIII

ff. 103-104b

### QUID SIT CARNIS AFFECTIO. ITEM EXEMPLA, QUO PACTO EA HOMINIS IUDICIUM EXCAECET.

Docent medici morbum esse affectionem contra naturam, quae affectio actionem impediat ut, si sit in oculis, prohibeat videre aut bene videre; in auribus audire; in pedibus ambulare. Sic est carnis affectio morbus animi alioquin peccatum appellatus, hoc est intemperies et perturbatio quaedam animi contra naturam, quae animi actionem hoc est officium impediat, hoc est prohibeat, quo minus bene iudicet et deum "toto corde"[1] et "alterum sicuti seipsum amet".[2]

Hic contradicet forsan aliquis[3] negans peccatum esse contra naturam et certos sacrarum literarum locos allegans, quibus ostendat peccatum homini esse naturale. Cui ego respondebo, si qui sunt aut esse videntur eiusmodi loci, eos non de natura, sed de corrupta natura esse. Ego vero de natura loquor, in quali hominem deus creavit videlicet recta et morbi experte. Supervenit deinde instinctu Satanae peccatum, qui dei temperatum opus intemperatum reddidit contra naturam. Neque enim ad peccandum creavit deus hominem, non magis profecto quam ad claudicandum aut febricitandum. Quod si Adamus aliquo casu leprosus evasisset et porro nos omnes leprosos progenuisset, non iccirco non esset lepra contra naturam. Quemadmodum si quis caecus natus est, non iccirco non est eius caecitas contra naturam. Hine fit, ut Christus eorum animi morbos tollat et sanet, qui in ipsum credunt, quemadmodum corpora sanabat etiam eorum, qui ab utero matris aegroti erant. Venit enim, ut aboleat opera Diaboli,[4] hoc est peccatum, quod profecto nequaquam faceret, si peccatum opus esset naturae ab ipsius patre conditum. Alioquin patris opus aboleret essetque patri contrarius.

Iam exempla afferre libet, quibus ostendam caecari perturbationibus animum et ab officio prohiberi.

Videmus saepe duos litigatores sic inter se contendere, ut uterque ius a se esse sibi certo persuadeat. Et tamen alter uter certe, nonnunquam uterque errat. Quid in causa est? Nimirum amor sui, animi carnalis

---

* [1] Deut 6:5.

* [2] Lev 19:18.

[3] See Calvin, *Institutes*, 1559, C.R. XXX, col. 184-185: "Dicimus ergo naturali hominem vitiositate corruptum, sed quae a natura non fluxerat... Vocamus tamen naturalem, ne quis ab unoquoque prava consuetudine comparari putet, quum haereditario iure universos comprehensos teneat...".

* [4] Jn 3:8.

affectio, quae efficit, ut uterque sua tantum iura spectans alterius vicissim iura non consideret. Id quod ex eo luce clarius perspici potest, quod neuter unquam ad dexteram errat aut deflectit, hoc est neuter sic errat, ut alteri plus, sibi minus aequo, sed semper contra alteri minus, sibi plus aequo vindicet. Nam certe, nisi huiusmodi errores ab amore sui proficiscerentur, non minus saepe ad dextram quam ad sinistram erraretur nec minus saepe uterque sibi quam alteri detraheret.

Similiter et disputantibus usuvenit, quorum saepe aliquis opinionem tuetur ita falsam, ita absurdam et ineptam, ut id nemo excepto uno ipso non videat. Et tamen eam putat verissimam et mordicus ita tuetur, ut mori malit quam cedere. Nimirum in causa est victoriae cupiditas (in qua est ambitio), quae efficit, ut alterius argumenta non perpendat.

Stulta indulgensque mater sic amat natos suos, ut, quamvis de eorum improbitate universa vicinia conqueratur, tamen putet insontes malitque universae viciniae testimonium damnare quam natorum suorum mores sano animo explorare. Est aliquis, qui uxorem suam sic amat, ut nullum tantum possit illius existere peccatum, quin id excuset. Rursus, alius suam ita odit, ut nulla tanta esse queat virtus, quin eam aut in vitium vertat aut certe supra modum extenuet. Et ut summatim dicam: *in omnibus contentionibus et bellis semper videre licet caecitatem et pertinaciam aliquam ab amore sui manantem*, quam plerumque soli ii, in quibus ea inest, non videant, caeteri apertissime perspiciant. Si invehitur concionator in avaritiam, ei contradicunt eumque odere foeneratores. Si in bellum, milites. Si in saltationes, adolescentes et puellae. Si de ieiunando loquitur, in eum conspirant et adversus eum disputant gulosi et ex sacris literis planum facere nituntur ieiunandi tempus praeterisse. Breviter mundi iudicium amore sui caecum est acciditque in animo, quod in corpore fieri videmus. Nobis minus foetet minusque sordet excrementum nostrum quam alienum. Si quis habet in sinu atque adeo in ore vomicam, ab ea haud usque adeo abhorret, eidem aliena nauseam parit. Audivi aliquando proverbium nullos esse foedos amores. Item domesticos pediculos non esse foedos. Item suum cuique avi nidum placere. Haec proverbia vera sunt. Licet videre hominem vindictae cupidum adeo abhorrere ab ebrietate, ut eam conspuat, at eidem fallere, mentiri, insidiari, inimicum ulcisci et simultatem viginti aut triginta totos annos fovere non est religio. Cur? Quoniam eius est vomica, non foetet ei. Rursus ebriosus ab aliorum vitiis abhorret, at ebriositatem pro nihilo ducit. *Breviter amor sui caecat homines. Quo circa homini discendum est odium sui, alioquin insanabilis est. Haec a me verissime dicuntur. Quare expue sordes tuas et tibi foetere incipient tanquam alienae.* Nam quandiu eas intus retinebis tuaeque erunt, foetere tibi non poterunt. Haec si feceris et animo veritatis cupido huc accesseris, eam, sive tuae opinioni quadrabit sive discrepabit, sequi paratus, spero hic te lucem veritatis nonnullam inventurum, ita ut de ea lucis patri deo gratias agas. Atque hic huius libri finis esto.

# LIBER SECUNDUS

## I ff. 105

Demonstravimus praeter caetera generaliter superiore libro, quae quaestiones sub sensus rationemque cadunt, de iis esse sensu et ratione iudicandum. Deinceps quaenam sint eae quaestiones, singillatim est ostendendum. Neque enim de iis inter omnes convenit, quippe cum nonnulli quaestiones quasdam a sensibus et ratione summoveant et solis literis componi velint, quas nos maxime sensibus et ratione diiudicandas esse, ut spero, planum faciemus. Sequemur autem rationem hanc docendi, ut primum unaquaque quaestione in medium proposita de ea ratione disputemus. Deinde rationi authoritates subiungamus ex sacris literis. Postremo quae contra dici vel solent vel possunt, non equidem omnia (quis enim omnia vel recordari vel excogitare aut queat aut necessarium putet?), sed praecipua et quae erunt eiusmodi, ut iis refutatis in caeteris facile futurum putemus certamen, diluamus. Illud autem praemonitum volo lectorem, morosioribus et sacrarum literarum verba pertinacius retinentibus, etiamsi falsissimam sequantur sententiam, eam non posse extorqueri. Itaque illis repudiatis ad aequiores provocamus et tales postulamus lectores, qui non res verborum, sed verba rerum serva esse et intelligant et patiantur. Tractabimus autem quaestiones non omnes, sed eas quae nobis videbuntur maxime tractatu necessariae et de quibus tam pertinaces sunt hodie controversiae, ut alii alios propter eas non dicam damnent et infestent, sed quantum in ipsis est in aeternos gehennae cruciatus deturbent. Quin ne eas quidem omnes, siquidem sunt quaedam nostro tempore ita agitatae atque explicatae et superioris aevi in iis errores ita luce palam confutati sint, ut, si quis cognitis illis de rebus disputationibus tamen in erroribus perseverat, eum ego ceu pertinacem missum esse faciendum existimem. Est enim de eorum numero, quos superiore libro dixi, quia claudunt oculos, non posse collustrari. Faciemus autem quaestionum classes duas, sicuti antea iam attigimus: unam earum, quae aut quarum certe pars aliqua sensibus potest et ratione diiudicari; alteram earum, quae sensibus et ratione diiudicari nequeunt.

## II

ff. 105b-108

## De Trinitate

Igitur ut hic quoque, sicuti superiore libro fecimus, a deo exordium ducamus, prima veniat in medium quaestio de trinitate.

Esse deum ratione percipitur, sicut et principio superioris libri demonstravimus et rationem secutae gentes omnes (nisi si qua prorsus fera, sylvestris et a bestiarum natura non multum distans fuit) persuasum habuere. Sed utrum unus deus an plures dii sint, id vero ratione aut non percipitur aut ita difficulter percipitur, ut pleraeque omnes gentes quamvis ratione praeditae, tamen quia patefacta divinitus doctrina carebant, plures deos coluerint. Sed Christi, lucis mundi, adventus effecit, ut unum esse deum Asia et Europa et Africa (quae tunc tres orbis partes commemorabantur) etiam hodie inter tot introductos postea errores et scelera tamen constanter credant: tanta est vis lucis etiam in tenebris lucentis.[1] Itaque hoc ex fide assumpto quod nemo negabit, videlicet unum esse deum, deinceps super hoc fundamento de trinitate an sit et quid sit, ratione quaerere licet. Quaestio est ardua et de qua certi aliquid statuere est periculosum. Quare ego de ea nihil affirmabo. Tantum huc apponam ad considerandum disputatiunculam cuiusdam viri nondum in vulgus aeditam, quae qualis sit iudicent lectores, consideratione quidem dignam esse ego iudico. Facit autem ille vir seipsum cum Athanasii Symbolo disputantem his verbis:

### Athanasius

Quicumque vult salvus esse, ante omnia opus est, ut teneat catholicam fidem, quam nisi quisque integram inviolatamque servaverit, absque dubio in aeternum peribit.

### Quidam

Oportet igitur, ut fides catholica talis sit, ut eam et omnes tenere possint et publicani illi et meretrices[2] atque adeo latro ille, qui in cruce pendens in Christum credidit[3] et salvus factus est, tenuerint, alioquin perierunt.

---

* [1] Jn 1:5.
* [2] Mt 21:32.
* [3] Lk 23:40ff.

Athanasius

Fides autem catholica haec est, ut unum deum in trinitate et trinitatem in unitate veneremur.

Quidam

Istam vero fidem ego publicanis illis et meretricibus notam fuisse non puto. Si tu putas, proba. In sacris quidem literis nullum de ea verbum comperio. Quod si tu vera scribis, illi omnes sine dubio in aeternum perierunt, nisi forte tu non de praeteritis, sed de futuris loqueris. Sed non est tuum, Athanasi, mutare tuo tempore tempora et efficere, ut quod ante te non fuit creditu necessarium, post[4] te fiat necessarium. Iam vero quaero, cuiusnam rei unitatem et trinitatem appelles. Est enim trinitas ternarius numerus, ut, si foliorum trinitatem dicas (ternionem Latini typographi, triadem Graeci vocant), intelligantur libri tres,[5] et, si librorum decadem (quae eadem loquendi forma est) dicas, intelligantur libri decem. Cuiusnam igitur rei unitatem et trinitatem appellas? Nam si dei, erit haec tua sententia: Unum deum in trinitate deorum, hoc est in tribus diis, et tres deos in uno deo veneremur.[6] Quam sententiam tu, credo, non approbabis. Sin personae, erit haec: unam personam in tribus personis et tres personas in una persona veneremur. Ac ne hanc quidem admittes. Vis enim tres non unam esse personam, sicut in sequentibus ostendis. Sin substantiae unitatem et trinitatem appellas,[7] sic accipienda erunt verba tua: Unam dei substantiam in tribus substantiis et tres substantias in una substantia veneremur.[8] Sed si est haec[9] mens tua, erunt tres dei substantiae, id est tres dii. Sin sic accipienda sunt: Unam dei substantiam in tribus personis et tres personas in una substantia veneremur,[10] obscure admodum et plane aenigmatice locutus es, id quod non decet scribentem fidei omnibus tenendae Symbolum. Quod enim scire omnes debent, id ita dici debet, ut ab omnibus intelligi queat.

Athanasius

Neque confundentes personas neque substantiam separantes.

---

[4] Copy: *per*.
[5] Copy: *folia tria*.
[6] Copy: veneramur.
[7] Copy: *appelles*.
[8] See note 4.
[9] Copy: *haec est*.
[10] See note 4.

Quidem

Et hic scire velim, quid personas voces. Si enim personam vocas ut Latini, dum Caesaris personam dicunt pro Caesare, erit idem persona quod substantia, ita inepte locutus eris. Sin personam sic appellas, ut cum dicimus in eodem homine, qui sit civis et sartor et pater, tres esse personas, videlicet civis et sartoris et patris, feceris nobis ex patre et filio et spiritu sancto unum et eundem. Ita fiet, ut, quod Christus iussit homines baptizari in nomine patris et filii et spiritus sancti, perinde sit ac si iussisset eos baptizari in nomine unius trinominis dei. Quod et falsum est et non minus absurdum quam si dicas aliquid factum esse in nomine Abrahamidae et Isaaci et patris Iacobi. Item, quod Christus patrem oravit, oraverit seipsum. Et quod pater filium genuit,[11] genuerit seipsum. Et quod filium misit et spiritum sanctum misit, miserit seipsum. Quae omnia nemo et inepta et falsa esse negaverit.

Athanasius

Alia est enim persona patris, alia filii, alia spiritus sancti: sed patris et filii et spiritus sancti una est divinitas, aequalis gloria, coaeterna[12] maiestas. Qualis pater, talis filius, talis spiritus sanctus. Increatus pater, increatus filius, increatus spiritus sanctus. Immensus pater, immensus filius, immensus spiritus sanctus. Aeternus pater, aeternus filius, aeternus spiritus sanctus.

Quidam

Istorum omnium pleraque nusquam invenio in sacris literis et tu plus a nobis exigis quam deus, qui, ista ut crederemus, nusquam iussit.

Athanasius

Et tamen non tres aeterni, sed unus aeternus, sicut non tres increati nec tres immensi, sed unus increatus et unus immensus. Similiter omnipotens pater, omnipotens filius, omnipotens spiritus sanctus. Et tamen non tres omnipotentes, sed unus omnipotens. Ita deus pater, deus filius, deus spiritus sanctus et tamen non tres dii, sed unus est deus. Ita dominus pater, dominus filius, dominus spiritus sanctus et tamen non tres domini, sed unus est dominus.

---

[11] Copy: *genuit filium.*

[12] Copy: *aeterna.*

Quidam

Ista vero perinde sunt ac si dicas: Senex Abrahamus, senex Isaacus, senex Iacobus et tamen non tres senes, sed unus est senex; aut si dicas:[13] Annosa palma, annosa cedrus, annosa quercus et tamen non tres annosae, sed una est annosa. Enimvero ut ista[14] credam, Athanasi, necesse est, ut omni rationi (quod dei donum est longe praestantissimum et quo homo potissimum a bestiis[15] differt) vale dicam atque ita in brutam naturam sensumque conversus eo ipso etiam caream, quo creditur. Credi enim non nisi ratione potest, quo fit ut, qui rationis sunt expertes, nihil credere queant. Extitit olim quidam Sophista Gorgias, qui ausus est contendere nihil esse eorum, quae sunt, cuius insaniam merito insectatus est Isocrates.[16] Sed tu mihi videris non minus insana dicere, qui tres, de quibus singulis dicatur: "hic est aeternus", neges esse tres aeternos. Me vero et deus et natura et omnium gentium consuetudo loquendi et grammatica et dialectica et arithmetica docuit[17] tres esse tres et unum esse unum, et si tres sunt, non esse unum, et si unus est, non esse tres, et qui haec negant, ii mihi non magis quam bestiae videntur esse docibiles.

Hactenus ille quidam, quae ego dumtaxat ad considerandum proposui. Equidem[18] si Athanasium possem defendere, facerem. Sed verum fatebor: non possum. Quod si quis potest, me perlibente fecerit. Absit enim, ut veritatem opprimi velim. Quod ad fidem meam attinet, Credo in unum deum patrem omnipotentem, creatorem coeli et terrae, et in Iesum Christum filium eius unicum dominum nostrum, et in spiritum sanctum. In hac fide et sum et ad finem usque, volente deo, esse pergam; atque hoc mihi persuadeo, qui hanc simplicem et quae nobis ab Apostolis tradita putatur fidem vere tenent, eos in via esse salutis, etiam si illas nescioquas inexplicabilitates in ecclesiam post apostolicae simplicitatis tempora curiosius introductas nec teneant nec credant. Quod si qui tam acuto sunt ingenio, ut illa percipiant, quae ego et mei similes non percipimus, bene est, non invideo. Sed idem ingenii acumen ab omnibus servandis

[13] *aut si dicas* not in copy.

[14] Copy: *ita*.

[15] Copy: *brutis*.

[16] Isocrates, 10,3. See Works ed. L. Van Hook, Cambridge: Harvard University Press, 1945, vol. 2, pp. 60-63.

[17] Copy: *docent*.

[18] Copy: *etenim*.

exigere est (ut mihi quidem videtur) viam salutis maximae hominum parti praecludere.[19]

## III ff. 108b, 109

### De fide. Eam videlicet voluntatis esse, non intellectus

Proximum est, ut de fide dicamus. Fidem non esse notitiam, ut quidam tradunt, supra demonstravimus et quid ea sit ostendimus. Atque id ipsius rationis iudicio facile percipi potest. Tam enim sciunt omnes ratione praediti, quid sit credere, quam quid videre, audire, cogitare estque id cognitu facilius quam definitu. Adducam exemplum, ex quo natura fidei plene et proprie perspici queat. Id erit ex Iohannis evangelio,[1] ubi narratur, quemadmodum Iesus illum caecum natum sanaverit, videlicet lutatis eius oculis et eo ire iusso ad Siloam piscinam ad lavandum, quo ille facto vidit. Quod enim iussus ivit, fuit credentis, videlicet se visurum. Nisi enim credidisset, non ivisset. Quod autem lotus vidit, fuit scientis, scilicet se videre. Atque hic illa eius fides finem habuit, videlicet in adventu scientiae. Est enim fides via ad scientiam eademque, ubi venit scientia, desinit. Neque sine magno mysterio factum puto, ut eum per tenebras, hoc est adhuc caecum, ire Iesus iusserit. Indicatur enim hoc facto vis fidei, quae homines ducit per tenebras, hoc est nondum ea scientes, quae credunt. "Sic Abrahamus, iubente deo, profectus est in locum, quem haereditate obtenturus erat, nesciens quo vaderet".[2] Sic denique totus ille nymbus testium, qui in epistola ad Hebraeos commemorantur, crediderunt quae non videbant. Et, ut paucis absolvam, Petrus in epistola secunda aperte ostendit fidem non idem esse quod scientiam, sed a fide oriri scientiam, dum dicit: "Acquirentes in fide vestra virtutem, in virtute scientiam.[3]

Est autem fides in voluntate non minus quam caetera, quae homini itidem ut fides praecipiuntur, id quod tum ratione tum authoritate confirmari potest. Ratio est haec, quod videmus "homines facile credere quae volunt", sicuti dicit Iulius Caesar,[4] contraque difficulter credere,

---

[19] I have recently been engaged in an extensive study of Servetus' writings. It seems to me that the *Quidam* in the dialogue on the *Trinity* expresses thoughts that are very close to but not identical with Servetus'. See esp. *De Trinitatis Erroribus*, ed. Frankfurt: Minerva, 1965, book I. We know, moreover, that Castellio was familiar with Servetus' writings. See *Introduction* n. 2.

[1] Jn 9.
[2] Heb 11:8.
[3] II Pet 1:5.
[4] *De bello gallico* III,18,6: "fere libenter homines id quod volunt credunt".

quae nolunt. Atqui si fides intellectus, non voluntatis esset, aeque facile crederent, quae nolunt, ac quae volunt. Aeque enim facile intelliguntur, quae aspera sunt ac quae dulcia. Exempla proferre facile est. Si quid boni aut fortunati nobis de uxore aut liberis aut amicis narratur, id protinus credere solemus, etiam si parum sit verisimile. Sin aliquid mali, aegre credimus, etiam si sit verisimile. Nimirum quia eorum bonum volumus, malum non item. Item si cui ebrioso aegrotanti dicas morbum ab ipsius intemperantia ortum fuisse, non facile credet, sin ab aere pestilente aut alia quapiam causa, facile.

Authoritas quoque est in promptu. Primum quod credere homini tam aut praecipitur aut interdicitur quam parentes amare aut alteri benefacere aut adulterare aut furari et huius generis alia. "Agite poenitentiam", inquit, "et credite evangelio".[5] Item: "Quicquid petetis a deo, creditote vos impetraturos, et impetrabitis".[6] Et sane vulgo sic loquimur, dum alicui credi aut non credi iubemus. Praeterea in corde fidem esse tradunt sacrae literae. Ut in Luca: "O tardi corde ad credendum".[7] Et in Actis: "Si toto corde credis".[8] Et ad Romanos: "Corde creditur ad iusticiam".[9] Et ad Hebraeos: "Cor incredulum".[10] Ex his apparet fidem sicut et caeteras iusticiae partes in corde, itaque voluntatis esse.

## IV ff. 10

### Argumentorum refutatio, quae ab iis adduci solent, qui fidem intellectus esse contendunt

Contra haec sic docent quidam.[1] Fides est actio intellectus. Intellectus autem nullas habet actiones nisi cognoscere: ergo fides est cognitio videlicet rerum probabilium, sive sunt verae sive falsae, ut cum dicit Turca: Scio per fidem Mahumetem esse vatem dei: illa eius fides et cognitio est rei falsae. Ad quod ego respondeo: rei falsae non esse cognitionem, sed cognitionis opinionem falsam, quae error appellatur estque in animo idem, quod in corporis oculis hallucinatio. Ut enim oculis non potest videri, quod non est, ita et animo non potest cognosci, quod non est. Itaque quemadmodum, qui sibi videtur videre duos soles,

---

* [4] Mk 1:15.

* [6] Mk 11:24.

[7] Lk 24:25. In his Bible Castellio uses *animo* instead of *corde*.

[8] Acts 8:37.

[9] Rom 10:10.

[10] Heb 3:12 In his Bible Castellio says: *prava diffidentiae mens*.

[1] Who is the quidam? St Thomas? A contemporary Arab writer?

non videt, sed hallucinatur, ita qui se putat scire Mahometem esse dei vatem, non scit, sed errat.

Addunt haec. Intellectus est facultas naturalis ideoque necessario assentitur aut dissentit aut dubitat, prout est evidentia rerum, quae ei obiiciuntur. Proinde sine evidentia non assentitur et porro neque credit. Respondeo. Imo saepe credit homo res minime evidentes minimeque probabiles, id quod de cognoscendo dici non potest.[2] Credidit Abrahamus se senem ex sene et sterili Sara suscepturum prolem,[3] id quod erat minime evidens minimeque probabile. Erat quidem probabile deum, qui promittebat, vera dicere. Sed res ipsa, quam promittebat deus, erat per se minime verisimilis. Nos autem hic non quaerimus, an Abrahamus deum cognosceret, sed an eam rem, quam illo promittente credebat, cognosceret, id quod negamus. Addam exemplum aliud. Narratur in tertio libro Regum, quemadmodum vates quidam dei iussu iusserit viro cuidam, ut se vulneraret, id quod ille facere recusavit.[4] At alius fecit. Hic eorum alter vati credidit, alter non credidit. Cur ita? An quia eadem res uni esset probabilis, alteri non item? Nequaquam. Erat enim eadem res eodemque modo iussa eaque minime probabilis. Quid enim improbabilius aut incredibilius quam dei vatem insontem vulnerari iuberi a deo? Itaque qui credidit, is non rei probabilitatem secutus est intellectu, sed vatis iusso credidit voluntate. Sic et nos in via saepe credimus ignoto homini viam nobis ostendenti nulla inducti probabilitate nullamque illo reddente rationem. Quin saepe credibile nobis videtur ad sinistram esse deflectendum et tamen ad dextram illo docente volentes et credentes, non intelligentes deflectimus, et postea, ubi in urbem pervenimus, tum demum illum verum dixisse, quod tum credidimus, cognoscimus.[5] Addam et aliud exemplum longe nobilissimum et nobis ad obediendum deo, etiam si res sit minime verisimilis, utilissimum. Cum a Chaldaeis obsideretur Ierosolyma iamiam expugnanda, praedixit Ieremiae[6] deus venturum ad ipsum Hananeelem quendam cognatum iussitque, ut ab eo fundum emeret, qui fundus erat apud Ieremiae patriam Anathotam, id quod factum est. Venit enim ille, ac tunc Ieremias illud esse Iovae mandatum intellexit, sicut ipsemet ibi narrat. Cur ergo ante non intellexerat? Nimirum quia res erat ipsi incognita; itaque tantum crediderat. Atque hic manifesto iam perspicitur, quemadmodum fidem

---

[2] See above chps. XIX,XX,XXIII.

[3] Gen, 18.

[4] I Kings 20:35ff.

[5] In margin reference to suppl. 8.

[6] Jer 32.

secuta fuerit cognitio. Sequitur continuo in eadem narratione aliud exemplum. Emit[7] enim fundum Ieremias contra omnem probabilitatem credens deo. Cum enim urbs iam iamque capienda foret, non erat credibile fundum illum in Ieremiae potestatem venturum esse. Sed ille rei ignotae (quia notus deus iubebat) credidit atque ita demum causam a deo quaesivit et cognovit, sicut ibi literis mandatum extat. Ita fidem eius secuta est cognitio.

Dices: At si ita foret, esset caeca fides crederetque homo aeque Satanae atque Christo. Respondeo: Non ita est. Non enim dico hominem ignorare eum, cui credat, sed ignorare eam rem, quam credat. Novit deum ideoque ei credit, sciens deum esse qui dicat. Sed rem, quam dicit deus, saepe ignorat.[8] Noverant Apostoli Christum et porro Christi patrem deum ideoque Christi dictis credebant. Sed ipsa dicta saepe non intellegebant. Apparet hoc ex illa Lucae narratione, ubi recenset, quemadmodum Christus praedixerit eis futurum, ut ipse "extraneis traderetur et illuderetur et contumeliis afficeretur et conspueretur et verberatus interficeretur et tertio die resurgeret. At illi (inquit Lucas) nihil horum intellexerunt ideoque tecta eis erat illa oratio, ut, quae dicerentur, ignorarent".[9] Credebant illi quidem Christo. Sciebant enim eum esse veracem, sed quod dicebat ignorabant. Idem dico de eo, quod, cum aliquando praeciperet eis, ut Pharisaeorum fermentum caverent,[10] putabant eum de panis fermento loqui, in quo quidem fidem habebant, sed hallucinabantur. Sicut et quod eum regnaturum esse credentes Zebedaei filii putabant humano more regnaturum. Quare in tota hac quaestione etiam atque etiam animadvertenda est haec distinctio, quam supra posui, aliud esse cognoscere eum, cui credas, aliud eam rem quam credas. Nam rem quidem, dum credimus, cognoscere non semper necesse est et saepe ne vult quidem deus. Magis enim honoratur eius veritas ab homine, si ei de re ignota credit homo (id quod paucorum est), quam si de re nota, id quod cuiusvis est. At eum cognoscere, cui credamus, debemus, ne videlicet ignoto credentes decipiamur. Hinc dictum illud Pauli ad Timotheum: "Scio, cui crediderim et persuasum habeo eum posse meum depositum (hoc est vitam) custodire ad illam diem".[11]

---

[7] *ibidem.*

[8] The same thought is expressed by M. Flacius, *Novum Testamentum Jesu Christi filii Dei ex Versione Erasmi*, gloss. 1011b: "... contra in sermone divino non tam, quid dicatur, quam, quis dicate, attendendum est..." And also Luther. See G. Moldaenke, *Schriftverständnis und Schriftdeutung im Zeitalter der Reformation* I, "Matthias Flaccius Illyricus", Stuttgart, 1936, ch. IV, notes 26, 27.

[9] Lk 18:32.

*[10] Mt 16:6.

[11] II Tim 1:12.

Dices: Si credere esset arbitrii voluntatisque nostrae, possemus credere, quando vellemus. Atque hoc falsum est, ergo et illud. Respondeo: Etiam comedere, bibere, ambulare, vigilare sunt arbitrii hominis, et tamen interdum ea facere non potest. Quod idem et in fide aliquo casu accidere potest: nec tamen iccirco non est fides arbitrii hominis.

## V ff. 111-112

### Locorum refutatio, qui ab iis allegari solent qui fidem volunt esse notionem

Allegant etiam sacras literas. Primum locum illum ad Hebraeos, in quo fides dicatur esse "sperandarum substantia rerum, argumentum non apparentium".[1] Quem locum sic interpretantur quidam, ut dicant substantiam[2] (quae ibi Graece hypostasis dicitur) esse quasi fulcrum, cui pia mens innitatur et incumbat. Perinde ac si diceret fidem ipsam certam quandam esse ac securam possessionem eorum, quae nobis a deo promissa sunt. Argumentum autem (qui Graece est Elenchus) esse iudicem, probationem aut, ut reddidit Augustinus,[3] convictionem rerum non praesentium, perinde ac si diceret evidentiam non apparentium rerum, visionem earum quae non videntur, perspicuitatem obscurarum, praesentiam absentium, demonstrationem occultarum. Hinc effici volunt, ut fides sit cognitio. Sed pace eorum dixerim: locum illum non vere interpretantur. Primum enim fides non potest esse fulcrum, cui pia mens innitatur. Alioquin ipsa fides inniteretur sibimetipsi, quod falsum est: innititur enim non sibi, sed vel deo vel dei promissis. Deinde tantum abest, ut sit fides possessio promissorum, ut cum ipsa possessione consistere non possit. Itaque ubi promissa possidebimus, iam non credemus, sed fruemur. Fides enim dux est ad possessionem, ad quam ubi perventum est, finem habet fides. Quare locum illum, dum sic interpretantur, rem alioquin non obscuram obscurant, felicius locum illum ex re ipsa quam rem ex loco intellecturi, si hoc rite considerassent. Proinde locus ille est diligentius perpendendus. Primum nomen hypostasis non est eo in loco proprie substantia. Nam si fides est substantia sive subsistentia rerum, quae sperantur, efficitur, ut rerum substantia sit antequam sint ipsae res. Nam quae sperantur nondum sunt. Ut quod

---

[1] Heb 11:1 In his Bible Castellio says: "*Est autem speratorum subiectio, rerum demonstratio, quae non cernuntur*...".

[2] Literally in Calvin, *Institutes*, 1536, C.R. XXIX, col. 57.

[3] *De Trinitate*, 13, 1, 3.

speramus resurrectionem mortuorum, ea nondum est; quod si fides est eius substantia, efficitur, ut iam substet, hoc est sit resurrectio aut certe ut substet, antequam sit id, quod fieri non potest. Praeterea efficitur, ut in iis, qui credunt resurrectionem aut diem iudicii aut Christi supplicium etc., sint illa omnia, cum sit in eis fides, id quod est absurdum. Item ut si illa non credantur, non sint neque esse possint extra credentes, quandoquidem sine subsistentia, hoc est sine fide, esse non possunt, id quod est absurdum. Adde quod nec substantiae nec argumenti sive demonstrationis nomen significat cognitionem. Est enim cognitio in eo qui cognoscit, substantia autem rei et demonstratio est extra ipsum. Quare Pauli locus ille sic accipiendus est, ut eum quidam converterunt his verbis: "Fides est speratorum subiectio, rerum demonstratio, quae non cernuntur".[4] Hoc est: fides nobis quasi sub oculos subiicit et demonstrat ea, quae non cernuntur efficitque non equidem, ut ea cernamus (cerni enim non possunt, quae non sunt), sed ut ea cernere videamur nec secus eis assentiamur quam si cerneremus. Sic dicit Paulus Galatis Christum apud ipsos fuisse crucifixum,[5] hoc est ita praedicatum et verbis depictum, ut ipsum cernere viderentur. Declaratur hoc in eodem epistolae capite, ubi de Mose sic scribitur: "Fide reliquit Aegyptum non veritus regis iram".[6] Tanquam enim inaspectabilem (videlicet deum) aspiceret, sic duravit.

Dicunt praeterea fidem esse ex auditione sermonis dei, sermonem autem dei esse lucernam accensam pedibus nostris,[7] ergo fidem esse cognitionem. Ad quod ego respondeo locum illum, ubi lucerna dicatur sermo dei, esse de praeceptis sicut cum ex toto Psalmo tum potissimum ex verbis illis patet, quod dicit "pedibus meis", videlicet ad ambulandum, hoc est ad ea facienda, quae mihi praecipiuntur. Itaque locus ille est de cognitione praeceptorum, quae certa et clara sunt. Sed non iccirco omnia cognoscuntur, quae creduntur. Praeceptum erat Abrahamo,[8] ut iret in terram, quam nesciebat. Illud praeceptum erat clarum: "Exi ex patria". Sed quonam iret, nesciebat faciebatque, quod nos solemus, dum fidelem aliquem ducem credentes sequimur nescientes, quo nos ducat. Sic et Israelitae per solitudinem columnam illam noctu lucentem per multas ambages sequebantur nescientes,[9] quonam ea duceret aut ubinam

[4] See n. 1.
* [5] Gal 3:1.
* [6] Heb 11:27.
[7] Ps 119:105 (Vulg. 118:105).
[8] Heb 11:8.
* [9] Ex 13:21.

quietura foret. Ducem enim sciebant et haec erat cognitio. Sed viam nesciebant et haec erat vis fidei per ignota locorum eos ducentis. Nam omnino quemnam sequamur scire debemus, alioquin periculum esset, ne quando angelum Satanae sequeremur, sed quonam sequamur scire nec semper e re nostra est nec semper ipse vult. Maior enim est et eius honos et nostra fides atque obedientia, si ei tantum tribuamus, ut eum per ignota subsequamur. Sic quibus plurimum tribuimus hominibus, eorum nudis dictis credere solemus eosque, quocumque ducant, sequi, etiam si quonam ducant ignoremus.

## VI

ff. 112-113b

Sed citantur loci quidam, in quibus sciendi verbum pro credendo poni videtur. Cuiusmodi est ille Iohannis in prima epistola: "Nos nunc dei filii sumus, tametsi nondum patet, quid simus futuri. Scimus autem, cum id patefactum fuerit, nos eius fore similes".[1] Item illud Marthae apud Iohannem: "Scio, quicquid a deo petiveris, daturum esse tibi deum" et mox: "Scio resurrecturum esse in resurrectione in novissima die".[2] Item illud Iobi: "Equidem scio vindicem meum vivere et postremo in terram surrecturum esse".[3] Item illud Pauli ad Thess.: "Cum ipsi praeclare sciatis Domini diem venturam esse ut furem noctu".[4] Ad quos et si qui alii illorum similes sunt locos respondeo scire ibi pro certo credere poni, sicuti nos vulgo loqui solemus, si quis nobis bonae fidei vir aliquid promisit. Sic enim dicimus: Scio eum venturum esse; promisit enim. Scio magistratum nostrum mihi stipendium hoc mense soluturum esse; promisit enim. Sed non iccirco, si sic loquimur, est haec vere scientia, sed est certa fides, qua ad agendum non minus movemur quam scientia, ideoque scientiam (sed non proprie) vocamus. Illud addo, interdum ex fide quodam modo fieri scientiam, ut quod superioribus diebus nunciabatur mors Enisii,[5] id si qui cum adhuc dubium esset credebant, ii proprie credere dicebantur. At nunc quod id credimus, cum iam dubitari non potest, id quamquam non nisi ex auditione habemus, tamen quodam modo non tam fides quam scientia est. Itaque iam id scire nos constanter affirmamus. Sic cum primum Israelitis Moses diceret se missum esse a deo,[6] id si qui credebant, ii proprie credidisse dicendi sunt. Sed ubi eius

---

[1] I Jn 3:2.
[2] Jn 11:22.
[3] Job 19:25.
[4] I Thess 5:2.
[5] Enisius could not be identified. It may be a fictitious name.
* [6] Ex 4:28ff.

missio tot iam miraculis et operibus confirmata fuit, ut de eo ne Aegyptii quidem aut Chananaei dubitare possent, id credere magis scire erat quam credere. Itaque Iudaei Christi tempore id non dubitant tanquam scientes affirmare. "Nos scimus" inquiunt "cum Mose locutum esse deum".[7] Ac talis fides, quae iam scientia est, non est virtus, quippe quae tum demum sit, cum iam non esse non potest. Nam id credere, quod non possis non credere, virtus non est, sed scientia, quae vel in invitos cadit neque quicquam prodest habenti.

Sed allegantur insuper quidam loci,[8] in quibus fides donum esse dei ostenditur, ex quibus effici videtur, ut ea non sit arbitrii hominis. Quod enim homini divinitus datur, id non ipse sibi homo sua voluntate parat. Neque vero huc adducere libet locum, qui in hoc argumento vulgo allegari solet, videlicet ex Pauli epistola ad Ephesios, ubi sic loquitur: "Beneficio servati estis per fidem idque non ex vobis. Dei donum est non ex factis, ne quis se iactet".[9] Ibi enim dei donum voçat non ipsam fidem, sed quod servati sunt, hoc est ipsam salutem, id quod ex tribus rationibus deprehendet, qui locum illum non inconsiderate (ut fit, dum vulgi opinioni temere assentimur), sed paulo attentius legerit. Primum quod ibi non de fide, sed de salute agitur estque locutio illa perinde ac si dicas: Daniel dei beneficio per fidem indemnis evasit leones, non ex se.[10] Dei donum fuit scilicet quod evasit. Deinde quod illa verba "non ex factis" non possunt ad fidem referri, sed ad salutem, quam non suis factis consecuti fuerant. Quis enim nescit fidem non esse ex factis? Tertio quod beneficium et donum ibi sunt idem et, cum beneficium de salute manifesto dicatur, de dono idem censendum omnino est. Adde quod paulo ante eandem sententiam dixerat, non addito nomine fidei: "Estis" inquit "beneficio servati",[11] ex quo perspicitur nomen fidei obiter adiectum fuisse. Sed longe apertissime hoc apparebit sententia, quae (ut saepe facit idem author) gemina est hoc pacto inter sese composita:

| | | |
|---|---|---|
| Beneficio servati estis per fidem | | Non ex vobis |
| | idque | |
| Dei donum est, videlicet quod servati estis | | Non ex factis |

[7] Jn 9:29.

[8] Augustine, Erasmus, Luther, Zwingli, etc.

[9] Eph 2:8ff.

*[10] Dan 6.

*[11] Eph 2:5 In the Vulgate *gratia* for *beneficio*.

Ne illum quidem locum ex Actis satis apte huc allegari puto, ubi scribitur "Dominum aperuisse animum Lydiae, ut Pauli orationem attenderet".[12] Illa enim verba non de fide, sed de attentione dicta sunt, quam deinde secuta est fides. Sed est Pauli locus in secunda ad Corinthios, in quo fidem vocat donum spiritus sancti. Verba Pauli sunt haec: "Huic per spiritum datur oratio sapientiae, illi oratio scientiae ex eodem spiritu, alii fides per eundem spiritum, alii dona sanationum, alii prodigiorum effectiones, alii vaticinatio, alii spirituum diiudicationes, alii genera linguarum, alii interpretatio linguarum".[13] Ad quem locum et si qui alii sunt huius generis respondeo omne quidem bonum esse donum dei. Sed habet deus duos modos donandi, unum naturalem, alterum miraculosum. Naturaliter donat homini panem terram colenti, pisces piscanti, aves aucupanti. Sed idem miraculo dedit Israelitis in illa solitudine panem, videlicet manna non colentibus terram,[14] item Eliae illos panes, quos ei misit per angelum,[15] item per corvum.[16] Idem igitur dico de donis illis, quae modo ex Pauli epistola recensuimus.[17] Ea nimirum illo tempore donabat quibusdam miraculo. Sed non iccirco eadem nunquam sine miraculo donantur. Nam et scientia sapientiaque pollent quidem sine miraculo, et morbos sanant interdum medici sine miraculo, et futura praedicunt interdum mathematici sine miraculo,[18] et linguarum cognitionem multi sibi non miraculo, sed longo studio compararunt. Quare in fide idem fieri dico, ut fidem interdum homo habeat miraculo, interdum non miraculo. Atque hanc distinctionem ego diligenter retineri cupio. Est enim magni ad multos locos momenti valetque adversus eorum, qui, si quid usquam de quopiam dictum est, idem ad caeteros omnes continuo transferunt, quod eorum argumentum non minus absurdum est quam si quis sic argumentetur: Paulus dicit quibusdam dari a spiritu sancto donum sanationum. Ergo quicumque morbos sanant, id habent a spiritu sancto itemque in caeteris: quicumque linguas interpretantur, id habent a spiritu sancto. Illud addam: si fides sic semper esset donum dei, ut isti volunt.[19]

---

[12] Acts 16:14.
[13] Rather I Cor 12:8ff. In the Vulgate *operatio virtutum* for *prodigiorum effectiones*.
*[14] Ex 16:4.
*[15] I Kings (Vulgate 3 Kings).
*[16] *ibid.*
[17] See above n. 13.
[18] In margin reference to suppl. 11.
[19] In margin reference to suppl. 25.

## De Iusticia[1]

### VII

ff. 113

*Post fidem proximum est ut de iusticia quatenus ea quoque in controversiam vocatur dicamus*.[2]

[Scripturus aliquid de Christiana[3] justitia imprimis confiteri volui me non alte causas justificationis nostrae repetiturum, sed statim ab initio rem qualis sit ostendere aggressurum: nemo enim nescit quin justificantis cognitu primum omnium sit necessaria praeteritorum peccatorum renunciatio et horror quidam cordis post auditam vocem violatae legis divinae in poenitente excitatus. Quae omnia postea sequatur fides in Christum Servatorem: deinde vero hanc comitetur justificatio seu Christiana justitia quae et a Christo in nos manet et nos vere justos in conspectu Dei efficiat. Quae cum hodie quoque in controversiam vocetur, nihil impedit quo minus et nos ea de re nostram in medium afferamus sententiam. Quam ego ita propono Christianis lectoribus ut si ipsi vi justificandi et sacris literis consona esse inventa fuerit approbetur; sin minus liceat saltem hoc mihi quoque quod permultis alijs licere video, liberam et non impiam sententiam in vulgus aliorum utilitatis gratia libere emittere. Ut autem jam de ipsa re dicere incipiam hoc primo tenendum est, me hoc loco justitiam vocare]...[4] Iusticiam autem hoc in loco vocamus non partem unam virtutis [uti philosophi tradunt], qua suum cuique reddatur, sed [loquens cum Theologis et sacris literis] virtutem ipsam quae partes omnes complexa est et a qua iusti, hoc est viri boni, denominantur; eamque dicimus esse in animo, quod est in corpore sanitas, ut sit iusticia, quasi animi[5] sanitas, videlicet affectio secundum rectam naturam. Iam Christum esse animarum medicum *in confesso est, ut nos superiore libro demonstravimus, et* sacrae literae testantur. Esaias quidem de eo scribit haec verba: "Ipse ob peccata vitiaque nostra peremptus atque contusus, poenas nobis salutares dedit, eiusque vibicibus sanati sumus".[6] Et Petrus in epistola priori ad eundem Esaiae locum alludens: "Peccata (inquit) ipse suo corpore sustulit in patibulum, ut peccatis defuncti[7] iusticiae vivamus, cuius vibice[8] vos estis sanati".[9] Sed

Quomodo sanet ani

[1] G: SENTENTIA VIRI PII DE IUSTIFICATIONE. See *Preface* p. 10.

[2] Words and sentences in asterisks *...* are in the MS. only.

[3] G: *Christiania.*

[4] All words or sentences in square brackets [...] are found in G only.

[5] G: *animae.*

[6] Is 53:5.

[7] G: *defunctis.* [8] G: *vibicibus.* [9] I Pet 2:24.

quomodo sanet, hoc est iustos reddat homines, acerrima est inter theologos[10] controversia. Quidam enim re vera sanari, alii imputatione contendunt: quod quale sit, postea dicetur. Haec controversia ratione dirimi facilime potest. Si enim sanare est morbum tollere, ut certe est, et animi morbus est peccatum sive iniusticia, non dubium est quin sanare animum sit iniusticiam tollere. Exempli gratia: animi morbi sunt invidia, superbia, avaritia et huius generis alia vitia. Hos morbos si Christus sanat, [tum certe] tollit, et ex avaro liberalem, ex superbo modestum, ex invido benevolum efficit. Aliud quid sit sanare nec natura, nec gentium loquendi consuetudo, nec grammatica, nec profanae nec sacrae literae sciunt; nec ego ne cogitare quidem aliud possum.[11] Probari hoc plurimis et authoritatibus et exemplis potest. Sed ego paucis contentus ero. In primis Iesus ipse quaerentibus Scribis et Pharisaeis qui fieret ut cum publicanis et improbis cibum caperet, respondit:[12] "Non egent valentes medico, sed male affecti. Non veni vocatum insontes, sed sontes ad frugem".[13] Ex his verbis apparet medicum ideo vocari Christum, quod sontes vocet ad frugem, hoc est ad vitae correctionem. Matthaeus quoque postquam narravit, quemadmodum omnes aegrotos sanasset, subiungit haec verba: "Ut fieret quod fuerat ab Esaia vate [prae] dictum his verbis: Is nostras infirmitates morbosque suscepit atque tulit".[14] Eum certe locum non de imputatione sanationis, sed de vera sanatione allegat Matthaeus. Neque enim imputative (utar [ut] istorum verbo) sed re vera sanaverat aegrotos Christus. Cumque de sanatis hominum corporibus locum illum Esaiae citet Matthaeus, in quo non solum de corporum verum etiam de animorum morbis sanandis agitur, sicuti quivis qui totum[15] locum perpenderit facilime perspiciet, dubitari non potest quin Esaiae mens haec sit, animos a Christo sicuti corpora sanatum iri. Atqui[16] corpora vere sanavit, ergo et animos; in quo perspicuum fit, quam graviter hic errent, qui locum illum accipiunt[17] quasi Christus in se tulerit morbos nostros, hoc est fecerit ut non nobis sed sibi imputarentur. Si enim ea mens esset Esaiae, Christus profecto aegrotos illos non vere sanasset, sed eorum morbos ipse portasset, hoc est ipse pro eis aegrotasset. Verum de his postea. Petrus quoque hac de re

---

[10] G: *homines.*
[11] G: *ne cogitatione quidem aliud assequi possum.*
[12] G: *respondet.*
[13] Mt 9:12f.
[14] Mt 8:17.
[15] G: *eum.*
[16] G: *atque.*
[17] G: *accipiant.*

scribit apertissime in priore[18] epistola his verbis: "Scientes non vos caducis rebus, argento aut[19] auro, ex vanis istis patrijs moribus esse liberatos, sed Christi pretioso sanguine".[20] Liberatos hic vocat sanatos a vitijs, sicut apparet mox ex eiusdem epistolae cap. 4 *quem locum in priore libro allegavimus in cap. 5 ad quod etiam caput hic lectorem remitto*.[21] Denique ut paucis absolvam Christus est agnus dei qui tollit peccatum[22] mundi, qui venit ut aboleret opera Diaboli, ut aboleretur corpus peccati: fortis armatus qui irrumpit[23] in aedes Diaboli, hoc est in hominem peccato emancipatum, et vincto Diabolo hominem a peccati servitute asserit in libertatem iusticiae: breviter credentium animos non minus vere sanat ab iniusticia, quam olim corpora sanabat a morbis.

## VIII

ff. 115

Sed sunt qui docent hominis Christiani iusticiam esse imputativam: hoc est eum propter Christi meritum pro iusto apud deum haberi. Christi enim[1] iusticiam ei imputari, ut licet in sese sit iniustus, at in Christo quidem sit iustus, hoc est peccatorum veniam propter Christum consequatur. Denique ita docent, ut fidei iustificationem dicant esse peccatorum remissionem, qua sola servemur nullo operum nostrorum respectu. Adeo quidem ut quendam non piguerit haec verba scribere: "Nullo opere nostro ad iusticiam et salutem opus est".[2] Atque haec in primis ex Urbanus 3 et 4 ad Romanos capite confirmant, ubi doceat[3] Paulus Abrahamum fide sine legis operibus fuisse iustificatum.

Hic ego non disputabo[4] utrum iustificari more Hebraico interdum sit idem quod peccatorum veniam consequi, aut absolvi. Id enim concedo; neque item utrum qui in Christum credunt veniam gratis consequahtur suorum peccatorum. Nam ne hoc quidem dubitatur. Sed quod fidei

---

[18] G: *prima.*
[19] G: *et.*
[20] I Pet 1:18f.
[21] See above p. 23.
[22] G: *peccata.*
[23] G: *erumpit.*

[1] G: *Christique.*
[2] Compare Urbanii Regii, *Dialogus Oder gespreche Urbanii Regii mit seiner Ehelichen Hausfrauen von der Predigt so Christus Luc XXIV den zweien Jüngern so gen Emaus giengen am Ostertag getan hat.* Wittenberg 1545. See fol. 138: "Nicht von der werck der Gerechtigkeit, die wir getan hatten, sondern nach seiner Barmherzigkeit macht er uns selig". Also fol. 139.
[3] G: *docet* Rom. 4:3.
[4] G: *disputo*

iustificationem dicunt isti veniam[5] esse peccatorum, id vero in controversiam voco. Ac primum ratione disputans dico ab eis[6] dimidium Christi beneficium aboleri atque adeo totum beneficium foedari. Dicunt enim hominem a Christo non iustum fieri, sed effici ut pro iusto habeatur et a deo admittatur. Quod quale sit hac similitudine perspicuum efficiam. Fingamus iniusticiam esse lepram. Iam lege cautum est ut leprosi ex Dei tabernaculo excludantur. Sed existit aliquis gratiosus qui suo beneficio obtinet a deo, ut leprosi non sanentur illi quidem, ut ita sanati secundum legem admittantur, sed sic leprosi pro sanis habeantur et intromittantur. Hic[7] ego quaero quale sit *hoc* illius gratiosi in leprosum beneficium. Certe non ita magnum. Quid enim *aegroto* prodest in sanorum habitationem admitti? Deinde polluit ille gratiosus leprosi introductione locum sacrum, contra legis institutum. Postremo ostendit suam vel infirmitatem si leprosum illum sanare non potest, vel malignitatem, si non vult. Iam confer totam similitudinem nihil similius. Christus est ille gratiosus: Is in regnum dei (in quod non nisi iustos ingredi lege sancitum est) iniustos tanquam iustos introducit[8] et a patre impetrat ut illorum iniusticiae rationem nullam habeat. Quale quaeso est hoc Christi beneficium? Certe non magnum. Quid enim iniusto prodest in iustorum habitationem admitti? Deinde polluit Christus iniustorum introductione sanctum templum dei. Postremo ostendit suam vel infirmitatem, si ex iniustis iustos facere non potest: vel malignitatem, si non vult. Nonne et verius et longe splendidius ac praeclarius et vero non putatitio, aut imaginario medico dignius foret, eos vere sanare atque ita sanatos in sanctum dei regnum (in quod iniusticiam intromitti nefas et profanum est) intromittere? Veniam ad singularia. Nonne Christo dignius ex impudico castum efficere, atque ita castum hominem in castum dei templum intromittere? Quid enim indignius aut immundius quam impurum profanumque hominem in locum sanctum inducere? Non ferebant hoc, ne gentium quidem templa aspectabilia, nedum Hebraeorum, quanto id minus feret dei templum inaspectabile? Enimvero si hoc Christus facit, similis est gratiosorum hominum qui corruptis iudicibus persuadent ut in civitatem admittant, quos leges vetant, et si pater patitur similis est ipsorum iudicum. At quanto rectius lex Mosis, quae leprosos, ne tum quidem, postquam sanati sunt, admitti sinit, nisi prius *sacerdotis iudicio* eorum sanitas fuerit comprobata. Qui nos cum sit rei spiritualis

---

[5] G: *tantum veniam.*
[6] G: *sic* for *ab eis.*
[7] G: *Huc.*
[8] MS: *introdicit.*

umbra, si Christus in re spirituali contra facit, is et patri, illius figurae authori, et sibi metipsi contrarius est, qui sanato a se leproso iussit ut se sacerdoti ostensum iret,[9] ut videlicet tum demum in mundorum consortium admitteretur, postquam non imputative sed vere et reipsa mundum esse constitisset.

## IX

ff. 116

Iam authoritates perpendamus, quibus isti se tuentur. Allegant Paulum ad Romanos, a cuius mente aberrant longissime. Ac verba eius trutinemus. Paulus primum ostendit omnes tum Iudaeos tum caeteros peccato subesse. Peccatum autem quid vocet declarat his verbis: "Non est iustus, ne unus quidem. Non est qui sapiat, non est qui deo studeat",[1] et caetera quae ibi commemorat flagitia. Deinde ut ostendat haec non solum de caeteris gentibus, verum etiam de Iudaeis dici, subiungit haec verba: "Scimus autem quaecunque lex dicit ijs loqui, qui[2] sunt in lege, ut omne os obmutescat obnoxiusque fiat totus orbis deo,[3] quod per legis opera mortalium nemo iustus fiet apud eum[4]".[5] Quasi hoc dicat: Ipsi Iudaei, qui legis operibus funguntur et sacra caeremoniasque obeunt, tamen illa[6] quae commemoravi flagitia perpetrant neque per illa legis opera eam iusticiam adipisci *non* [7] possunt, quae apud deum valet; hoc est, non possunt veri dei cultores effici, nisi[8] qui deum in spiritu et veritate colant ambulentque non in vetustate literae, sed in novitate spiritus. Subiicit deinde haec verba: "Nunc absque lege divina iusticia patefacta est, a lege ac[9] vatibus testata: divina inquam iusticia, quam fide Iesu Christo habenda consequantur et obtineant omnes fidentes".[10] Quamnam autem iusticiam divinam[11] lex *aut*[12] vates testantur, perspicuum fit apud Lucam ex illo Zachariae carmine ubi sunt haec verba: "Ut

---

* [9] Lk 17:14.

[1] Rom 3:9-11.
[2] G: *quae*.
[3] G: *soli Deo*.
[4] G: *Deum*.
[5] Rom 3:19f.
[6] G: *ea*.
[7] MS: *non* added by the other hand.
[8] *nisi* added by the other hand.
[9] G: *et*.
[10] Rom 3:21f.
[11] G: *divina*.
[12] changed by the other hand to *et* for *aut*, and also in G.

utatur (videlicet deus) clementia erga maiores nostros et sui sancti foederis recordetur. Qui iureiurando promiserit Abrahamo patri nostro daturum se nobis ut intrepide ex hostium nostrorum manu liberati ipsum coram pie iusteque colamus toto vitae nostrae tempore".[13] Nam deum per Christum pie iusteque colere divina iusticia est, quam Iudaei sine fide nunquam adipisci potuere. Sequuntur deinde Pauli illa verba: "Non est enim discrimen ullum. Nam omnes peccaverunt, divinaque gloria carent et gratis iustificantur[14] eius beneficio per liberationem quae fit in Christo Iesu".[15] Deinde quonam pacto fiat illa liberatio declarat his verbis: "Quem proposuit deus placamentum per fidem in eius sanguine collocandam, ad demonstrationem iusticiae dei".[16] Hoc est: Quem Iesum deus fecit hostiam pro peccatis, ad suam in sontes iram placandam, ut qui in Iesum credant,[17] iis placetur veniamque det deus, atque ita *demonstret, hoc est*[18] exhibeat iusticiam suam, hoc est eos iustos efficiat ea iusticia quae apud deum valet,[19] de qua supra verba feci.[20] [Eandem sententiam dicit in capite 4. his verbis: "Qui (Iesus) propter nostra peccata traditus (hoc est ut nobis impetret veniam peccatorum) propter nostram iustitiam resurrexit",[21] hoc est ut nos iustos redderet. Hic certe venia peccatorum et iustitia non idem sunt. Idem dicit ad Col. 2: "In quo (sc. Christo) circumcisi estis, circumcisione non manufacta, exuto humanorum peccatorum corpore in Christi circumcisione una cum eo sepulti in baptismo, in quo etiam simul resurrexistis per collocatam in Dei vi fiduciam, qui eum ex mortuis suscitavit. Qui idem vos delictis et vestri corporis praeputio mortuos in vitam una cum eo revocavit".[22] Hic in vitam revocatos spiritualiter vocat justos factos. Est enim vita haec profecto morti contraria. Quod si non opinione, sed vere eorum animi peccato erant mortui, ijdem profecto non opinione, sed vere justitia revixerunt. Cujus enim generis fuerit mors, ejusdem vita sit necesse est: Sed longe et copiosissime et apertissime in 6. cap. ad Rom. in quo vel citando vel explanando ne sim prolixior, perlegatur, nam hac de re

[13] Lk 1:72-74.
[14] G: *iustificamur gratis*.
[15] Rom 3:22-24.
[16] Rom 3:25.
[17] G: *credent*.
[18] not in G.
[19] MS: *valeat*.
[20] In margin reference to suppl. 9. See the following insertion in square brackets.
[21] Rom 4:25.
[22] Col 2:11-13.

nominatim disserit, ut quasi dedita opera contra istorum imaginariam justitiam disputare videatur. Idem et ad Hebraeos docetur his verbis: "Si enim taurorum et hircorum sanguis juvencaeque cinis pollutos aspergens lustrat ad corporis puritatem: quanto magis Christi sanguis, qui per aeternum spiritum seipsum libavit innocentissimum Deo, purgabit nostram conscientiam a mortuis operibus, ut viventem colamus Deum?"[23] Sed jam ad 3. cap. revertamur.] Pergit Paulus eadem aliis verbis enucleare: "Qui pro sua facilitate" inquit "praeteritis peccatis veniam det, ut hoc tempore suam iusticiam demonstret".[24] Quod ante dixerat Christum esse placamentum, id nunc dicit deum peccatis veniam dare, scilicet Christi sacrificio placatum; et quod dixerat: Ad demonstrationem iusticiae dei, idem nunc dicit: Ut *hoc tempore*[25] suam iusticiam demonstret.[26] [Quod si veniam dare et justitiam demonstrare sive justos facere idem esset, tunc absurde locutus esset Paulus, perinde ac si dixisset, peccatis veniam dat, ut peccatis veniam det.] Sequitur deinde: Ut sit ipse et iustus, et qui Iesu fidem habentes iustificet, scilicet ea iusticia qua ipse iustus est. Ut enim bonus bonos et sanctus sanctos, sic et iustus iustos non opinione sed vere facit. Haec est Pauli mens, ex qua planissimum fit[27] aliud esse iusti ficationem quam peccatorum remissionem, quod quo magis elucescat, rem totam ex Pauli sententia verbis meis sic ob oculos exponam: Deus Iesu sanguine placatus veniam dat praeteritorum peccatorum credentibus in Iesum, eosque iustos facit non legali sed divina veraque iusticia.[28] Ac ne quid adhuc restet scrupuli, idem ostendam et ex alijs locis. Scribit idem in eiusdem epistolae cap. 8 haec verba: "Nulli iam damnationi sunt obnoxij, qui in Christo Iesu non carnis sed spiritus arbitrio parent".[29] Parere spiritus arbitrio idem vocat quod in cap. 4 appellavit iusticiam dei. Pergit deinde: "Nam lex spiritus vitalis in Iesu Christo liberavit me a lege peccati atque mortis".[30] Hoc ipsum est quod in tertio dixerat: "Per liberationem quae fit in Christo Iesu".[41] Legem autem peccati atque[32] mortis vocat legem Mosis, cui qui serviliter obediunt sunt emancipati peccato, sicut dixit in cap. 7 in

[23] Heb 9:13.
[24] Rom 3:25.
[25] *hoc tempore* not in G.
[26] In margin reference to suppl. 12. See the following insertion in square brackets.
[27] G: *sit*.
[28] *Rom 3:26.
[29] Rom 8:1.
[30] Rom 8:2.
[31] Rom 3:24.
[32] G: *et*.

persona hominis qui est sub lege, qui ita loquitur: "Ego vero carnalis sum, peccato emancipatus. "Et paulo post: "Aliam video legem in membris meis, repugnantem legi mentis meae, quae me captivum reddat legi peccati,[33]quae lex est in membris meis".[34] Ab hac inquam lege, hoc est, a peccandi servitute liberatum se, hoc est Christianos, docet in capite octavo, quo magis patet eorum error qui eum[35] de se loqui putant *in* illis verbis: "Ego sum carnalis, emancipatus peccato"[36] cum liberatum esse et emancipatum esse plane pugnantia sint. Exponit deinde cuiusnam beneficio et opera sit liberatus: "Quod enim", inquit, "a lege fieri non poterat, quoniam ipsa in eo propter carnem infirma erat"[37] (id ipsum est quod [in] capite tertio dixerat, "per legis opera neminem iustum fieri apud deum"), hoc est, quam iusticiam lex homini conferre non poterat, eam[38] deus praestitit suo ipsius filio misso carni[39] sontis simili" (idem dixerat aliis verbis *in* capite tertio, Christum appellans placamentum)[40] "et *pro* peccato peccatum damnavit in carne",[41] hoc est, ad delendum peccatum nobis veniam dedit in Christo, "ut legis iustificatio in nobis perageretur", hoc est, ut illa in lege promissa iusticia, de qua supra ex Zachariae carmine disseruimus[42] nobis conferretur, "qui non carni obtemperamus (ut faciunt qui sunt sub lege), sed spiritui",[43] hoc est, qui a Christo iusti facti iusticiae operibus fungimur. Nam qui iusta facit, iustus est. "Etenim qui ad carnis arbitrium vivunt (ut qui sunt sub lege) carnalia sapiunt", hoc est, secundum carnem affecti sunt. "Qui vero ad spiritus, spiritualia. Carnis autem studium sive affectus, est mors"; peccat enim et porro mortem parit. "At spiritus studium vita est atque pax";[44] recta enim facit ideoque vitam parit. "Caro enim inimica deo, dei legi nec paret nec parere potest",[45] ideoque necanda est. "Qui sunt autem in carne (ut sunt ij de quibus paulo ante illa verba dixerat: "Ego sum carnalis, emancipatus peccato"[46] deo placere nequeunt. At vos non estis in carne sed in spiritu (animadverte hic discrimen eorum qui

[33] G: *vitiositatis.*
[34] Rom 7:14.
[35] G: *illum.*
[36] Rom 7:14.
[37] Rom 8:3.
[38] G: *jam.*
[39] G: *carne.*
[40] Rom 3:25.
[41] See note 37.
[42] Lk 1:75, see p. 106, l. 132.
[43] Rom 8:4.
[44] Rom 8:5-6.
[45] Rom 8:7.
[46] Rom 7:14.

sunt sub gratia ab ijs qui sunt sub lege) si modo dei spiritus habitat in vobis",[47] hoc est si modo eum spiritum habetis qui vos iuste vivere faciat. "Quo spiritu si quis caret, is Christi non est".[48] Animadverte quonam evadat imputativa[49] istorum iusticia. Nam qui Christi spiritum illum iustificum non habet, qui efficiat ut spiritui obediat, is Christi non est. "Si vero Christus in vobis est, corpus quidem mortuum est per peccatum", hoc est caro sive carnalitas (ut ita loquor) mortua est, videlicet ideo interfecta, quia legi dei non parebat. "Sed spiritus vivus est per iusticiam".[50] Ut enim peccatum mortem, ita et iusticia vitam parit. Deinde post aliquot verba eadem dicit: "Nam si carnis arbitrio", inquit, "vixeritis, moriemini. Sin spiritu corporis[51] actiones peremeritis, vivetis".[52] Haec toties inculcat Paulus, ut quasi de industria imputativae isti iusticiae obviam ire videatur. Quod enim dicit: vivere secundum spiritum, perimere[53] corporis actiones, et huius generis alia, tantum non dicit: Serio loquor, non de opinione iusticiae, sed de vera iusticia, qua vere perempta carne, vere vivat spiritus. Nolite errare: doceo ambulandum esse, sive vivendum secundum spiritum, doceo carnem necandam esse, quod qui non facit, is Christi non est. "Nam ij demum dei filii sunt qui dei spiritu aguntur. Non enim servitutis spiritum accepistis *rursus ad metum (qualem habent qui sub lege sunt), sed spiritum accepistis* adoptionis per quem clamamus Abba, pater",[54] hoc est, cuius ope deum intrepide (ut canit Zacharias) in sanctitate et iusticia[55] per omnem vitam colamus, et non metu sed amore verae iusticiae (qua praediti sumus) opera obeamus.[56] Eadem sententia est et *in* Petri epistola prima his verbis: "Igitur Christo pro vobis *carne* supplicium passo vos quoque eadem mente armamini. Siquidem qui carne[57] supplicium tulit", (hoc est cuius caro, sive vetus homo necatus est) "is peccare desiit, ne deinceps ad hominum cupiditates sed ad dei voluntatem reliquum in carne[57] tempus vivat".[58] Item Paulus ad Galatas: "Qui sunt Christi, inquit, *ii* carnem

---

[47] Rom 8:8f.
[48] Rom 8:9.
[49] G: *imputationis.*
[50] Rom 8:10.
[51] G: *carnis.*
[52] Rom 8:13.
[53] G: *primere.*
[54] Rom 8:14.
[55] After iusticia *Deum* added by the other hand.
[56] Lk 1:74-77.
[57] G: *corpore.*
[58] I Pet 4:1f.

una cum libidinibus et cupiditatibus crucifixerunt”.[59] Et ut in pauca conferam, talibus sententiis plenum est novum foedus; ex quibus luce clarius fit quidnam sit vera et apud deum valens iusticia quae fidei iusticia nuncupatur.

## X

ff. 118-120

Iam revertamur ad quartum caput ad Romanos quo isti unice nituntur. Docet ibi Paulus Abrahamum eam, de qua loquimur iusticiam non legis operibus (quippe cum lex nondum lata foret), sed fide fuisse consecutum. Fide enim assecutum veniam peccatorum ita demum iustum fuisse factum. Sunt enim haec ordine consequentia: fides, venia peccatorum, iusticia. Fuisse autem Abrahamum non opinione[1] sed re ipsa iustum facile est vel ex hac ipsa Pauli disputatione ostendere. Facit enim Paulus hic[2] duo hominum genera: Unum iniustorum, de quibus illa dixit: “Omnes pariter deflectunt, nequamque sunt: non est qui recte[3] faciat, “et cetera,[4] quae ibi commemorat. Alterum iustorum, de quibus modo disseruimus in quibus fuisse Abrahamum nemo mihi non confitebitur. Neque enim profecto dicere audebunt, credentem Abrahamum fuisse praeditum illis, quae Paulus commemorat flagitijs. Nam illa sunt non credentium. Et Abrahamum, Paulus allegat non solum ut credentem sed etiam ut patrem credentium, quorum iusta opera passim et alibi et in hac maxime epistola recenset. Ex quo facile apparet, credentes[5] non esse in illorum numero, de quibus citat Paulus illa: “Non est qui recte[3] faciat”. Nam credentes certe iusta faciunt, et qui iusta facit iustus est. Ne quid interim dicam quod Christus ipse Abrahami iuste facta [opera] commendat, dum Iudaeis dicit: “Si [vos] Abrahami nati essetis, Abrahami opera faceretis”.[6] Nec non deus ipse, dum dicit ei: “Quoniam fecisti, ut te ne[7] ab unico quidem filio abstineres”.[8] [Et sequitur: “Quoniam dicto mihi obediens fuisti”.] Itemque Isaacum alloquens “[Omnes gentes terrae in semine tuo benedicentur] quoniam mihi, inquit, dicto audiens fuit Abrahamus meaque instituta, praecepta, decreta, leges conserva-

[59] Gal 5:24.

[1] G: *opinarie*.
[2] G: *haec*.
[3] G: *recta*.
[4] Rom: 3:12.
[5] G: *credentem*.
[6] Jn 8:39.
[7] G: *non*.
[8] Gen 22:16-18.

vit".[9] Adde quod in illo *ipso* Psalmo (ut taceam alios complures) ex quo Paulus illa verba "Non est qui recte[10] faciat" allegat, manifesto[11] fit proborum et improborum mentio, quorum hi *illos comedant* [commemorata illa flagitia perpetrent], illi in Iova fiduciam habeant et Iovae populus appellentur.[12] Ex quo obiter animadvertitur quantopere errent qui illa flagitia de omnibus promiscue, nullo credentium et infidentium[13] discrimine citare solent. Quaero igitur illa Abrahami iusta opera, nonne erant opera fidei? Fatebuntur. Et erant opera iusticiae? Et hoc fatebuntur, nisi volent appellare iniusticiae, quod nunquam sobrij facient, cum et res et sacrae literae sexcentis locis vocent opera iusticiae. Ex quibus unus ille in praesentia satis erit ex epistola ad Hebraeos, ubi dicitur: "Sancti per fidem operati sunt iusticiam".[14] Cum igitur haec opera vocet sanctus spiritus opera iusticiae, et haec iusticia valeat apud deum, quippe qui eam in Abrahamo commendet[15] et remuneretur, et haec iusticia non sit venia peccatorum sed sequatur veniam peccatorum, sitque non aliquid extra hominem (ut est venia peccatorum) sed penitus[16] in homine, videlicet animi sanitas et habitus iniusticiae contrarius, et actiones pariens iniusticiae actionibus contrarias, non possum satis mirari, quid istis in mentem venerit, ut hanc iusticiam doceant esse veniam peccatorum, ex duabus rebus unam facientes et iusticiae divinum donum, sine quo deum nemo videbit, abolentes. Nam si beatos praedicat Christus eos qui mundo sunt corde[17] (quae haec ipsa est de qua hic verba facimus iusticia), quoniam[18] deum visuri sint, consequens est, ut qui immundo sunt corde deum non sint visuri. Sed inest in ijs quos Paulus allegat locis nonnulla difficultas. Dicit enim: "Credidit Abrahamus deo, id quod ei iusticiae ductum est".[19] Et mox haec verba subiungit: "Quemadmodum David quoque hominis beatitatem in eo statuit, si ei deus iusticiam tribuit sine operibus. Beati quorum remissa [sunt] delicta, quorum obducta peccata. Beatus homo cui non imputat[20] Dominus peccatum".[21] In his

---

[9] Gen 26:4f.
[10] G: *recta.*
[11] G: *manifeste.*
[12] Ps 14.
[13] G: *infidelium.*
[14] Heb 11:33.
[15] G: *commendat.*
[16] G: *aliquid.*
[17] *Mt 5:3ff.
[18] G: *ut qui modo.*
[19] Rom 4:3.
[20] G: *imputavit.*
[21] Rom 4:6-8.

verbis videtur Paulus iusticiam appellare peccatorum veniam, quae res istis occasionem dedit ita docendi. Sed cum et[22] ratio quae peccatorum veniam iusticiae nomine appellari non patitur, et antecedentia, et caeteri tot loci quorum nonnullos iam allegavimus repugnent, debuit hic locus diligentius perpendi. Igitur quod dicit Moses, fidem Abrahamo ductam fuisse iusticiae, hoc nihil ad veniam peccatorum. Nam fides est hominis, at peccatorum venia est dei. Et fides est vera iusticia, id quod isti fatentur, *nam* qui [in] deo credit, hoc ipso deum honorat et eius praecepto obedit,[23] qui hominem ipsi credere iusserit. At peccatorum venia non est hominis iusticia, sed est hoc ipsum tantum quod dicitur, videlicet peccatorum venia. Et fides homini praecipitur, et iusticia praecipitur non minus quam agricultura; at peccatorum venia nec praecipitur[24] nec praecipi potest, non magis *profecto* quam pluvia. Iam cum hic fides iusticia vocetur, et iusticiam isti velint esse peccatorum veniam, efficitur, si verum sentiunt, ut non solum illa duo quae supra diximus, videlicet iusticia et venia, verum etiam haec tria, videlicet fides et venia et iusticia sint idem. Quod cum sit absurdum, apparet verba Mosis non sic esse ad vivum resecanda, neque sic uti sonant a Paulo allegari.[25] Paulus enim in capite tertio sicuti supra ostendimus de iusticia disputat non quae sit fides, sed quam fide consequatur homo.[26] Quod si aliud est (ut certe est) quod homo consequitur, ab eo quo sive cuius ope id consequitur, necesse est, ut iusticia quam homo fide consequitur aliud sit, quam fides qua iusticiam consequitur. Quare hic locus sic erit interpretandus, ut etiam ad Galatas ponitur: "Abrahamus iusticiam fide adeptus *est*".[27] Quanquam enim fides est ipsa quoque pars iusticiae, at hic non de parte agitur iusticiae, sed in universum de ipsa iusticia, quae partes omnes complexa est. Hanc esse Pauli sententiam videre est in tertio ad Galatas capite, in his verbis: "Hoc tantum volo a vobis discere, utrum per legis opera spiritum acceperitis, an per orationem[28] fidei?"[29] Ibi enim de spiritu loquitur iustifico, cuius *porro* opera carnis operibus contraria recenset in capite 5 his verbis: "At spiritus fructus est charitas, gaudium, pax, *clementia, benignitas, bonitas, fides,* lenitas, continentia. Contra talia non est lex". Deinde continuo ostendit eos qui fidem

[22] G: *ea.*
[23] G: *praecepta obit.*
[24] *nec praecipit* added by the other hand.
[25] G: *allegata.*
[26] See above p. 102, ls. 16-18.
[27] Gal 3:6.
[28] G: *auditionem.*
[29] Gal 3:2.

habent habere et illa opera spiritus interfecta carne, dum dicit: "Qui sunt autem Christi, ij carnem una cum libidinibus[30] et cupiditatibus crucifixerunt. Si spiritu vivimus etiam spiritu gradiamur".[31] Hic certe non de imputatione, sed de vera iusticia, iniusticiae contraria loquitur, quam Galatae sicut et Abrahamus fide, non legis operibus, consecuti fuerint.[32] Eamque ob causam mox eundem de Abrahamo locum allegat, quem allegavit ad Romanos: "Quemadmodum, inquit, credidit Abrahamus deo, id quod ei iusticiae ductum est".[33] Quasi hoc dicat: quemadmodum Abrahamus, sic et vos iusticiae spiritum non legis operibus sed fide consecutis estis.

## XI

ff. 120,

Sed habet locus alter[1] ex Psalmis[2] a Paulo allegatus etiam plus difficultatis, ubi dicit: "Beatus homo cui non imputat deus peccatum".[3] Sed animadvertendum est locum a Paulo mutilum citari et minus in eis verbis quae allegat quam in ipsius positione contineri. Est enim eius positio haec: David hominis beatitatem in eo statuit, si ei deus iusticiam tribuit sine operibus. At verba Davidis quae allegat non de iusticia, sed de venia sunt peccatorum. Qua re decepti isti putarunt[4] ibi beatitatem soli peccatorum veniae tribui, quod non est. Nam nec Paulum id censere ex ijs quae iam recensuimus, satis patet, nec Davidem id sentire, ipsemet[5] David optimus erit interpres. Nam eius verba sunt haec: "Beatus homo cui non imputat Iova[6] culpam et cuius in animo dolus non est".[7] Haec verba: "Cuius in animo dolus non est" a Paulo omissa sunt, tamen intelligenda. In ijs enim continetur illud ipsum quod Paulus docet de iusticia, ut sit haec Pauli sententia: beatus homo cui deus iusticiam tribuit, sive imputat sine operibus, condonatis ei peccatis; hoc est, quem iustum fecit non motus[8] ipsius operibus eumque[9] a se iustum factum pro

---

[30] G: *libidine.*
[31] Gal 5:22-25.
[32] G: *fuerant.*
[33] Gal 3:6.

[1] G: *ille.*
[2] G: *ad Rom ex Psal.*
[3] Ps 32:2; Rom 4:7-8.
[4] G: *putabant.*
[5] G: *ipse.*
[6] G: *Jehova.*
[7] Ps 32:2.
[8] G: *reputatis.*
[9] G: *cumque.*

iusto habet, sicuti re vera iustus a deo factus iustus est. Patet hoc non solum ex ijs quae dixi verbis: "cuius in animo dolus non est", sed etiam ex ipsius Psalmi ultimis verbis: "Gaudete in Iova et exultate, iusti; ovate[10] omnes probae mentis", sive (ut fert hebraismus) recti cordis hominis.[11] Ibi enim iustos et recti cordis homines eosdem vocat, ex quo luce clarius fit iusticiam illam de qua in hoc psalmo loquitur non imputationem esse, sed cordis rectitudinem de qua dixerat: "cuius in animo est dolus", et de qua Petrus in prima epistola *loquitur* his verbis: "Ergo deposito omni vitio omnique fallacia et simulationibus et invidijs et omnibus maledicentijs, ut recens nati infantes rationale et[12] infraudulentum lac appetite ut eo grandescatis ad salutem",[13] et caetera quae[14] ibi graviter, aperte copiose [que] disseruntur.[15] [Neque vero in eo quod a Paulo mutilam citari sententiam videmus, quae tamen tota sit intelligenda, ulla debet esse offensio. Id enim ab auctoribus tum sacris tum profanis saepe fit in locis manifestis, et in quibus sciunt auditores facile per sese suppleturos, quod in allegando omittitur. Sic certe legem de cupiditate in hac eadem ad Rom. Epistola mutilam allegavit Paulus, ubi dicit: "Cupiditatem nescirem nisi diceret lex: ne concupiscito".[16] Neque enim dicit lex: ne concupiscito, sed: ne concupiscito uxorem aut quicquam alterius. Non est enim cupiditas peccatum, quinimo, interdum est virtus, ut cupere justitiam, cupere regnum Dei, cupere salutem alterius. Interdum non est vitium, ut cupere panem tum cum esurias, cupere asinum tuum cum equitare velis; sed alieni cupiditas vitium est, et hanc lex vetat. Sed cum id omnibus notum esse sciret Paulus, non expressit. Sic igitur in hoc Psalmo mutilam sententiam allegavit.] Quae cum ita sint, sic iam constanter legis iusticiam a fidei iusticia definiendo distinguere audeo. Iusticia legis est externa obedientia a metu servili proficiscens.

Legis iustitiae quid sit, fidei iustitia quid sit.

Iustitia fidei est animi virtus iniustitiae, sive vitio contraria, quam deus credentibus gratis dat, condonatis eorum praeteritis peccatis.

---

[10] G: *orate*.
[11] Ps 32:11.
[12] G: *ac*.
[13] I Pet 2:1-2.
[14] G: *qui*.
[15] In margin reference to suppl. 10. See the following insertion in square brackets.
[16] Rom 7:6.

## XII

ff. 120 (121b cancell by Cas 122-12

Loci Io 16 natio de s reprehensi

Atque illud addam videri Iesum de hac iusticia loqui apud Iohannem, in illo alioquin[1] obscuro et hactenus parum intellecto et tamen[2] magni momenti loco, ubi sic suos alloquitur: "E re vestra est ut ego discedam. Nisi enim discessero, confirmator ad vos non veniet. Sin abiero, eum ad vos mittam: atque ille ubi venerit mundum arguet de peccato, *et* de iusticia, et de iudicio. De peccato quoniam mihi fidem non habent. De iusticia quoniam ad patrem discedo nec me videbitis amplius. De iudicio quoniam huius mundi princeps iudicatus est".[3] Huius loci quae *nam* sit sententia nolo audacius affirmare. Tantum dicam meam opinionem de qua lectores iudicent. Quamdiu [in] corpore praesens versabatur *in terris* Christus, eum agnoscebant apostoli secundum carnem, hoc est illi aspectabili homini Iesu Mariae filio sic adhaerebant, ut coelestia minus saperent aut sentirent. Eam ob causam expediebat eum ab illorum praesentia corpore discedere, ut eum misso ad ipsos confirmatore spiritu discerent secundum spiritum cognoscere,[4] et coelestia sapientes ac sentientes coelestem iusticiam haberent. Sed animadvertendum est *(id quod supra etiam annotavimus)* eius spiritus duo esse genera donorum. Quaedam enim affert quae non sunt omnium, ut *sunt dona illa quae in prima ad Corinthios epistola vocat spiritualia. Alia quae sunt omnium, ut est* haec ipsa de qua hic agimus iusticia, sine qua nemo Christianus est. Nam qui Christi spiritum non habet, videlicet iustificum, is non est eius.[5] Est igitur iusticia donum spiritus, non unius temporis, aut certis ac non omnibus concessum, sicut illa dona quae die pentecostes largitus est discipulis Christi,[6] sed omnium et temporum et [tam Iudaeorum quam] Christianorum, ut ea quisquis careat, is sit reprehendendus. Itaque illa de qua hic agimus reprehensio spiritus ad nostrum quoque tempus pertinet, quippe cum idem spiritus qui apostolos et reliquos illo tempore iustos fecit, nunc quoque iustos faciat eos qui credunt [in Christum], et idem facturus sit ad extremum. Mundum igitur reprehendit spiritus de peccato, quia non credunt in Christum. Qui enim in eum non credit, non habet[7] *hanc* quae fide paratur iusticiam, ideoque peccat et in

Cap. 6

[1] G: *alioqui.*
[2] G: *tam.*
[3] Jn 16:7-11.
[4] added by the other hand above the original 'scire'.
[5] Rom 8:9.
[6] G: *suis Christus.*
[7] G: *tenet.*

[eo]peccato manet. Sed cum habeat aliquam tamen sive legis sive imputativam iusticiam *et ea non sit vera iusticia fit* eam reprehendit spiritus, quia vera non est iusticia.[8]

*Quam autem causam Christus affert huius reprehensionis ea est admodum obscura et quae primo aspectu plane aliena absurdaque esse videatur. Sed si ea teneas quae diximus est aptissima. Dicit enim: Quoniam ad patrem discedo nec me videbitis amplius. Sed quorsum hoc? Nimirum sit: Ego ad patrem discedo non versaturus amplius inter vos corpore, ut vobis mittam spiritum hunc iustificum qui credentes vere iustos reddat. Id quod non fieret, si apud vos corpore semper versarer, quippe vobis in res aspectabiles, non in spirituales, interentibus. Atqui mundus non hanc spiritus habebit iusticiam, eamque ob causam reprehendendus erit*.[9]

Sequitur tertia spiritus reprehensio quae superioribus consentanea est. Reprehendit spiritus mundum de iudicio, quoniam princeps huius mundi, hoc est Diabolus, iudicatus est, hoc est damnatus, et potestate sua in credentibus privatus. Est enim Diaboli potestas in peccato posita. Haec potestas ei iudicio dei adimitur dum homo per fidem liberatur a peccato. Atque ita a Diaboli ad dei potestatem transfertur. At mundus id negat. Iudicat enim hominem non liberari a peccato, quod perinde est ac si neget damnatum esse Diabolum, in quo quidem male iudicat, et de eo iudicio reprehenditur a spiritu, et sic de Diabolo, *ut* et de Christo, male iudicat. Nam et Diabolum non vere damnatum, et Christum non vere resurrexisse ac de Diabolo victoriam reportasse iudicat, qui suos adhuc in Diaboli potestate hoc est in peccato reliquerit. Nam "qui peccatum committit, servus est peccati",[10]et porro Diaboli. Atque hoc loco obiter animadvertatur illius[11] Pauli ad Romanos loci[12] sententia: "Ne dixeris cum animo tuo: Quis ascendet[13] in coelum? Hoc est Christum devocare".[14] Quasi hoc dicat: Doceo hominem divina iusticia iustum fieri oportere. Quaeret aliquis an fieri hoc possit dicetque non minus esse difficile sic iustum fieri quam in coelum ascendere. Respondeo: Quod ab hominibus fieri non potest, id a deo fieri potest. Et Christus ideo in

---

[8] Castellio clearly differs from Calvin and Luther.

[9] This paragraph comes after Castellio has crossed out one page and a half and it is followed by the deletion of another half page. This may account for the fact that the printer has overlooked it.

[10] Jn 8:34.

[11] G: *illa*.

[12] G adds: *10. cap*.

[13] G: *ascendit*.

[14] Rom 10:6.

coelum ascendit ut hoc faceret, hoc est ut iusticiae spiritum suis mitteret, per quem hoc praestaret eosque sic iusticia renovaret ut servarentur, videlicet per Christi mortem peccatorum veniam consecuti et per eiusdem resurrectionem et in coelum ascensionem, iusticiam, qua praediti fungantur operibus iusticiae et ijs defuncti regnum quod obedientibus promissum est obtineant.

## XIII

ff. 123-

Haec est solida, certa, invicta, et rationi et sacris literis consentanea doctrina de iusticia fidei, quam iusticiam isti in imputationem iusticiae, hoc est in non iusticiam, sive in opinionem iusticiae convertentes sustulerunt. Ita eis usuvenit idem quod simulachricolis, qui pro dijs simulachra colentes, ea deorum nominibus nuncupant, atque ita deos colunt non deos, hoc est qui re vera nulli sunt. Sic isti iusticiam sibi tribuunt, quae re vera nulla est, sed tantum inane nomen iusticiae. Ut enim illi dei aures habent et tamen non audiunt; oculos habent et non vident; manus habent et non tangunt; pedes habent et non ambulant; ora habent et non loquuntur: Sic istorum iusticia nomen habens[1] iusticiae, rem ipsam non habet nec operibus iusticiae fungitur. Vocantur, exempli gratia, sobrii, cum re vera non sint[2] sobrii, sed Christi sobrietas eis imputatur, hoc est a deo pro sobriis, cum ebriosi sint, habentur, et patientes, cum sint impatientes, et modesti, cum sint superbi, et amantes, cum odio laborent, et liberales, cum sint avari. Certe hoc fert eorum doctrina, quanquam non sic singillatim[3] partes recensent, (pateret enim prima statim fronte falsitatis[4] absurditas), sed cum in universum Christi iusticiam sibi imputari contendant, et iusticiae quasi corpus constet ex partibus, *necesse est in partibus* ea [liquet] fieri quae diximus, hoc est Christi singulas virtutes eis[5] non habentibus imputari. Alioquin quid sit homini iusticiam Christi imputari, ne cogitari quidem potest. Neque vero haec a me de illis finguntur:[6] ipsorum scripta sunt in manibus, ad quae dum recurro, (ne quid forte temere de ipsis allegem), invenio hanc esse eorum doctrinam, atque adeo[7] haec ipsa eorum[8] verba: "gratis nos esse

---

[1] G: *habet.*
[2] G: *sunt.*
[3] G: *singulatim.*
[4] G: *falsitas et.*
[5] G: *eas.*
[6] G: *a me illis affinguntur.*
[7] G: *ideo.*
[8] G: *ipsorum.*

iustos propter Christum, quem solum invocet fides in omni invocatione, etiamsi nos iniusti atque indigni simus. Hominem non in se ipso iustum esse, sed quia Christi iusticia imputatione cum illo[9] communicetur".[10] Quae istorum verba, si iusticiae singulis partibus accommodes, necesse erit ut sic interpreteris: Hominem non in se ipso castum esse, sed ei Christi castitatem imputari; quod idem dico de caeteris iusticiae partibus. Neque vero non credo eis errore, non malicia labi, quo fit ut eorum peccatum sit levius. Sed non *idcirco* minus nocet doctrina [haec] populis; itaque refellendi sunt, ut populi si fieri potest in viam revocentur. Sperarem eos refutationem hanc modeste esse laturos, nisi vererer ne (sicuti fert ipsorum doctrina) Christi modestia quoque (sicut et caeteris virtutibus) careant et pro modestia opinionem habeant modestiae. Neque vero haec iocans sed maxime serio dico. Et ut dicam, eorum scriptis quibusdam in quibus parum modestiae animadverto moveor. Parum enim est eis[11] opinionem suam docere, nisi *id* insuper faciant cum dissentientium contumelia. Certe non puduit eorum quendam (cuius nomen modestiae gratia taceo), cum in hoc ipso de iusticia argumento recenseret argumento recenseret argumenta adversariorum, haec verba scribere: "sed omnibus his[12] sententiis astute ac[13] perfide utuntur ad veritatem de industria depravandam falsis collectionibus".[14] haec sunt illius verba imitantis nimirum magistrorum immodestiam, qui eos qui ab ipsis dissentiunt ausi sunt aeternis poenis confidentissime destinare. Enimvero si Christiana modestia praediti essent, ac *non* moribus eam ipsam quam verbis profitentur doctrinam referrent, didicissent profecto ab eo ipso cuius imaginariam iusticiam sibi vendicant Christo, modestius de aliena et soli deo cognita pronunciare conscientia. Sed ita est, similes arbor fructus, similes parit doctrina mores. Illi suae doctrinae consentanea faciunt et nos nostrae faciamus: et eorum errorem, quia errore, non voluntate labuntur, modeste, quia tamen labuntur, refellamus. Et quidem satis iam alioquin hactenus refutavimus, si quis nostra perspiciat. Sed quoniam in multorum animis alte radices egit error iste, et est alioquin carni suavis, quippe cui aliena virtute niti[15] sit dulcius quam

---

[9] G: *illis*.

[10] Calvin, *Institutes*, Corp. Ref. XXX, bk. III, XXIII, 2-5. In the following chapters Castellio refutes Calvin's views.

[11] G: *eos*.

[12] G: *hic*.

[13] G: *et*.

[14] See n. 10.

[15] G: *cum alienae virtuti inniti*.

suis renunciare vitiis, extirpandus est potentius et ita in lucem[16] exponendus, ut abs quivis[17] qui modo non claudat oculos perspici queat. Primum autem ostendam eos ipsos secum pugnare, ac quod verbis et voluntate negant idem reipsa victos videlicet veritate fateri. Deinde, quibus causis ad sic docendum[18] impellantur eas non esse idoneas. Postremo quos ex sacris literis locos ad sententiae suae confirmationem allegant, non vere allegare.

## XIV

ff. 124
126b-1

Igitur primo docent Christi iusticiam credentibus non dari sed imputari: et tamen fatentur in eis per fidem novas virtutes excitari eosque per spiritum non imputatione sed re ipsa sanctificari. Fatentur enim de vera non imaginaria sanctitate illa Pauli ad Corinthios verba dici: "Et tales quidem nonnulli eratis, sed abluti[1] estis, sed sancti, sed iusti facti[2] per nomen Domini Iesu perque dei nostri spiritum".[3] Ibi enim ablutos expiatosque dicit Paulos Corinthios ab iis quae modo commemoraverat vitiis, quae vitia uno iniusticiae nomine comprehenderat. Sic enim dixerat: "An vos latet iniustos *non esse* divinum regnum [non] adepturos"?[4] Et continuo quosnam vocet iniustos declarans[5] "Ne errate, inquit, nec impudici, nec deastricolae, *nec adulteri*, nec molles etc. divinum regnum consequentur".[6] Subiungit deinde: "et tales quidem nonnulli eratis, sed abluti estis, "hoc est, iam tales esse desiistis. Neque enim hic profecto imaginaria ulla ablutio cogitari potest, quasi non re vera ab illis[7] vitiis expiati essent Corinthii; sed adhuc essent tales, videlicet impudici, deastricolae, etc. Nam si tales adhuc erant,[8] male diceret Paulus: Tales eratis, cum dicendum esset: Talis estis. Deinde male negaret tales regnum esse dei adepturos, si de imaginaria illa ablutione aut iustificatione loqueretur, cum illis respondere esset in promptu: Tales quidem sumus, sed id nobis non imputatur, itaque dei regnum nihilo

[16] G: *luce.*
[17] G: *quovis.*
[18] G: *dicendum.*

[1] G: *absoluti.*
[2] G: *sanctificati estis, sed iustificati.*
[3] 1 Cor 6:11.
[4] I Cor 6:9.
[5] G: *declarat.*
[6] G: 1 Cor 6:10f.
[7] G: *iis.*
[8] G: *essent.*

minus adipiscemur. Fuit[9] igitur illa, sive ablutio, sive iustificatio, sive sanctificatio (his enim tribus utitur Paulus) non imputativa,[10] sed re vera, vereque illi ex simulachrorum cultoribus dei cultores, ex impudicis casti, ex furacibus liberales, ex ebriosis sobrii facti fuere. Et hoc isti confitentur. Atqui[11] illa iusticia erat fidei, quippe quam illi fide adepti essent. Ne hoc quidem negare audebunt. Est ergo fidei iusticia non imputativa sed vera et, ut eam quidam appellant, "inhaerens". Hic ego si scribendi finem faciam, necesse est *ut* huic veritati vel iniquissimi iudices victoriam concedant.

Adducam[12] alterum argumentum ex ipsorum[13] confessione depromptum. Docent veterem hominem in hac vita semper quidem necari,[14] sed ante mortem nunquam prorsus extingui. At in morte extingui et prorsus in nihilum redigi. *Fatentur* quam quidem confessionem ab eis veritas extorsit invitis. Cum enim veterem hominem in credentibus mori sacrae literae subinde tradant et isti *id* in hac vita fieri nollent, post resurrectionem autem fieri dicere non auderent, in mortem saltem distulerunt; et nobis *novum* nescio quod purgatorium, quod superiores post mortem collocaverant, isti in ipsa[15] morte, non equidem[16] nomine, sed re ipsa certe commenti sunt. Quos enim a peccato fides in Christum purgare viventes non potuit, eos a morte purgari finxerunt. Sed fingamus ita esse. Quaero ex istis: iudicium dei nonne *demum* post resurrectionem fiet? Fatebuntur. Atqui post resurrectionem[17] exstinctus erit vetus homo eruntque Christiani vera non imputativa iusticia iusti. Et hoc negare non poterunt. Valebit ergo apud deum illa iusticia; et deus in eam non *in* imputativam (quae tunc nulla erit) intuens sententiam feret et hominem qualis tunc erit, non qualis olim fuerit iudicabit. Ita corruit ex vestra, o impudentes, confessione vestra doctrina qui hominem imputatione iusticiae tutum deo sistere velitis. Si enim re vera iustus erit homo, re vera deo ob suam iusticiam placebit: id quod vosipsi fatebimini. Docetis enim hominem, si ab omni peccato mundus esset, sua iusticia placiturum esse deo, sed quia mundus non sit non placere. Nunc

Novum purgatorium.

---

[9] G: *Fit.*
[10] G: *imputative.*
[11] G: *Atque.*
[12] G: *Adjiciam.*
[13] G: *eorum.*
[14] MS: *neccari.*
[15] G: *sua.*
[16] G: *quidem.*
[17] G: *mortem.*

mundum tunc fore vosipsi fatemini, quo fit ut vestra ipsi confessione refellamini.[18]

Iam quaero porro: quod in morte morietur vetus homo, quanam vi id fiet? Utrum vi fidei an vi mortis corporis? Vi fidei dici non potest. Nam sive intellectus, sive voluntatis fidem esse vultis, in morte nec intellectus nec voluntas vires habent; id quod nos saepe in morbis (qui sunt tanquam mortis suburbia) experimur, dum debilitatis et corporis et animi sensibus, ne ad precatiunculam quidem vires *nobis* suppetere sentimus. Ne quid interim de iis dicam, quos repentina mors extinguit, in cuius momento certe nulla vis esse potest fidei. Taceo quod uno temporis puncto vi fidei fieri, quod eadem fide per omnem hominis vitam fieri non potuerit, absurdius est quam ut cuiquam in mentem venire debeat. Superest ut vi mortis extingui velitis veterem hominem, hoc est peccatum qui morbus est animi, quia quemadmodum *ut* est in proverbio: "Homo mortuus non belligerat", sic qui mortuus est non peccet.[19] Sed istud quidem non est hominem sanari sed mori. Alioquin et latrones hominem aeque sanarent interficiendo atque Christus ipse curando. Et impiorum non minus quam piorum animae in ipsa morte ab omni peccato expiarentur, atque ita et nulli perirent et Christus homini nihil ad salutem conduceret. Sin dicetis a Christo veterem hominem sed in ipsa demum morte interfici, mirabimur cur non potius in ipsa vita interficiat maiore et patris et sua[20] gloria et efficaciore ad alios ad imitationem permovendos exemplo. Ad viventium enim non ad mortuorum exempla provocari solemus. Deinde eodem relabentes quaeremus utrum per fidem [Christus] an per mortem an neutro adhibito interficiat [veterem hominem]? Per fidem dici non potest, nam in morte fidem non esse supra ostendimus. Per mortem si dicetis, Christo mirum socium[21] mortem adiungetis, qui cum veneri ut mortem aboleret, peccatum non nisi mortis auxilio abolere vel possit vel velit. Sin neutro adhibito efficitur ut salus fidei non debeat ascribi, cum tamen hominem[22] fide servari, nulli magis quam vos affirment. Postremo quaero ex vobis unde nam didiceritis peccatum in morte aboleri? Nam ratio reclamat, sacrae literae reclamant, et passim in hac vita fieri id vociferantur id quod si negabitis, obruere vos

---

[18] Here Castellio has added something in French: "ils diront ici qu'il les iugera selon les iniures(?)passées qu'il aura...".

[19] G: *peccat*, also MS, corrected by the editor to *peccet*.

[20] G: *sui*.

[21] G: *inimicam sociam*.

[22] G: *homines*.

possum multitudine testimoniorum quorum nonulla iam superius allegavimus.

## XV

ff. 127b, 128, 125b, 126

Venimus nunc[1] ad causas quibus impulsi ita docent.[2] Eae sunt tres. Prima quia nemo omnibus dei praeceptis obediat. Altera quia quibus [praeceptis] obediunt credentes imperfecte obediant. Tertia quia non semper obediant, sed saepe in ea delinquant. Iam cum deus sit perfectus sibique *et* in omnibus et perfecte et semper obediri velit, [apparet] neminem coram eo insontem esse. Hinc fieri[3] ut hominis iusticia qua apud deum iustus habeatur non [inhaerens] iusticia sit, sed imputatio iusticiae. Harum trium causarum nullam idoneam esse contendo, propter quam sic docere debuerint. Ac priusquam singulas refello, fingo[4] omnes esse veras *et* respondeo ne sic quidem effici quod volunt. Non enim valent haec argumenta:[5] Nemo omnibus praeceptis obedit, ergo nemo re vera obedit. *Nemo perfecte obedit, ergo nemo re vera obedit. Nemo semper obedit, ergo nemo re vera obedit*. Nam obedientia etiamsi nec in omnibus nec perfecte nec semper sit, tamen obedientia est. *Quod si obedientia, iusticia est, ut certe est*. Et si fideles non imputatione sed re vera obediunt, efficitur ut eorum obedientia non imputatione sed re vera sit iusticia. Et si iusticiam hanc non operibus sibi pepererunt, sed a deo eam per fidem consecuti sunt, efficietur ut sit iusticia fidei, eaque non imputatione sed re vera sit iusticia. Itaque hoc adhuc constanter tenemus iusticiam fidei non imputatione constare nec ei verae iusticiae nomen eripi patimur. Nunc singulas causas ponderemus. Prima causa est, quia etiamsi quis aliquibus dei praeceptis obediat, at omnibus neminem obedire, ideoque neminem non a lege damnari, quae execrabilem pronunciet quicunque non omnia quae praecepit lex praestiterit. Et allegant Iacobi locum illum: "Si quis quamvis alioquin totam legem observet, tamen in uno delinquit, is omnibus tenetur".[7] Hinc statuunt omnes quamvis credentes tamen non re vera iustos esse *sed haberi*.

Obedientia[6].

An quisquam omnibus dei praeceptis obedire queat.

Ad quod ego respondeo, idque ex ipsius Iacobi sententia: si nemo omnibus dei praeceptis obedit, neminem salvum fore. Sunt enim aperta

[1] G: *jam.*
[2] G: *doceant.*
[3] G: *fit.*
[4] G: *finge.*
[5] G: *valet haec argumentatio.*
[6] By the other hand.
[7] Jas 2:10.

verba Iacobi: Si quis in uno delinquit is omnibus tenetur, hoc est poenas perinde dabit ac si omnia praecepta violasset. Exempli gratia: Si [quis] hominem occidit, licet non sit adulter, poenas dabit non minus quam si adulter quoque foret et caetera omnia praecepta violasset. Neque vero est quod hic quisquam eum putet de imputatione loqui iusticiae. Alioquin, quaeram ex eo, num putet adulteros aut homicidas dei regnum consecuturos. Quod si negabit (ut certe negandum erit, cum sacrae literae tales homines tot locis tam aperte excludant a regno dei), necesse erit, ut fateatur vere, non imputative, abstinendum *esse* ab homicidio et adulterio ut salutem consequare. Ac quod in his duobus dei praeceptis concesserit, idem et in caeteris concedat necesse est. Quam enim rationem affert Iacobus in illis duobus, eandem et in caeteris [locis] licebit afferre. Nimirum, qui dixit: ne occidito, idem dixit etiam: parentem utrumque honorato, et: ne furator, et: falsum testimonium ne dicito, itidemque in caeteris. Itaque quisquis in ullum istorum praeceptorum peccaverit, is non minus damnabitur quam[8] si in omnia peccasset. Itaque quod isti negant, quenquam omnibus dei praecaeptis obedire, id si verum est, eo valet non ut (quod isti volunt) inobedientes serventur, sed ut nemo servetur. Ita fit, ut dum etiam iniustos *et inobedientes servare volunt, nec iniustos* servent, et insuper iustos etiam a salute excludant. Sed non ita est, nec isti vere dicunt neminem omnibus dei praeceptis obedire, quin et seipsos et alios perniciose decipiunt. Sunt enim qui omnibus obediant id quod isti, si tam exemplorum quam praeceptorum verba perpenderent et dei spiritum praeceptorum authorem eorundem in exemplis interpretem admitterent, facile cognoscerent. Idem enim spiritus, qui iussit deum toto corde diligi eiusque praecepta servari, idem inquam suorum verborum et mentis interpres testatur cum alios multos multis in locis tum in primis Iohannis Baptistae parentes Zachariam et Elizabetham id praestitisse: "Erant, inquit, ambo apud deum iusti sese in omnibus Domini[9] praeceptis ac institutis gerentes inculpatos".[10] Quod dicit "apud deum iusti" ostendit eorum iusticiam apud deum valuisse, ne quis forte illam referat ad hominum iudicium. Quod dicit "in omnibus praeceptis" nullum excipit. Quod dicit "inculpatos" interpretatio est iusticiae quae talis erat ut in ea nihil esset culpandum. Cum igitur haec de illis testetur sanctus author, nos authoris sancti testimonium et interpretationem sequamur et[11] aliquos esse credamus qui omnibus dei praeceptis et

[8] G: *ac*.
[9] G: *Dei*.
[10] Lk 1:6.
[11] G: *ut*.

institutis obediant divinaque iusticia vere, non imputative iusti sint. Neque vero me latet, quid[12] hic[13] nonnulli contra dicant. Videlicet Zachariam non credidisse Angelo eamque ob incredulitatem (quae peccatum sit) fuisse mutum factum. Neque enim dum dicimus eum iustum fuisse, dicimus peccare non potuisse, sicuti dum dicimus aliquem sobrium esse non sic accipiendum est quasi nunquam postea possit inebriari. Quemadmodum quod dicit Christus eum qui in luce ambulat non impingere, non sic interpretandum est quasi nunquam possit impingere.

## XVI ff. 126, 128-130b

Secunda causa est quia quibus obediunt credentes, imperfecte obediant. Imperfectionem autem esse peccatum cum deus perfectionem exigat, quippe qui se toto corde diligi iubeat. Itaque omnia[1] hominum opera, si sua dignitate censeantur, nihil nisi inquinationem et sordes esse, et quae iusticia vulgo habetur[2] eam apud deum esse iniquitatem: quae integritas, pollutionem; quae gloria, ignominiam. Denique nullum unquam extitisse pii hominis opus quod, si severo dei iudicio examinetur, non sit damnabile.

Hic ego non iam de perfectione disputabo, videlicet utrum possit homo per dei spiritum in se habitantem[3] perfecte obedire legi dei qua de re suo loco volente deo disseremus, sed de imperfectione, videlicet an ea sit peccatum et an quisquis deo imperfecte obedit in eo ipso peccet eiusque inchoata obedientia dei iudicio sit vitiosa. Imperfectionem autem hoc loco ex istorum sententia accipiam, videlicet quicquid eiusmodi est ut non sit summum, hoc est ut aut ipsum[4] maius esse possit, aut eo maius sit aliud.[5] Ut huius ignis calor est imperfectus, quia est aliud calidior. Et lunae candor est imperfectus quia est aliquid[6] candidius. Sic isti omnem hominis iusticiam in hac vita imperfectam et porro vitiosam esse tradunt, quia vel ipsa fieri maior possit, vel alia maior inveniatur. Hanc ob causam nullam cuiusquam in hac vita iusticiam dignam esse quae in dei

---

[12] G: *quod.*
[13] In margin it is said: suppl. 19 deest, sed ex Sn. Hermanni libro suppletum. See *Preface* pp. X-XI.

[1] G: *omnium.*
[2] G: *habeatur.*
[3] G: *inhabitantem.*
[4] G: *idipsum.*
[5] G: *aliquid.*
[6] G: *aliud.*

iudicio iusticiae nomen obtineat. Hanc ego sententiam et dico et (ut spero) ostendam esse plusquam Stoicam, prodigiosam, monstrosam, barbaram, et naturae atque[7] rationi et omnibus tum sacris tum profanis, atque adeo ipsis sui authoribus repugnantem.

Ac primum quod ad naturam attinet, quis est tam vel a natura degener, vel naturae ignarus, qui nesciat in rebus bonis non ea solum quae summa sunt carere vitio, sed etiam quae multis gradibus sunt inferiora? Est mel pomis dulcius; an iccirco poma non sunt dulcia? aut[8] pomorum dulcedo non nisi cum venia dulcedinis nomen obtinebit? Est[9] caro carne melior; an iccirco illa quae alterius bonitati caedit, bona non est? Est[9] sol luna splendidior; nunquid propterea luna non splendet? Est aliquid brassica viridius; numquid[10] iccirco brassicae nomen viridis adimemus? Quid *authores* allegem? profanos an sacros? In profanis[11] quidem[12] [docent medici eos quoque sanos esse, in quibus tamen non est perfecta illa et magis cogitata quam inventa quatuor humorum temperatio, modo nulla insit affectio naturae contraria quae laedat actionem. Sanitatem enim latius patere quam ut sit illa uno puncto metienda; alioquin in innumeris hominum millibus vix, ac ne vix quidem, quisquam sanus esset, quod idem de animi valetudine censendum est. Item] deridentur ab aliis et merito deridentur Stoici qui peccata volebant esse paria, quod quidem[13] non minus absurdum erat quam si dixissent morbos omnes esse pares, qui error vel a grammaticis facilime et optime refellitur, qui docent substantiva (ut ipsi vocant) non comparari, *at adiectiva comparari*. Hoc est piscem nullum (ut hoc exemplo utar) magis esse piscem quam alterum: at[14] majorem esse aut magis celerem[15] aut album. At isti pene absurdius faciunt qui virtutes docent esse pares. Nulla enim eis proprie virtus est, nisi quae summa est. Caeterae omnes quae virtutes appellantur proprie vitia erunt appellanda et quod est omnium absurdissimum etiam fugienda, nisi forte vitium negabunt esse fugiendum.

Quid de sacris loquar authoribus? Primus Moses scribit a deo creata fuisse imparia luminaria, videlicet solem, lunam et stellas, "solem"

---

7 G: *et.*
8 G: *ac.*
9 G: *et.*
10 G: *num.*
11 G: *Inprimis.*
12 MS: in margin reference to suppl. 29. *suppletus est locus* added by the other hand.
13 G: *equidem.*
14 G: *sed.*
15 G: *rubrum.*

vocans "maius luminare, lunam minus".[16] Cur lunam vocat luminare, cum non esset eius perfecta lux aut solis luci par? Neque vero est quod hic ut solent subterfugiant dicantque non dei iudicio luminare dici. Nam ipsemet deus suo certe non alieno iudicio illic luminare vocat. Quid quod in eadem mundi creatione scribit haec verba Moses? "Animadvertit[17] deus omnia quae fecerat esse admodum bona".[18]Atqui non erant omnia aeque bona et tamen etiam ea quae caeteris minus bona erant ipsius dei iudicio non solum bona verum etiam admodum bona vocantur. Possum huius generis exempla allegare innumera, sed quia est hoc evidentissimum, satis esse debet. Ut enim qui in luce unius solis non videt, ne in mille quidem (si mille essent soles) videret. Ita si quem unum evidentissimum et[19] irrefutabile exemplum non movet, vereor ne frustra plura afferantur. Igitur quod de luminibus et rerum a deo creatarum bonitate dixi, idem et de iusticia dico, videlicet quamvis minorem iusticiam, tamen re vera et ipsius dei (qui eam non minus quam illa luminaria et caetera creavit) iudicio esse iusticiam; ipsique deo per sese non minus quam illa quae diximus eius opera placere. Nihil enim creavit quod non ipsi per sese, ut bonum opus, placeat. Quod si iusticiam creavit, iusticia ei per sese ut bonum opus placet. Et qui hoc negant, ii dei opus vituperant. Et si ei luna, quamvis sole minus clara tamen ut luminare placet et probatur, quod idem de stellis dico; etiam homines iusti quamvis non iustissimi ei et iusti placent et probantur.[20] [Et certe Christus in iudicio sic pronunciabit: "Venite beati Patris mei, nam esurienti mihi dedistis comedere, sitienti bibere",[21] et caetera quae ibi habentur: ex quibus perspicitur apud eum valere eorum iusticiam]. "Alius est solis splendor", inquit Paulus, "alius lunae, alius stellarum; nam stella alia aliam splendore antecellit. Talis est etiam mortuorum resurrectio".[22] Hic certe sanctos in altera etiam vita cum coelestium luminarium impari splendore confert. Ex quo fit perspicuum etiam in altera vita fore splendoris inaequalitatem. Quod idem et in Daniele videre licet, qui fore docet ut periti fulgeant ut fulgor aethereus, *utque qui* multos reddiderint[23] iustos sint stellarum similes in omnem aeternitatem[24] Id quod convenit et cum illo dicto

[16] Gen 1:16.
[17] G: *Animadverti.*
[18] Gen 1:31.
[19] G: *atque.*
[20] MS: reference to suppl. 23. *Suppletus locus* added by the other hand.
[21] Mt 25:35.
[22] I Cor 15:41f.
[23] G: *et multos reddiderunt.*
[24] Dan 12:3f.

Christi: "Vos qui me secuti estis *in* renovata vita sedebitis in duodecim tribunalibus iudicantes duodecim tribus Israelitarum".[25] Hic certe erit inaequalitas, nec omnes erunt pares apostolis. Quod si non summum esse vitiosum est, haerebunt et in altera vita (*in*[26]) piis vitia, quod quam pie dicatur isti viderint. Quod si in altera vita inaequalitatem sine vitio admittunt, patiantur et in hac. In Apocalypsi quidem hoc scriptum est: "Iustus iustior fiat et sanctus sanctior".[27] Hic certe iustum appellat eum qui tamen iustior fieri potest. Quid quod de Christo scripsit Lucas: "Iesus sapientia et aetate et gratia tum[28] apud deum proficiebat tum apud homines".[29] Et hic certe Christi sapientia nondum summa erat: quod si imperfectio vitium est, in Christo fuit vitium. Sin in Christo nullum fuit vitium (ut certe nullum fuit) imperfectionem vitium non esse fatendum est. Idemque dico de eiusdem Christi infirmitate, quae in illis mortis pavoribus et angoribus tanta fuit, ut sanguinem sudaverit et in patibulo exclamaverit: "Mi deus, mi deus, cur me dereliquisti"?[30] Illa enim infirmitatis esse negari non potest. Et Paulus Christo infirmitatem aperte tribuit *in secunda ad Corinthios*, ubi dicit: "eum crucifixum fuisse per infirmitatem".[31] Quod si infirmitas (quae certe imperfectionis est) vitium est, in Christo fuit vitium. Illa vero tantum abest, ut sit vitium, ut etiam Domini fortitudo in ea perficiatur, sicut ipsemet Paulo[32] in eadem epistola, paulo ante illum locum dicit infirmitatem *suam* sibi eximi cupienti [Dominum dixisse]: "Satis est tibi mea gratia, *inquit* nam mea fortitudo in infirmitate perficitur".[33] Quare facessat haec opinio quae imperfectionem vitium esse statuit.

## XVII ff. 130b

Ostendi hanc opinionem et naturae et omnibus tum sacris tum profanis authoribus repugnantem. Nunc libet ostendere etiam ipsismet qui eam tuentur esse contrariam ipsosque suo ipsorum gladio iugulari, et quidem in limine statim eorum ipsorum verborum quibus eam oppu-

---

[25] Mt 19:28.
[26] *in* put in MS by the other hand.
[27] Rev 22:11.
[28] G: *cum*.
[29] Lk 2:52.
[30] Mt 27:46.
[31] II Cor 13:4.
[32] G: *Paulus*.
[33] II Cor 12:9.

gnant. Vocant enim inchoatam iusticiam. Atqui[1] si inchoata iusticia est, iusticia est, et si iusticia bonum est (ut certe est) etiam inchoata iusticia bonum est, idque *eius* iudicio, qui eam inchoavit, videlicet dei. Quod si bonum est, vitiosum non est. Ita fit ut inchoata iusticia vitiosa non sit. Possum hoc Mosis testimonio facile planum facere. Scribit in opere quinti diei: "Creavit deus ingentia cete et omne genus fluitantium animalium et alatarum volucrum, quaecunque ex aqua originem trahentia[2] moventur. Quam rem cum videret esse bonam ea foecundavit his verbis: (*adduc verba*)[3] [crescite et multiplicamini et replete aquas maris]".[4] Ex his verbis Mosis apparet animalia adhuc inchoata (quippe nondum foecundata) tamen[5] dei iudicio rem bonam fuisse. Id quod etiam si Moses non scripsisset tamen negare nemo auderet omnia dei opera, licet inchoata, tamen esse bona et omnis vitii expertia. Itaque et de homine inchoata, videlicet cum ex humo creatus nondum spiritum vitalem haberet,[6] idem dicendum erit, videlicet fuisse rem bonam. Alioquin dei opus malum fuisset, quod vel cogitatu impium est.Quod si iusticia quamvis inchoata opus dei est (ut certe est), eam bonam et vitii expertem esse fatendum est.

Quid quod fidem isti (qua sola servari contendunt hominem) inchoatam esse confitentur? Atqui si inchoata quae sunt, vitiosa sunt, fides est vitiosa, itaque fide servari homo non potest. Ita fit ut non solum iusticia sed etiam fides ipsa homini sit imputanda; itaque[7] non magis fide quam operibus iustificetur homo neque fide sua (quod tamen docet Habacuc) vivat.[8] Quod si hoc falsum est (ut certe est) illud quoque falsum sit necesse est.

Superest tertia causarum quae istos ad sic docendum impulerunt. Videlicet quod Christiani in ea ipsa quibus obediunt praecepta nonnunquam delinquant. Qua quidem in re sciendum est nos dum de iusticia loquimur, non de uno aut altero facto, sed animi habitu loqui, a quo rectae actiones efflorescant. Quod ut planius fiat, similitudene enucleabimus. Sanavit Christus claudum aliquem, hoc est vitioso habitu sive affectione naturae contraria liberavit quae clauditas appellatur. Hic sic

---

[1] G: *Atque.*
[2] G: *habentia.*
[3] *adduc verba* put in MS. by the other hand.
[4] Gen 1:21f.
[5] G: *tum.*
[6] Gen 2:7.
[7] G: *atque.*
[8] Hab 2:4.

sanatus, iam claudus non est, nec aliorum nec ipsius sanatoris iudicio. Sed accidere potest ut incautius ambulando impingat in stipitem et eo casu concusso pede claudicet per aliquot passus. Hic ego quaero num sit claudus? minime vere, non enim habet clauditatis habitum et tamen claudicat. Idem dico de muto sanato, cui usuvenire potest casu quopiam ut per unam aut alteram horam loqui nequeat; nec tamen mutus iccirco censendus est. Idem accidere *dico* in animi morbis. Crediderant[9] in Christum Corinthii[10] et illius fidei ope erant iustificati, hoc est ex ebriosis sobrii, ex mendacibus veraces redditi. Sed accidere poterat ut eorum quispiam[11] cum esset negligentior aliquando inebriaretur. Hic ego quaero num esset ebriosus? Minime vero. Nam si ebriosus *iam* factus erat, iam regno dei exclusus[12] erat, quod ebriosis claudunt sacrae literae. Erat sobrius, sed in virtutem sobrietatis peccaverat. Ipsam tamen sobrietatem non amiserat. Itaque dei iudicio[13] adhuc sobrius erat. Sic iustos appellant sacrae literae ab habitu, non ab una aut altera actione, ut apparet in Noha, in Abrahamo, in Davide et caeteris. Qui non ideo iusti vocantur, quia nihil unquam committerent reprehendendum, sed quia habitum sive (ut Hebraeo more loquar) spiritum haberent iusticiae. Iam quemadmodum nos hominem alioquin sobrium, sed quia forte semel aut[14] iterum ebrius fuit, tamen sobrium et vere et proprie appellamus, eique peccatum illud ignoscimus: sic et deus. Ita fit ut aliquis et vere proprieque sit iustus, et tamen ei venia detur. Hac distinctione solvitur illa quae tam multos hodie vexat quaestio, qui fieri possit, ut *et* aliquis re vera sit iustus et tamen dicat: "ignosce nobis peccata nostra". Non enim ita iustum reddit hominem *Christus*, ut non possit peccare, sed ut possit non peccare. Quemadmodum non ita sanabat claudos, ut non possint claudicare, sed ut possent non claudicare. Ita fit ut quod isti propter eiusmodi delicta negant credentium iusticiam coram deo consistere male negent. Deo enim re vera iustus et est et habetur is, in quo inest spiritus iusticiae, etiam si quid aliquando delinquat.

## XVIII

ff. 132-

Superest de illis tribus quae supra *pro* posueram tertium, videlicet ut ostendam ab istis sacras literas ad sententiae suae confirmationem non

Supra XII

---

[9] G: *crediderunt.*
[10] G: *Corinthei.*
[11] G: *quisquam.*
[12] G: *reclusus.*
[13] G: *justitia.*
[14] G: *atque.*

vere allegari. Et quidem iam obiter eorum, quae allegant partem refutavimus; sed restant loci quidam quos hic tractabimus, non equidem singillatim[1] omnes, ne simus prolixiores, sed praecipuos, et eos qui tales sunt ut iis cognitis de caeteris eorum similibus eadem opera constet.

Primus omnium et maximi momenti locus sunt verba legis, quibus iubet deus "se toto corde, toto animo, totis viribus diligi".[2] Hic exultant et quicquid est infra hanc perfectionem, quam verba legis exigunt, vitium esse et eo vitio mortales omnes semper in hac vita teneri contendunt, quippe nemine deum sic amante. Sed pace eorum dixerim mentem legis non assequuntur. Nam ipse legis author deus verba illa "toto corde, toto animo, totis viribus" non aliter interpretatur, quam nos cum dicimus aliquem toto corde totoque animo amare divitias, id quod faciunt multi, non tamen ita ut nihil *prorsus* ad amorem illum addi possit. Item dum dicimus aliquem toto corde amare natos suos, etiam si aliquis extet qui eos amet propensius. Sic toto corde amare deum is dicitur qui eum impense et supra omnia amat, etiam si amor ille non ita sit magnus, quin possit esse maior. Hanç esse mentem legis, ipsius legislatoris *ipsius dei* clarissimo et inconfutabili testimonio probabo. Qui sic in Deuteronomio loquitur: "Cum haec omnia tum fausta tum infausta a me proposita vobis evenerint, et vos ad eum[3] reversi eius dictis una cum natis vestris toto corde atque animo parebitis: tum Iova deus vester vicissim vos[4] ex captivitate revocabit et tum vestra tum vestrae sobolis corda circumcidet, ad Iovam deum vestrum toto corde totoque animo amandum ut vivatis".[5] Hic certe ad verba legis alludens "toto corde totoque animo" in ea notione ponit quam nos diximus. Alioquin frustra et absurde poneret futurum exemplum eius rei quae fieri non posset, si verba illa legis "toto corde atque[6] animo" tantam perfectionem necessario exigerent quantam isti in ullum mortalium in hac vita cadere negant. Ac perinde esset ac si diceret: Si vos deo toto corde atque animo parebitis, deus vos ex captivitate revocabit. *Sed nunquam id facietis (fieri enim non potest), itaque nunquam vos revocabit*. [, at vobis impossibile est ita obedire Deo, idcirco Deus vos nunquam liberabit. An non ridicula et veteratoria esset haec promissio?] Similis est locutio et in libro regum,

---

[1] G: *singulatim*.
[2] Deut 6:5.
[3] G: *Deum*.
[4] G: *vox*.
[5] Deut 30:1-6.
[6] G: *totoque*.

cap. 2. ubi David Solomonem filium suum alloquitur.[7] Sed longe apertissimus est locus ille in eodem libro, ubi deus ipse de Davidis obedientia testatur his verbis: "Mea praecepta executus est mihique tota mente obsecutus ea demum fecit quae mihi accepta forent".[8] Huius generis multi sunt loci quos ego brevitatis gratia praetermitto et ipsius dei suae[9] legis interpretationem sequens hoc dico: Quos deus ipse suae legi obedivisse pronunciat, eos nemo inobedientes pronunciet, quin potius legis eam esse mentem credamus, quam ipse deus (cui magis quam istis credendum est) interpretatur.

Sed allegant in primis locum illum ex Iobo: "Cum in eius oculis ne luna quidem splendeat neque sidera niteant, nedum mortalis et homine natus, qui putredo et vermis est".[10] Itemque alterum ex eodem: "Scilicet deo et creatore suo innocentior erit et purior mortalis homo. Ille ne suis quidem servis credit, et genios suos temeritatis insimulat, nedum cretacearum domorum incolas et c".[11] Sed in his locis allegandis suam causam (si adsit aequus peritusque iudex) plane evertunt et quidem ita ut praevaricari videantur. Allegant enim eorum dicta quae ipse deus totius disputationis iudex damnat: videlicet amicorum Iobi, qui eandem quam isti tuebantur sententiam nimirum Iobum non esse re vera iustum. Iobus vero contra. Et deus iudex ad extremum secundum Iobum contra illos fert his verbis sententiam: "Irascor tibi ", inquit, Elipham[12] alloquens, illius quam posterius allegavimus authorem sententiae, "tuisque duobus amicis, quoniam de me non recte locuti estis sicut meus Iobus. Quamobrem sumite septem tauros et totidem arietes et Iobum meum adite et sacrificium pro vobis facite, et Iobus meus pro vobis orabit, et ego in eius gratiam non agam vobiscum ut vestra meretur insania, qui non recte de me locuti sitis, sicut meus Iobus".[13] Haec est dei aperta sententia aperte illorum dicta damnantis, Iobi vero approbantis, ad quam sententiam si quid forte in totius disputationis statu controversum est, debet referri et secundum eam exponi. Nunc isti non Iobi contra illos dicentis neque dei item contra eosdem iudicantis, sed illorum[14] dicta pro veris allegant et in eo tum deo tum Iobi iudicio illorum iudicium anteponunt. Quod quidem non minus absurdum est quam si Pharisaeorum dictum aliquod ex

[7] I Kings 2:4.
[8] I Kings 9:4.
[9] G: *sive*.
[10] Job 25:5f.
[11] Job 4:17-19.
[12] G: *Elephan*.
[13] Job: 42:7-8.
[14] G: *eorum*.

euangelio desumptum contra Christi sententiam alleges. Neque vero hoc ita dico quasi velim in tota illa disputatione *singula* vel Iobi dicta approbari vel illorum improbari. Sed de causae statu loquor, videlicet utrum[15] re vera iustus esset Iobus an contra. Iustum esse ipse Iobus contendit: Iobi orationem deus approbat, illorum autem damnat. At isti contra dei Iobique iudicium damnant, illorum autem et Satanae (qui et ipse Iobum iniustum esse contendebat)[16] iudicium approbant. Itaque postquam isti Iobi librum allegant, nos nullum iudicium malumus et ex illo libro sic contra *istos* argumentamur. Deus Iobum iustum esse iudicat. Atqui vos neminem dei iudicio iustum esse docetis: ergo vos falsum docetis.

## XIX

ff. 133b-135

Iam ipsa quae isti allegant verba perpendamus. Baldadi *verba* ex cap. 25 sunt haec: "Cum eius "(scilicet dei)" et agmina sint innumera et lux in nullum non oriatur, scilicet innocens sit homo apud deum? scilicet purus sit foemina natus? Cum in eius oculis ne luna quidem splendeat, neque sidera niteant, nedum mortalis et homine natus, qui putredo et vermis est".[1] Horum verborum sententia est haec: Dei lux (hoc est sol; qua forma in quodam psalmo[2] Dei vox sive sonitus appellatur tonitru) in nullum non oritur, hoc est mortales omnes collustrat adventu suo tanto splendore, ut ne luna quidem aut caetera sidera (quae sunt alioquin caelestia luminaria et quidem ita clara, ut eo absente terras collustrent) eo praesente luceant. Tantum abest ut terrestre lumen ullum (ut sunt faces et caetera) in luce solis lucere possit. Iam vero iusticia est quasi lux quaedam, et dei iusticia appellari potest sol iusticiae. Sic igitur rem conferamus. Quemadmodum solis tanta lux est ut ne stella quidem aut luna, nedum candelae si cum eo conferantur, luceant, ita[3] dei tanta iusticia est, ut ne angeli quidem qui sunt agmina coelestia, nedum homines si cum eo conferantur, iusti esse videantur. Hanc sententiam veram esse *nec nos* nec Iobus negat. Sed non ideo refellitur Iobus. Non enim dum de Iobi iusticia agitur quaestio est, utrum Iobus sit aeque iustus atque deus, sed utrum sit re vera iustus. Quemadmodum si de stellarum splendore agatur, non quaeritur utrum stellae sint aeque

---

[15] G: *an*.
[16] Job 1,2.

[1] Job 25:3-6.
[2] MS: in margin Psal. 77 and by the other hand *et 104*.
[3] G: *illa*.

splendidae atque sol, sed utrum sint re vera splendidae. Iam quemadmodum luna, stellae, faces re vera lucidae sunt, quamvis cum solis luce minime conferri queant, ita angeli, Iobus et eius similes sunt re vera iusti, quamvis cum dei iusticia minime conferri queant. Et quemadmodum ipse sol, si loqueretur, diceret lunam et stellas et speculum, a se collustratum, esse re vera lucida, sed cum ipso nequaquam conferenda. Ita deus ipse angelos et pios homines dicit pronunciatque esse re vera iustos, sed cum ipso nequaquam conferendos. Et quemadmodum luna, stellae, faces non ideo reprehendi possunt, quia solis splendorem non aequant (neque enim fecit ea deus ut aequarent), ita homo si ea iusticia iustus est, quae cadit in hominem, reprehendi non potest; non enim a deo ad iusticiam divinae iusticiae parem creatus est. Et qui hominem reprehendunt quia dei iusticiam non aequet, ipsum[4] deum hominis conditorem, et ipsius iusticiae authorem reprehendunt, qui talem non creaverit. Nam ne Adamus quidem talis ante peccatum fuit, neque pii post hanc vitam (quos tamen isti tunc fore re vera iustos non negant) tales erunt. Enimvero deus homini non nisi ea praecepit quae caderent in hominem, sicut nec[5] caeteris animalibus, non nisi ea quae caderent in ipsa. Nec divinae legis ea mens est, ut velit deus eum qui homo est dei iusticiam habere non magis quam aut stellam solis lucem, aut bestiam hominis iusticiam. Itaque deus in iudicio suo (quod certe secundum legem ipsius fiet) non plus exiget ab homine quam quantas ei vires dederit. Quemadmodum ille in evangelio dives non plurium ab unoquoque talentorum rationem exigit quam quot ei dedit.[6]

Quod ad alterum locum attinet in quo Eliphas loquitur, idem respondemus; at quod etiam angelos a deo temeritatis accusari dicit, id *nos* aut[7] plane falsum, et Eliphae non veritatis sententiam esse dicimus,[8] aut non proprie sed comparate dictum interpretamur, sicuti de stellarum luce disseruimus quae quamvis alioquin sit re vera lux, tamen cum solis luce collata lucis nomen amittit. Nam angeli iustos esse et dei voluntatem exequi testantur sacrae literae. Sic enim de eis canit David in Psalmis: "Collaudate Iovam eius Genii virtute praestantes, [et] eius exequentes iussa auditis eius mandatis".[9] Sed fingamus verum esse quod dicit Eliphas. Efficietur ut nec Adamus ante peccatum iustus fuerit neque nos

[4] G: *ipsi.*
[5] G: *ne.*
[6] G: *dederat.* In margin from the other hand: *Matth. 25.*
[7] G: *autem.*
[8] G: *dicemus.*
[9] Ps 103:20.

post hanc vitam iusti simus futuri. Numquam[10] enim ad perfectionem veniemus quam etiam[11] in angelis desiderat Eliphas, quippe angelorum similes futuri. Ita fiet ut falsum sit quod docent isti in morte aboleri peccatum. Quinimo ita fiet ut peccatum non sit opus Diaboli. Nihil enim vel in angelis vel in Adamo ante lapsum operatus est Diabolus. Ita fit ut isti, postquam rem falsam semel defendendam susceperunt,[12] *et* in multa absurda incurrant et ipsimet sibi adversentur.

## XX

ff. 135b-136b

Allegant et Esaiae locum illum: "Cuncti ut immundi sumus, nostraeque virtutes omnes menstruati panni similes".[1] Sed imperite allegant. Quod enim vates ibi in persona impii Israelitarum populi dicit (sicut ex tota eius oratione perspicuum est) id isti etiam de piis citant, quod quidem non minus absurdum et falsum est, quam si quae de piis scripta sunt ea de impiis alleges. Nec obstat quod dicit "cuncti". Est enim locutio illius similis: "Non est qui recte faciat, ne unus quidem".[2] Excipiuntur enim pii qui etiam in eodem Psalmo "dei populus, qui ab impiis comedatur"[3] vocantur. [Ubi etiam Propheta versu 7 loquitur: "non est qui Deum invocat",[4] et in tribus proxime subsequentibus versibus Propheta ipse Deum invocat. Si igitur omnes homines putat oportet ipsum aut non fuisse hominem, aut in versu 7 mentitum. At homo erat nec mentiebatur. Ergo de impiis hoc totum dicit, qui ita sunt immundi et quorum nemo Deum invocat.][5] Alioquin si de piis quoque illa dicerentur, efficeretur ut omnes piorum virtutes, omnia sancti spiritus in piis opera quae recenset Paulus ad Galatas,[6] ipsa denique piorum sacrificia quibus seipsos hostiam sanctam et incontaminatam deo libant, ipsae piorum preces quae suffitus appellantur, cuius nidore[7] deus recreatur, ipsa denique Christi opera quae in credentibus facit dicente Paulo: "Vivo autem non iam ego sed vivit in me Christus"[8] non magis

---

[10] G: *neque*.
[11] G: *rem*.
[12] G: *susceperint*.

[1] Is 64:6.
[2] Ps 14:3 and 53:3.
[3] G: *comeduntur*.
[4] Is 64:7.
[5] *ibid.*. 64:8.
[6] Gal 5:22.
[7] G: *nitore*.
[8] See Gal 2:20.

deo placerent quam menstrua, ideoque piis essent fugienda et menstruorum instar abominanda. I nunc et pios ad recte facta exhortare, videlicet ut[9] suis rectis et a deo iussis[10] factis deum etiam irritent.

Allegant et Solomonis locum illum ex Proverbiis: "Sui cuique mores probantur, sed Iova mentes componit".[11] Verum locus ille nihil ad rem. Indicat enim non omnes esse iustos qui suo iudicio iusti sunt. Non enim nos sed deus de iusticia nostra iudicabit.

Item illum ex eodem: "Quis se corde purum, quis mundum a peccato dicat"?[12] Hinc effici volunt neminem esse qui sit corde purus. Sed hanc loquendi formam Solomonis non recte accipiunt. Non enim neminem, sed paucos tales esse indicat. Nam et in eodem capite tribus ante versibus similis est *et* sententia et locutio: "Multi homines viri pii vocantur, *sed* fidelem virum quis inveniet"?[13] Hoc est: Nomine multi sunt pii, sed re ipsa pauci. Esse autem aliquos ipsemet protinus sequente versu docet his verbis: "Qui sincere se gerit iustus, [est] beatos habet successores liberos".[14] Similis est et in cap. 31 locutio: "Strenuam mulierem quis inveniat?"[15] Non enim nullam sed paucas innuit. Item Esaiae locus ille: "Quis credit[16] orationi nostrae"?[17] Id quod de nullis, sed *de* paucis dictum esse interpretatur Paulus ad Romanos.[18] Idem igitur *et* de mundo corde censendum[19] est. Alioquin si nemo est mundo corde, nemo deum videbit. Sic enim pronunciat Christus: "Beati *qui mundo sunt* corde [puri], nam ipsi[20] deum videbunt".[21] Quod si quis hanc quoque cordis mundiciam imputativam esse putat, nihil causae est cur non et ipsam dei visionem imputativam esse putet. Cum enim ipsius cordis oculis videndus sit deus, non nisi mundis videri potest. Sicuti lucem non nisi mundis oculis videmus. Quod si non re vera sed imputative deum videbimus, non re vera sed imputative beati erimus: quandoquidem beatitas est videre deum. Ita fit ut dum isti omnibus

---

[9] G: *nt.*
[10] G: *iustis.*
[11] Prov 21:2.
[12] Prov 20:9.
[13] G: *invenit* Prov 20:6.
[14] Prov 20:7.
[15] Prov 31:10.
[16] G: *credidit.*
[17] Is 53:1.
[18] Rom 10:16.
[19] G: *dicendum.*
[20] G: *ii.*
[21] Mt 5:8.

modis imputativam, hac est imaginariam faciunt iusticiam, etiam beatitatem imputativam faciant.

Eiusdem erroris est quod[22] allegant Esaiae locum illum: "Omnes nos ut oves erravimus, suam quisque viam secuti".[23] Eumque non ad seculum unum, sed ad omnia pertinere contendunt. In quo licet eorum, dicam libere, caecitatem admirari, qui eos qui Christi sunt iisdem erroribus et sceleribus subiiciant, quibus eos qui sub lege. In quo plane perspicitur Christianos istorum iudicio nihil a Iudaeis carnalibus nisi imputatione differre. Quod si Esaiae locum illum vel mediocri diligentia considerassent, vidissent in eo loco hanc ipsam quam nos docemus iusticiam fidei aperte demonstrari. Ibi enim haec verba sunt: "Ipse ob peccata vitiaque nostra peremptus poenas nobis salutares dedit" (animadverte peccatorum veniam nobis hac piaculari victima partam), "eiusque vibicibus sanati sumus.[24] Quaeso quid est sanari? Estne hoc quoque imputativum aut[25] Christus morbos aegrotorum imputative sanavit? At Petrus in epistola prima hunc ipsum Esaiae locum citans de vera sanatione interpretatur his verbis: "Qui peccata nostra ipse suo corpore sustulit in patibulum, ut peccatis defuncti iusticiae vivamus, cuius vibice vos estis sanati. Eratis enim quondam quasi palantes oves, sed nunc ad pastorem *vos* et animorum vestrorum curatorem convertistis.[26] Hic aperte videmus Christianos errasse, non errare; aegrotasse, non aegrotare; iusticiae non vixisse, sed vivere. Idque iam declaverat ipse Petrus in capite primo illis[27] verbis: "Non caducis rebus, argento aut auro ex vanis istis patriis moribus estis liberati".[28]

Eiusdem generis est quod illum ad Philippenses locum citant: "Quinimo omnia damnum esse puto propter cognitionis Christi Iesu Domini mei praestantiam, propter quam omnium iacturam feci eaque pro stercoribus habeo ut Christum lucrer, et mihi in eo suppetat, nec habeam iusticiam meam quae a lege pendeat, sed in fide Christo habenda positam, pendentem a Deo iusticiam in fide sitam, eum eiusque et resurrectionis vim et suppliciorum communitatem cognoscendo".[29] Ex his Pauli verbis statuunt Pauli iusticiam non in Paulo sed in Christo extra

---

[22] G: *quum*.
[23] Is 53:6.
[24] Is 53:5.
[25] G: *an*.
[26] I Pet 2:24f.
[27] G: *his*.
[28] I Pet 1:18.
[29] Phil 3:8-10.

Paulum esse. Quod non minus absurdum est, quam si dicas: sanati sanitatem non in sanato, sed in medico extra sanatum esse. Docet enim ibi Paulus habere se non legis (ut olim), sed fidei iusticiam, qua factum sit ut cum Christo mortuus, scilicet mundo, quemadmodum alibi saepe docet, cum eodem vivat in novitate vitae. Quod enim dicit "cognoscendo vim eius suppliciorum et resurrectionis" idem est quod "moriendo et resurgendo cum eo", sicut apparet ex sexto capite ad Romanos.[30] Cognoscere enim aut "videre" pro "habere" aut "potiri" ponitur Hebraeorum more. Sic "videre corruptionem" pro "corrumpi" Psalmo 15.[31] Et mox: "Facies me scire viam vitae"[32] pro "facies me vivere". Et Ps. 91: "Faciam eum videre salutem meam"[33] hoc est "servabo". Et Ps. 27 "videre bona" pro "potiri".[34] Et Luc. 1: "ad dandam salutis cognitionem eius populo",[35] hoc est "ad praestandam salutem".

## XXI ff. 136b

Citant et Iacobi dictum illud: "Nolite multi esse magistri, fratres mei, scientes nos[1] graviores esse poenas daturos. Multa enim delinquimus omnes".[2] Hinc statuunt etiam Iacobum, nedum [etiam] alios multa deliquisse. Sed male locum hunc interpretantur. Loquitur enim Iacobus, sicut [et] Esaias in loco illo quem supra allegavimus:[3] "Cuncti ut immundi sumus nostrae *que* virtutes omnes [sunt] menstruati panni similes".[4] Cum tamen ipse Esaias non immundus esset. Sic et Iacobus haec non de se aut sui similibus apostolis dicit, sed de vulgo magistrorum, qui multa peccabant. Alioquin non debebat ne ipse quidem esse magister, si multa delinquebat, *cum alios hanc ob causam vetet fieri magistros. Adde quod erat graves poenas daturus, si multa delinquebat*, quod tamen isti nolunt. Contendunt enim fideles (qualem fuisse Iacobum nunquam negabunt) non esse poenas daturos, quippe cum Christus poenas pro ipsis dederit. Quid quod non solum poenas, verum etiam aeternas poenas daturus erat, si sic delinquebat? Loquitur enim de

[30] Rom 6:4.
[31] Ps 16:10.
[32] Ps 16:11.
[33] Ps 91:16.
[34] Ps 27:13.
[35] Lk 1:77.

[1] G: *vos*.
[2] Jas 3:1f.
[3] Cast. refers to chap. 20.
[4] Is 64:6.

linguae delictis, qua magistri peccent, sicut apparet ex eius verbis sequentibus, propter quae sint in Gehenna poenas daturi. Sic enim dicit: ["Lingua quae parvum membrum est magnas vires habet. Et quantulus ignis quantam materiam incendit. Et] lingua ignis est, scelerum mundus. Sic se habet in membris nostris lingua, totum corpus contaminans et aevi cursum inflammans, et ipsa[5] a Gehenna inflammanda".[6] His certe verbis explicat quas poenas daturi sint magistri qui multa peccant. Ita fit ut istidum pios quoque multa peccare contendunt, etiam Apostolos Gehennae subiiciant. Enimvero si Iacobi verba recte perpendissent, facile profecto animadvertissent, eum de duobus magistrorum generibus loqui, quorum uni mali sint et poenas daturi, quorum sapientiam terrestrem et humanam ac[7] daemoniacam appellat. In quorum numero si Iacobum fuisse putant, non debent eius authoritatem, utpote terrestris magistri, allegare. Alteri sunt boni, de quibus illa verba dicit: "At superne oriens sapientia primum casta est, deinde pacifica, aequa, obsequiosa, misericordia bonisque referta fructibus, severa et minime simulatrix.[8] Haec[9] sapientia si praeditus erat Iacobus (ut certe erat) non multa delinquebat neque[10] graves poenas daturus erat.

Urgent et dictum illud Solomonis ex libro regum 3: "Nemo est qui non peccet".[11] Sed totus ille locus sententiam nostram etiam confirmat, tantum abest ut evertat. Convenit enim cum illo Deuteronomi quem supra allegavimus, ubi docet Moses Israelitas peccaturos eamque ob causam exulaturos, deinde ad Iovam se conversuros, et Iovam tum eos iustos esse facturum eorum cordibus circumcisis.[12] Sic hoc in loco Solomo deum orat, ut si Israelitae peccaverint ideoque in exilium pulsi fuerint et ibi toto corde atque animo ad deum se converterint, ignoscat eosque revocet. Et obiter per occasionem hanc sententiam interserit: "nemo est qui non peccet".[13] Sed hanc sententiam [si] sic interpreteris ut dicas: Ergo nemo unquam in hac vita erit, qui re vera a peccando desistat iustusque fiat, a mente Solomonis plane alienum est, cum ipsemet mox de iis loquatur qui se ad deum toto corde atque animo converterint. Similis

---

5 G: *ipsam.*
6 Jas 3:17.
7 G: *et.*
8 Jas 3:17.
9 G: *Haec.*
10 G: *nec.*
11 I Kings 8:46.
12 Deut 30:1-6.
13 See n. 11.

est et[14] in Iohannis epistola prima sententia: "Si nos peccati expertes esse dicimus, fallimus nos ipsos nec est in nobis veritas. Si[15] confitemur peccata nostra, ille ita fidelis et iustus est ut nobis peccatorum veniam det nosque ab omni culpa expiet. Si nos peccasse negamus, mendacem facimus eum, nec est in nobis eius sermo".[16] In his verbis aperte docet nos ex iniustis iustos fieri. Et quod primo dixerat:[17] "Si nos peccati expertes esse dicimus", idem mox aliis verbis explicat: "Si nos peccasse negamus", nimirum de praeteritis peccatis loquens, quorum nobis[18] veniam det deus et nos ab eis expiet, hoc est iustos faciat.

## XXII

ff. 137

Sed in primis precatione[1] dominica nituntur, in qua deum docemur orare ut nobis peccata ignoscat.[2] Hinc effici volunt ut nunquam a peccatis in hac vita expiemur. Ad quod quidem dictum supra respondimus in fine capitis 17, atque illud nunc addimus. Primum non ita praescribi a Domino precationem hanc, ut semper sic sit orandum, quamvis id eius verba ferre videantur. Alioquin peccassent discipuli, si aliter orassent; quos tamen aliter orasse literis proditum est. Quinimo eos praescriptis illis verbis orasse nusquam invenimus. Deinde non *ita* praecepit ut semper omnia quae ibi praescribuntur peterent, sed quod tempus et necessitas postularet id peterent. Apparet hoc *in Actis* in eorum precibus super Matthiae in Iudae locum surrogatione. In quibus precibus nulla fit vel victus[3] necessarii, vel veniae peccatorum mentio.[4] Quod idem dico et de illis quibus postea usi sunt, cum eis interdixisset Iudaeorum senatus, ne deinceps Iesum praedicarent.[5] Quinimo in universo *novo* foedere nusquam quod sciam veniam orant[6] peccatorum suorum, quod tamen alicubi facturos fuisse valde verisimile est, si partem illam precationis omni tempore, ut isti, necessariam esse iudicassent.[7]

---

[14] *et* put in by the other hand.
[15] G: *Sin.*
[16] I Jn 1:8-10.
[17] G: *dixit.*
[18] G: *vobis.*

[1] G: *oratione.*
[2] in margin: Mat. 6 Luc. 11.
[3] G: *ad vitam.*
[4] Acts 1:23-25.
[5] Acts 4:18.
[6] G: *oravit.*
[7] Reference to suppl. 13. See the following insertion.

[Quin neque neque Christus dum pro illis orat veniam eis peccatorum orat, quippe quos iam mundos esse pronunciasset: "Ego pro eis oro", inquit, "Pater sancte, conserva per tuum nomen eos quos mihi dedisti".[8] Et paulo post: "Non oro ut eos ex mundo tollas, sed ut a malo tueare".[9] At idem in cruce dum pro iis qui peccabant orabat, veniam illis orabat peccatorum: "Pater ignosce" inquit "eis, nesciunt enim quid faciant".][10] Atque hinc obiter perspicere est, quanta sit quorundam imperitia, qui precatione illa ad omnia utuntur adeo, ut si pro aegroto, pro pace, pro rebus secundis sit orandum semper illam adhibeant, id quod mihi aeque absurdum videtur, ac si quis uno medicamento ad omnes morbos utatur. Tertio animadvertendum est ex hac de orando Domini praeceptione[11] non posse id quod isti[12] volunt statui, videlicet in perpetuum *sic* orandum esse. Non enim de temporis perennitate, sed de re praecipit Dominus, videlicet ut ea orent quae cupiant; cupiant[13] autem ea quibus *et* quando[que] sit opus. Est autem opus venia peccatorum si quis aliquando peccat. Itaque tunc oranda est. Sed hinc statuere, omnes semper peccare semperque nova venia egere, hominum est Christi beneficium et peccatorum expiationem ignorantium; neque hoc Christianae iusticiae natura patitur, neque Christi verba cogunt. Alioquin ex simili Christi locutione argumentari liceret,[14] nusquam nisi in cubiculo cuique suo idque clauso ostio orandum esse, quia Christus iusserit[15] ut "oraturus intres in cubiculum tuum et clauso ostio patrem ores in occulto".[16] Ita fiet ut si quis cubiculum non habebit orare non possit.Ita et Apostoli peccarunt qui Deum saepe palam oraverint, et omnium Ecclesiarum publicae preces erunt illicitae. Quod idem dico et de Eleemosina, quam cum Christus clam fieri iusserit, nefas erit publice facere. Item argumentari erit,] miracula a Christi discipulis semper nova esse facienda, quia *eis* dixit Christus: "Aegros[17] curate, leprosos purgate, suscitate mortuos".[18] Item parentes et cognatos et amicos semper odio habendos esse quia id fieri praeceperit;[19] quasi vero non

[8] Jn 17:11.
[9] Jn 17:15.
[10] Lk 23:34.
[11] G: *Dominum precatione.*
[12] G: *illi.*
[13] G: *cupiunt.*
[14] G: *licet.*
[15] In margin reference to suppl. 34. *Suppletus locus* added from the the other hand.
[16] Mt 6:6.
[17] G: *aegrotos.*
[18] Mt 10:8.
[19] Lk 14:13f; 26.

sint interdum tales parentes, ut sint amandi, aut quasi nemo parentibus careat ideoque illos odisse nequeat. Item neminem unquam fore sine adversario quia iusserit ut cum adversario componamus, dum sumus in via cum eo. Sic enim licebit istorum more argumentari. Iussit Christus ut cum adversariis componamus. Atqui componere cum adversariis[20] non possimus, nisi sunt[21] adversarii: ergo semper habebimus adversarios, quasi vero nullus unquam esse possit sine adversario. Atqui simile est istorum argumentum. Iussit Christus ut veniam oremus peccatorum;[22] atqui veniam orare non possumus, nisi sunt[23] peccata. Ergo semper sumus in peccatis. Enimvero non sic, sed sicuti dicam accipienda sunt huiusmodi dicta: diligite inimicos vestros, videlicet si habetis inimicos; compone cum adversario, videlicet si habes adversarium; honora patrem et matrem, videlicet si habes patrem et matrem; ora deum ut tibi veniam det, videlicet si peccasti. Sic Iohannes loquitur in prima epistola: "Filioli, haec vobis scribo ut non peccetis. Quod si quis peccaverit, patronum habemus ad patrem".[24]

Illud addo precationem hanc esse generalem: "Ignosce nobis peccata nostra". Itaque[25] cum in ipso genere sint peccata, hoc est cum inter Christianos sint qui peccent, non mirum est, si sic in genere iubemur orare. Sic Daniel orabat:[26] "Peccavimus, culpam commisimus impie et contumaciter a tuis praeceptis deflectentes, neque servos tuos vates audivimus[27]".[28] Quae omnia peccata in Danielem non cadunt. Nam ut eum aliquando peccasse confiteamur, at impie et contumaciter deflexisse et vatibus dicto audientem non fuisse, non confitemur. Sed quia in genere de populo loquitur ea confitetur, quae fuerant a populo perpetrata. Sic et nos loqui solemus dum ita dicimus: Non est mirum si nos deus punit, cum pleni simus avaritia, luxuria, denique omni[29] flagitiorum genere. Et tamen qui sic loquuntur, saepe sunt ab huiusmodi sceleribus alieni.

---

[20] G: *adversario.*
[21] G: *sint.*
[22] Mt 6:12.
[23] G: *sint.*
[24] I Jn 2:1; G: *apud patrem.*
[25] G: *Atque.*
[26] G: *orebat.*
[27] G: *andivimus.*
[28] Dan 9:5f.
[29] G: *omnium.*

## XXIII

ff. 138b-139b

Est et Pauli ad Romanos locus in quo isti magnifice exultant, ubi sic loquitur: "Non quod volo facio bonum, sed quod nolo malum, id ago".[1] Sed in eo loco graviter et magno cum periculo errant. Non enim de se illa dicit Paulus, sed in persona hominis legi subiecti; quod ut intelligatur, suadeo lectori ut nihil praeiudicati afferens diligenter perpendat eius epistolae totum[2] caput sextum et septimum et octavum. Inveniet eam ipsam, in qua explicanda iamdudum versamur, sententiam[3] ita enucleari ut nihil desideret, videlicet eos qui non sub lege, sed sub gratia sunt, mortuos esse peccato vivereque iusticiae. Et quidem hanc Pauli sententiam viderunt et alii et in primis Sebastianus Castellio, qui istorum errorem[4] in sua translationis novi foederis defensione satis refutavit, ad quam ego refutationem lectorem (si quis desiderat[5]) remittens plura de hoc Pauli loco non dissero, tantum ad illius refutationem hoc addo, Paulum etiam alibi sic loqui, ut personam sustineat eorum de quibus verba facit. Sic certe ad Galatas loquitur in his verbis: "Atqui si quae abolevi eadem redintegro, sontem me praebeo. Ego enim per legem legi mortuus sum, et c."[6] Haec enim de iis dicit de quibus ante plurali numero dixerat: "..si studentes[7] per Christum iusti fieri.."[8], hoc est de Christianis. Sic et in illo ad Romanos loco: "Nam[9] cupiditatem nescirem, et c."[10] de iis loquitur[11] de quibus ante plurali numero dixerat: "Cum essemus in carne"[12]quasi[13] hoc dicat: eorum qui in carne sunt is status est quem iam dicam, videlicet quod carnales sunt, emancipati peccato, hoc est servi peccato, utpote peccantes. Nam qui peccat servus est peccati. At eorum qui in spiritu sunt (de quibus mox agit in cap. 8) status est huic contrarius, quippe qui peccato mortui vivant secundum spiritum.

Non est praetereundus locus ille ex Solomonis proverbiis: "Septies in

---

[1] Rom 7:19.
[2] G: *totam.*
[3] G: *sententia.*
[4] G: *errorum.*
[5] G: *desideret.*
[6] Gal 2:18f.
[7] G: *studeatis.*
[8] Gal 2:17.
[9] G: *Num.*
[10] Rom 7:7.
[11] G: *dicitur.*
[12] Rom 7:5.
[13] G: *quibus.*

die cadit iustus et septies resurgit",[14] quem locum isti subinde habent in ore et in eo bis peccant. Primum quod hebraismi ignoratione (quem in latino sermone retinuit vetus interpres) locutionem perperam accipiunt; deinde quod labendi verbo peccatum significari[15] opinantur. Nam locutio illa sic accipienda est ut eam reddidit qui sic locum illum convertit. Licet septies cadat iustus, resurgit (nam illa quidem verba "in die" in Hebraeo non sunt), cui locutioni non dissimilis est illa Matthaei: "Quoties peccabit in me frater meus, et ignoscam ei?"[16] Hoc est: Quoties peccanti ignoscam? aut: Quoties ignoscam si peccaverit? Qui hebraismus citra interrogationem hic[17] erit: Septuagies septies peccabit in te frater tuus et ignosces[18] ei. Hoc est etiamsi septuagies septies peccaverit, ignosces. Atqui hic obiter animadvertere licet, quanti sit periculi Hebraismos in translatione retinere. Nam hic locus perperam propter hebraismi ignorationem acceptus ad falsam et quidem magni momenti sententiam tuendam subinde citari solet, nec nisi cognito hebraismo refelli potest: qua cognitione in bona translatione nihil opus est. Atque haec de Hebraismo. De casu vero sciendum est cadendi verbo in illo Solomonis dicto non peccatum, sed periculum aut res adversas, quas et latini casus appellant, indicari,[19] sicuti patet ex tota sententia. Sic enim loquitur Solomo:[20] "Ne insidiare impie mansioni iusti, ne vasta eius cubile. Nam licet septies[21] cadat iustus, resurgit, cum impii corruant in malum".[22] Quorum verborum haec est mens: Etiam si in plurima pericula cadant iusti (qualia eis impii creare solent) tamen evadunt. Itaque frustra eis insidiere.[23] Quin et continuo post illum versum casus nomen in eadem notione ponit, dicens: "Inimici tui casu ne gaudete, ne id videns Iova improbet et ab illo iram suam avertat".[24] Casum enim ibi vocat non peccatum, sed malum aliquod dei ira illatum.

### XXIII, 2 ff. 139

Hi sunt et huius generis alii sacrarum literarum loci, quibus isti male

---

[14] Prov 24:16.
[15] G: *significare*.
[16] Mt 18:21.
[17] G: *sic*.
[18] G: *ignosce*.
[19] G: *judicari*.
[20] G: *Solomon*.
[21] G: *saepius*.
[22] Prov 24:15f.
[23] G: *atque frustra ab eis insidiantur*.
[24] Prov 24:17f.

interpretandis falsam de fidei iusticia sententiam tuentur, quos equidem omnes, ne longior essem, mihi refellendos non putavi. Ac ne eos quidem quos recensui refutassem, nisi obviam eundum putassem errori et magno et pernicioso. Nam et dei gloriam diminuit, ne dicam abolet, et hominum moribus supra quam dici potest officit. Dei enim gloria est hominem ex iniusto iustum reddere. Haec gloria perit, dum non reddere sed putare iustum traditur. Sicuti Christi gloria periret, si quis aegrotos ab eo non reipsa sanatos, sed morbum eis non imputatum[1] fuisse doceret. Accedit eo quod deo [desit] vel[2] bonitas, vel potentia detrahitur. Potentia si non potest, bonitas si non vult hominem *vere* iustum reddere. Neque est quod hic quisquam mihi tritum illud alleget, ideo nolle ne homo peccato[3] liberatus superbiat. Quod perinde est ac si dicas deum nolle ut *homo* peccato liberatur, ne peccet. Quasi vero eum a superbia quoque, sicut et a caeteris, expiare vel nolit vel nequeat. At Paulo relictus est stimulus carnis ne superbiret. Credo. Sed si stimulum illum vultis esse peccatum, mirum nobis facitis deum, qui in discipulo suo peccatum relinqueret ne discipulus peccaret. Quod non minus absurdum est quam si dicatis[4] Christum noluisse sanare aegrotum ne aegrotus aegrotaret.[5] Non videtis locum illum totum esse contra vos. Dicit enim ei Dominus: "Sufficit tibi gratia mea. Virtus mea in infirmitate perficitur".[6] Quaeso quid est perfici? Nonne perfecte praestari? Quasi hoc dicat: Nisi tentarere vincere non posses. Nunc tentatus[7] vincis beneficio meo. Et ista demum Christiana virtus est, vincere certantem. Nam sine pugna non venit victoria, sine pugna non vicit David Goliathum. Ipse Christus in cruce sensit non vulgarem infirmitatem et tentationem, nec tamen iccirco peccavit, quin in eo ipso tanto maior *eius* virtus emicuit,[8] quod in tanta infirmitate victor evasit.

De moribus[9] vero quid dicam, quantum eis hic error officiat?[10] Deterruerunt olim decem illi exploratores Israelitas ab occupanda terra Chananaea, quod dicerent *eam* esse bonam illam quidem et fertilem,

---

[1] G: *morbos...imputatos.*

[2] G reads from here: *potentia, si non potest, vel bonitas, si non vult.*

[3] G: *peccatis.*

[4] G: *dicas.*

[5] G: *aegrotet.*

[6] II Cor 12:9.

[7] G: *tentatur.*

[8] G: *enituit.*

[9] Castellio had orginally planned to start a new section here entitled *De Moribus*, but he has later crossed it out. G kept the title.

[10] G: *officiet.*

sed inexpugnabilem; neque a Iova ideo eductos fuisse ex Aegypto ut terram illam occuparent, sed ut in solitudine perirent. Nonne[11] incredulitas et dehortatio illa deum usqueadeo offendit ut et illos decem protinus[12] interfecerit et hominum sexcenta milia in solitudine miserabiliter[13] perdiderit? Confer illos cum istis: nihil est similius. Viderant illi dei[14] in Aegypto inaudita miracula, et postea non credebant eum in expugnandis Chananaeis similia in posterum praestare vel velle vel posse. Sic vos vidistis (pro visis enim habenda sunt quae certo creduntur) eiusdem dei in Christi operibus inaudita miracula, usqueadeo ut etiam quatriduanos mortuos vitae reddiderit, et postea non creditis eum in expugnandis peccatis (ob quae abolenda a patre missus est [Christus]) similia in posterum praestare vel velle vel posse. Illi terram fatebantur esse bonam et fertilem, sed gentem inexpugnabilem. Sic vos iusticiae statum fatemini beatum[15] esse, sed peccata inexpugnabilia. Illi populum deterrebant, et vos deterretis, nisi forte hoc deterrere non est: negare fieri posse, ut homo per fidem peccatum[16] expugnet. Populus sic deterritus Iosuam et Chalebum [et] (qui deo confidentes officium suum praestabant) lapidare voluit;[17] et vester idem facit a vobis incitatus. Nam si quis Iosuae et[18] Chalebi imitator existit, non caret periculo. Ille populus postquam ab exploratoribus rem[19] fieri non posse audivit, conari desiit, cum tamen secundus adesset deus. Idem facit et vester. Quis enim id conetur, quod fieri non posse credat? Quis peccata oppugnet, quae expugnari[20] non posse, vobis magistris, sibi persuaserit? Itaque deest conatus, quia spes deest: neque quisquam unquam strenue peccata oppugnabit nisi qui expugnari posse credat.[21] Quid igitur superest nisi ut et vobis et populo vestro idem quod [et] illis usuveniat?[22] Videlicet ut postquam deo volente non vultis, eodem postea nolente neque favente velitis, et vos exploratores primi[23] saeviente deo pereatis, et populus eodem averso hostes, hoc est peccata, adortus vincatur? Neque enim frustra vel haec

[11] G: *Sed.*
[12] G: *omnes penitus.*
[13] G: *miserrime.*
[14] G: *Domini.*
[15] G: *bonum.*
[16] G: *peccata.*
[17] G: *volunt.*
[18] G: *aut.*
[19] G: *id.*
[20] G: *expugnare.*
[21] G: *credit.*
[22] G: *usu veniet.*
[23] G: *primo.*

umbra futurorum scripta sunt, vel Christus fore praedixit ut multi quaerant intrare, neque[24] possint.[25] Sed hactenus de huius erroris incommodis.

## XXIV ff. 141-142

Reliquum est ut ad quaestiones duas respondeamus, quarum una est haec: si vere iustus per fidem redditur homo, eamque iusticiam deus aeterna salute remuneratur, qui possit hoc consistere cum eo quod totius tradunt sacrae literae, "hominem gratuito dei beneficio servari[1] eamque salutem donum et haereditatem esse"?[2] Si enim donum et haereditas est, non videtur esse merces. Sin[3] merces est, non videtur donum et haereditas.

Ad quam quaestionem explicandam sciendum est et iusticiam et salutem donum esse dei, sic tamen, ut salus modo merces modo donum appelletur, iusticia vero (sicuti *disputat* Paulus ad Romanos) gratis homini conferatur. Cuius discriminis causa est haec, quod deus utriusque (sicut et caeterorum omnium bonorum) dator alterum, videlicet iusticiam donat homini sine ipsius *hominis* opera, ideoque proprie donum appellatur; alterum, videlicet salutem, donat ille quidem eamque ob causam donum vocatur, sed non nisi operanti, ideoque merces dicitur. Itaque ut proprie loquamur, dicemus hominem sine suo vel opere vel merito iustificari, at servari non item. Servatur enim sine suo ille quidem merito, at sine suo opere aut[4] labore non servatur; ideoque salus, eius operis merces dicitur. Hoc quale sit facilime cernetur ex duabus, quas iam dicam similitudinibus. Docet Paulus in priore ad Corinthios epistola eos qui in curriculo rite currunt assequi certaminis precium.[5] Et illud precium assimilat Christianorum saluti quae non nisi operantibus contingat, sicuti precium illud non nisi currentibus. Iam illud precium donum est munerarii. Frustra enim curras, nisi ille donum victori proponat. Sed quia non nisi currenti donat appellatur praemium laboris. Idem dico de agricola, cui (sicuti docet idem Paulus) laborandum est priusquam fructum[6] percipiat;[7] quique, ut docet David labore manuum

---

[24] G: *nec.*
*[25] Lk 13:24.

[1] G: *sanari.*
* [2] Rom 3:24.
[3] G: *Si.*
[4] G: *et.*
[5] G: *praemium* — and three more times. I Cor 9:24.
[6] G: *frumentum.*
[7] II Tim 2:6.

suarum vescitur.[8] Et tamen fructus ille donum dei est. Frustra enim terram colas, conseras, irriges, nisi deus det incrementum. Quo fit ut agricola fructum sine suo ille quidem merito, at non sine suo sudore consequatur. Hinc fit ut agricolae de frugum hubertate deo *datori* gratias agere soleant, quamvis deum sciant non fuisse daturum nisi ipsi laborassent. Sic est igitur salus, et sic ed ea subinde loquuntur authores sacri, videlicet eam[9] homini contingere non merenti illi quidem, sed laboranti. Quoniam igitur non nisi laborantibus contingit,[10] merces laboris rite vocatur, neque nos ab hoc loquendi genere debemus abhorrere, cum sit in sacris literis frequentissimum. Hinc Christus dicit eos salvos fore qui usque ad finem perseveraverint.[11] Hinc mercedem suis huberem in coelis repositam esse docet.[12] Hinc Paulus salutem vocat coronam iusticiae.[13] Haec est vera, plana, explicata et minime impudita[14] doctrina, qua fit ut et deo suus donandi honos et homini suum laborandi officium tribuatur. Neque [vero] est quod hic quisquam locos alleget, si qui verbis contra facere videntur, cuiusmodi est ille ad Ephesios: "Beneficio servati estis per fidem, idque non ex vobis. Dei donum est, non ex factis, ne quis se iactet".[15] Ibi enim servatos dicit non quia re vera iam salutem quam sperant Christiani fuissent adepti. Alioquin ipse sibi contradiceret qui toties sperari,[16] non iam adesse doceat[17] illam salutem. *Et ad Romanos hac de spe copiose disserens tandem aperte haec verba dicat:*[18] "Spe servati sumus. Spes autem eorum, quae cernuntur spes non est. Quod si quod non cernimus id speramus, per patentiam expectamus".[19] Sed illic servatos dicit Ephesios quia essent adoptati et ex gentilibus[20] Christiani facti, sicuti mox declarat, quae via erat ad salutem. Nam qui tales sunt, *salvi sunt: hoc est* certo[21] salvi erunt, si eo in statu ad finem[22] usque perseveraverint.[23] Sed sine perseverantia

[8] Ps 128:2.
[9] G: *etiam.*
[10] G: *contingat.*
[11] Mt 10:22.
[12] Mt 5:12.
[13] II Tim 4:8.
[14] G: *impedita.*
[15] Eph 2:8f.
[16] G: *sperare.*
[17] G: *docet.*
[18] G continues: *Etiam dicit.*
[19] Rom 8:24f.
[20] G: *gentibus.*
[21] G: *certe.*
[22] G: *fidem.*
[23] Mt 10:22.

salvos fieri tales si quis putat, is dictum illud Christi vel non perpendit vel non verum esse credit: "Qui perseveraverit usque ad finem salvus erit".[24] Non dissimile est huic locutioni quod dicere solemus:[25] Salvus sum, pro certo[21] salvus ero. Ut si aegrotus ita loquatur: Postquam mei curam suscepit tantus medicus, salvus sum: hoc est, sine dubio convalescam. Item quod lethaliter vulneratus aliquis dicit: Perii, hoc est, sine dubio peribo. Sic et Christus dicebat: "Nec iam sum in mundo, at hi in mundo sunt, et ego ad te venio".[26] Item paulo post: "Dum cum eis in mundo eram, eos equidem tuo nomine conservabam". Atqui et in mundo et cum eis adhuc erat. Sed quia iamiam migraturus erat, sic loquitur quasi iam migrasset.

Idem dico de haereditate. Est omnino haereditas donum patris. Sed quia ad eam haereditatem non nisi in recte factis ad finem usque perseverantes perveniunt, et contumaces exhaeredantur, merces appellatur. Ipse Christus est haeres patris, Christiani vero sunt Christi cohaeredes. Sed [cum] eam haereditatem ille adeptus obedientia sua, sicuti videre licet in secundo ad Philippos capite, [oporteret discipulum digniorem esse magistro, si citra obedientiam suam Christi haereditatem adipisceretur].[27]

## XXV ff. 142b-143b

Altera quaestio est, quid iis futurum sit qui inchoato opere, credentes illi quidem, nondum tamen plane necato veteri homine ex hac vita discesserint.[1] *Ad quam respondeo, si ad finem, hoc est ad mortem usque perseveraverint* suumque officium pro virili fecerint, salvos fore. Atque ut ita respondeam tum ratione tum authoritate moveor. Ratio est haec: quod si qua arbor insita est, quamvis nondum adoleverit ideoque nondum adultae arboris fructum tulerit, tamen bona et est et habetur. Quanquam enim de arbore iudicamus ex fructu, tamen non fructus arborem, sed fructum arbor facit*. Nec ideo bona est arbor quia bonum fructum fert*, sed contra, quia bona est, ideo fert fructum bonum. Et agricola etiam novellas, dummodo insitas arbores, non pro sylvestribus *sed pro cicuribus*, ut sunt, sic habet, etiam si fructum nullum adhuc tulerint: tulissent enim si per aetatem potuissent, et si adoleverint, ferent.

---

[24] See previous note.
[25] G: *solent*.
[26] Jn 17:11f.
[27] Phil 2:12.

[1] G: *decesserint*.

Idem igitur in homine quoque fieri dico. Si insitus est, hoc est, si in Christum credendo institutum vitae mutavit Christique spiritum habet, Christi est, et si forte praemature moritur, tamen salvus evadet. Talis enim et est et habendus est, qualem spiritum habet. Et deus qui hominem non solum ex operibus, ut nos, sed *etiam* ex ipsius spiritu et natura (quam nos citra opera nosse non possumus) novit, talem iudicabit. Atque haec de ratione. Authoritas autem Christi est, qui in illa de vinitoribus parabola docet[2] eos quoque, qui hora undecima operari coeperant, accepisse denarium. Bonus enim paterfamilias non pro horarum multitudine, sed pro perseverantia in opere mercedem dedit. Omnes enim ad finem usque diei perseveraverant, et qui serius venerant, si citius[3] venissent, perseverassent ipsi quoque sicut et priores. Neque enim ideo serius venerant quia caeteris essent ignaviores, sed quia eos nemo conduxisset, sicuti narratur in ipsa parabola.[4] Altera [autem] authoritas est eiusdem Christi, qui pendenti in cruce latroni et iamiam morituro paradisum promittit. Caeterum quonam pacto tales sint servandi, et quod in eis inchoatum in hac vita fuit perficiendum, deus sit ego neque scio neque mihi scitu necessarium existimo. De viventium enim officiis et factis disserimus ipsi viventes, et haec nobis ad sciendum scripta invenimus in literis. Sed de mortuis generaliter promissa tantum invenimus, quibus credentes fide contenti scientia carere[5] nos earum rerum quas deus nobis non aperuit, haud moleste ferimus. Interea si quis eas novit, ei non invidemus. Hoc in loco illud dissimulandum non puto, quod dixi de promissa iis salute, qui vel serius venerint, vel citius ex hac vita migraverint, id non sic accipiendum esse ut iis patrocinari et salutem promittere videatur, qui hac spe freti per ignaviam procrastinant vitaeque correctionem differunt. De strenuis enim et simulatque vocati sint ad opus euntibus illa dicta sunt, non de pigris et procrastinatoribus, quales si ille invenisset, videlicet qui hora tertia vocati, ire tunc noluissent[6] sed in horam undecimam, videlicet ne diei onus aestumque ferrent opus distulissent, non placuissent ei et eosdem undecima fortasse non vocasset. Et illi, si non vocati tamen in vineam inissent, frustra inissent.[7] Non enim cuivis, sed iis demum quibus promissum est, datur[8] merces. Promissa est autem nonnisi iis qui vocati eunt. Omnino perniciosae et

---

[2] G: *doceat*.
[3] G: *ocius*.
[4] Mt 20:1-16.
[5] the other hand added *nos* before *carere*.
[6] G: *tum nolussent*.
[7] G: twice *ivissent*.
[8] G: *data*.

periculosae socordiae est, in crastinum differre opus, cum hodie voceris: Cras enim aut non vocaberis, irato videlicet et averso ob ignaviam tuam paterfamilias,[9] aut fortasse mortuus eris, aut eadem quae est hodie segnitia opus detrectabis, aut interea tot te negociorum spinae obsederint ut non vacet, ac ne quidem ad semel serio de salute tua cogitandum sit ocium, aut[10] si et ocium sit et voluntas, *at* vires desint,[11] videlicet eas tibi denegante deo, sicut olim denegavit egressis ex Aegypto Israelitis, qui cum iubente et vires promittente ipso Chananaeam[12] invadere noluissent, eodem postea non iubente aggressi succubuere.[13]

## XXVI ff. 143b-145

Quoniam autem superius facta est insitionis mentio, et ea similitudo ad explicandum iustificationis negotium est aptissima, libet in ea versari copiosius. Tractabo autem eam non ut Paulus ad Romanos qui non usitato inserendi more oleastrum in oleam dixit insitum, cum contra faciant[1] omnes agricolae, idque postulet inserendi utilitas, quae nulla est si illo Pauli more fiat.[2] Sed servivit ille[3] instituto suo, sicuti rite annotatum est a quodam: et sunt[4] alioquin huiusmodi similitudines liberae, easque[5] semper licet ad instituti rationem accomodare. Itaque nos hic similitudinem ducemus a vulgari et usitata inserendi consuetudine quae sic habet. Exsecatur sylvestris arboris truncus, abiectisque ramis in truncum inseruntur sumpti ex arbore mansueta surculi, qui ubi coaluerunt arborescunt, fitque ex sylvestri trunco cicuribusque surculis arbor una, non sylvestris sed cicur, quae sylvestre alimentum a sylvestribus radicibus haustum per sylvestrem item truncum sursum transmittit in ramos cicures ibique ramorum vi cicuratum parit fructum cicurem. Ramorum enim non trunci naturam refert fructus. Arborem hic quinque figuris quo universa inserendi ratio ponatur ob oculos depingam, ut si quis forte est ab agricultura remotior vel ex pictura percipiat.

---

[9] G: *patrefamilias.*
[10] G: *at.*
[11] G: *vires fortasse deserint.*
[12] G: *Chananaeos.*
[13] G: *occubuere.*

[1] G: *faciunt.*
[2] Rom 11:17.
[3] G: *iste.*
[4] G: *sicut.*
[5] G: *eas.*

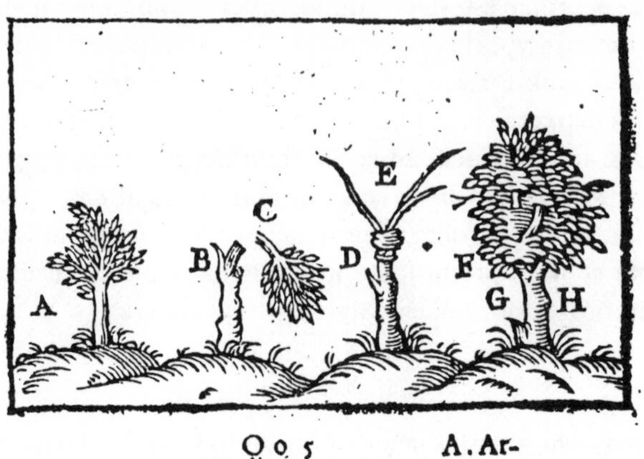


a. Arbor est sylvestris, inserenda. b. eiusdem truncata caudex inserendus. c. Rami execti et humi ad arescendum proiecti. d. Caudex insitus, cuius calami sunt e, aliunde[6] videlicet ex arbore cicure decerpti et in hanc insiti. f. Eadem arbor inolitis et incrementum adeptis calamis. Constat autem haec arbor ex duabus dissimilibus partibus, videlicet ex inferiore[7] sylvestri g, quantum scilicet est infra eum locum in quo insita fuit signatum litera h, et [ex] superiore cicure signata litera i. Sed tota cicur appellatur propter partem superiorem quae sola fert fructum eumque cicurem. Est autem animadvertendum solere in insita arbore antequam surculi vel inoleverunt,[8] vel inoliti adoleverunt,[9] a radice aut trunco pullulare stolones sylvestres (quippe ex trunco sylvestri) qui nisi decerpantur, ita succum arboris exhauriant et absumant, ut eo alimento privata pars superior languescat, nonnunquam et moriatur, atque ita iterum sylvescat arbor. Sed postquam adolevit insita arbor, ita fertur in partem superiorem tota vis humoris, ut deinceps rarissime si tamen unquam pullulent stolones. Huiusmodi arbor quicquid fructus fert, id bonum est et eiusdem naturae cuius fuit surculus. Ac quam habuit ante insitionem generositatem, eandem insita retinet, quasque vires ante in sylvestrem fructum insumpsit, easdem insita in cicurem insumit. Sed sciendum est non eandem omnium esse fertilitatem. Nonnullae enim fertilissimae sunt, aliae non usqueadeo; sunt et quae steriles. Omnes quidem quem fructum ferunt, cicurem ferunt. Steriles quae sunt, eae

---

6 G: *alicunde.*
7 G: *inferiori.*
8 G: *inoleverint.*
9 G: *inditi adoleverint.*

interdum cultura, ut[10] ablaqueatione, stercoratione, conclucatione[11] redduntur fertiles. Quod si non succedit, extirpantur, ne solum inutiliter occupent. Illud praetermittendum non est, solere eiusdem generis arbores in alias inseri, ut sylvestres pyros aut malos in cicures, et oleastros in olivas, itemque castaneas minus bonas in meliores. Nonnunquam etiam in diversi generis, ut malos in paliuros, quinimo fertiles in eos quae sunt natura steriles, ut malos in salices. Quin et quamvis in quamvis inseri posse, sed non eo quo diximus pacto Columella contendit.[12] Haec est insitionis et insitarum arborum ratio atque[13] natura qua nihil invenit agricultura solertius, et qua nihil est ad totum iustificationis negotium explicandum accommodatius. Quare animo adeste lectores et quae dicturus sum cognoscite, invenietis rem esse similimam: neve vos moveant dicta quorundam qui talia repudiant, nonnulli[14] etiam derident dicentes velle nos in theologia philosophari.[15] Nos vero philosophamur, sed coelesti et a Christo tradita nobis philosophia, qui coelestia rerum terrenarum similitudinibus explicare solitus nobis ad eadem[16] viam aperuit. Possemus equidem rem ipsam nudam et citra similitudines eloqui, sed quia ad coelestia hebetiores sunt et tardiores homines, movendi sunt rebus aspectabilibus, et earum similitudine ad inaspectabilium contemplationem cognitionemque deducendi. Hoc deus ipse in hoc mundi opificio aspectabili fecit, sicuti docet Paulus ad Romanos.[17] Hoc idem postea seipsum imitans fecit in legis ritibus et caeremoniis, quibus coelestia adumbraret, sicuti docet author ad Hebraeos.[18] Idem et Christus secutus est qui coelestem doctrinam totam similitudinibus illustravit. Denique ad docendos homines nihil est similitudinibus aptius: tantum[19] illud caveatur ne quae dissimilia sunt, ea assimilentur, id quod nos[20] cauturos esse confido. Nihil[21] enim dicemus quod non cum sacris literis convenire planum faciamus, ut etiam si rem ipsam nulla adhibita similitudine diceremus, eam nemo repudiare posset.

---

[10] G: *aut*.
[11] G: *confricatione*.
[12] Columella was a Roman writer on agriculture who lived at the time of Seneca.
[13] G: *et*.
[14] G: *aut*.
[15] Reference to Calvin.
[16] G: *eandem*.
[17] Rom 1:20.
[18] Heb 8:5.
[19] G: *tamen*.
[20] G: *ad quod vos*.
[21] G: *Nil*.

## XXVII

ff. 145-

Homines si divina disciplina careant[1] esse quasi sylvestres, hoc est vitiosos, res indicat. Tollitur haec vitiositas, dum dediscunt malum; haec est quasi sylvestris arboris exectio sive mutilatio. In sacris literis vocatur modo cordis circumcisio, olim in corporis circumcisione adumbrata, modo veteris hominis, hoc est vitiositatis exutio, modo carnis crucifixio sive interfectio, et si quae aliae sunt huius generis loquendi formae. Huic vitiositati succedit virtus quam sacri authores vocant iusticiam, dum discunt bonum: id quod fit divina et sancta quadam vi atque[2] natura, quae in hominem sic vitiis mutilatum atque exutum tanquam cicur quidam surculus in truncatae sylvestris arboris caudicem inseritur. Haec vis sive natura in sacris literis solet appellari spiritus qui in hominem ita inseritur ut postquam coaluit pro sylvestribus vitiorum cicures virtutum fructus aedat.[3] Ipsa autem mutatio qua *homo* ex iniusto iustus tanquam ex arbore sylvestri cicur efficitur, vocari solet a Paulo modo iustificatio, modo novi hominis indutio, modo cum Christo resurrectio.[4] Ipse deinde iusticiae habitus qui mutationem hanc consequitur, vocatur iusticia, nova vita, novus homo, nova creatura, quae est quasi insitae arboris nova cicurque natura. Iam quemadmodum arborem non natura, sed ars inserit agricolarum, ita hominem non natura, sed dei (quem agricolam Christus alicubi vocat) sapientia ex iniusto iustum facit.[5] Utque insita arbor, licet caudice sylvestri, tamen non sylvestris ab inferiore et iam infructuosa, sed cicur a superiore fructuosaque parte nuncupatur: *Ita* sic iustificatus homo, licet humana in eo natura, quae *caro vocatur, remunerat, tamen non ab ea natura, quae* iam infructuosa est, carnalis,[6] sed a spiritu, qui fructum in eo fert et secundum quem ipse vivit, spiritualis appellatur. Item sicut recens insita arbor non ita facile comprehendit, eademque postquam comprehendit, sed nondum adolevit, plerumque a caudice stolones gignit, qui cura coercendi sunt agricolarum, quorum stolonum causa est, quod rami cicures qui sylvestribus succressere[7] adhuc minores sunt, quam ut totius caudicis humorem possint admittere: ita fit et in spiritu. Nam recens renati hominis pars inferior tantas adhuc habet vires, ut eae in superiorem, qui novus

---

[1] G: *carent.*
[2] G: *et.*
[3] G: *edat.*
[4] Rom 3:24.
[5] Jn 15:1-8.
[6] G: [*non*] *carnalis.*
[7] G: *succrescunt.*

homo et adhuc tener et infans est, vix totae[8] possint absumi. Hinc fit ut subinde erumpant tanquam stolones quidam affectus carnales, qui nisi coerceantur, paulatim sic convalescunt, ut novus homo relanguescat, et nisi continentur affectus illos coercens[9] tandem etiam moriatur. Sed idem si adhibita cura assidua tandem adolevit, superat solusque in homine fert fructus iusticiae, totasque naturae hominis vires in se allicit. Exempli gratia: Valuit aliquis antequam Christianus factus est ingenio, idque ingenium ad peccandum applicuit, ad nocendum adversario, ad fraudandum, ad corruptelam uxoris alterius. Idem nunc Christianus factus eodem ingenio utitur ad virtutem, ad iuvandum alios, ad patrocinandum insontibus, ad honeste lucrandum, quo possit et familiam pie alere et egentibus opem ferre. Et quidem, quo maiore est ingenio, eo magis et tunc peccando nocuit et nunc recte faciendo prodest. Quemadmodum arbor quo generosior est eo plures et generosiores fructus, ut ante insitionem sylvestres, sic insita cicures aedit. Atque hoc ipsum est quod disserit Paulus in 6 cap. ad Romanos copiose, quod caput ut haec de qua dissero hominis insitio percipiatur, diligenter perlegi velim, tandemque in haec verba evadit: "Ut enim vestra membra[11] impuritati ac sceleri serva praebuistis ad scelus, ita nunc quoque membra vestra serva praebete iusticiae ad sanctimoniam".[12] Quod perinde est ac si translata ad insitionem similitudine dicas: Ut arbor ante[13] insitionem vires suas insumpsit in fructus agrestes,[14] eademque post insitionem easdem insumit in cicures. Sic homo ut antequam Christianus factus est 'omnes' vires suas insumpsit in *opera iniusticiae*,[15] *sic easdem*[16] Christianus factus [est vires suas] insumit in opera iusticiae. Utque nonnullae insitae arbores steriles sunt, ita et nonnulli Christiani ignavi sunt, et nemini nocent illi quidem neque flagitiosi sunt, sed neque prosunt aut recte faciunt. Ii diligenti doctrina et exercitatione redduntur interdum operosi. Sed si id non succedit, interdum a deo exciduntur. Non enim solum sylvestris arbor, sed etiam sterilis, quamvis cicur, displicet agricolae. Ita non solum improbus homo, verum etiam ignavus, quamvis improbitatis expers, displicet deo. Sicut et nos non solum improbos

---

[8] G: *tota.*
[9] G: *coerceat.*
[10] G: *Equidem, quo maior.*
[11] G: *umbra.*
[12] Rom 6:19.
[13] G: *ad.*
[14] MS: *agrestres* G: *agrestes.*
[15] G: *peccata.*
[16] G: *ita postquam.*

famulos, verum etiam[17] ignavos, quamvis alioquin probos, repudiamus. Haec quae recensui omnia in spiritu aeque atque in carne sic fieri et ratio docet et experientia testatur. Sed in spiritu pauci testes sunt experientiae. Pauci enim sibi renunciarunt deoque vivunt. Hinc fit ut huic qua nihil verius est doctrinae multi repugnent. Quoniam enim renati non sunt ideoque non novi, sed veteris hominis fructus ferunt, et tamen novi nomen sibi vendicant, sic statuunt: Ego sum novus homo et tamen iusticiae fructus non fero, ergo novus homo iusticiae fructus non fert. Cum potius sic ratiocinari debeant: Novus homo fructus fert iusticiae, atqui ego non fero, ergo non sum novus homo.

## XXVIII

ff. 146

Ex hac similitudinis explicatione universum iusticiae negocium licet perspicere, et quae sunt in hoc genere controversiae excutere atque dirimere. Cum enim tria sint hominum genera, videlicet irrenati, renascentes et renati, hic omnia perspiciuntur. Irrenati in arbore sylvestri, renascentes in recens insita, renati in eadem adulta. Hac distinctione adhibita patescit universum negocium. Loquuntur enim[1] authores sacri interdum de irrenatis quorum plena sunt omnia. Tunc dicunt omnes esse perditos, nullum esse qui recte faciat, sicuti nulla sylvestris arbor fructum parit cicurem. Interdum de renascentibus, ac tunc luctam describunt carnis et spiritus, vitiorum et virtutum in eodem homine, sicut in eadem insita sed nondum adulta arbore pugna est sylvestrium ramorum, hoc est stolonum, qui certatim erumpunt in parte inferiore ut agrestes fructus pariant, et cicurum, hoc est superiorum, qui caudicis succum omnem ad se conantur allicere, ut cicures fructus aedant. Interdum de renatis, ac tunc docent eos qui ex deo nati sunt non peccare, quin carnem suam cum cupidinibus[2] et perturbationibus crucifixisse mundoque mortuos deo vivere. Hanc distinctionem qui non intelligunt, ii in erroribus et versantur ipsi et alios detinent, dum quae de irrenatis aut etiam de renascentibus dicta sunt ea de renatis interpretantes omnes in uno ordine collocant; atque ita sublato discrimine omnes una sententia condemnant, et abolito in renatis divino dono, hoc est iusticia, hominem nescio qua imputatione falso securum reddunt. Neque non illud patet quemadmodum bona arbor est quae bonum fructum parit, etiam si non omnis eius fructus vitio

---

[17] G: *et*.

[1] G: *autem*.
[2] G: *cupiditatibus*.

careat, aut ad maturitatem perveniat. Ita et hominem iustum esse qui iusta faciat, etiam si non omnia eius facta vitio careant aut perfectionem adipiscantur. Nonnulli enim fructus arboris in flore inchoati mox arescunt, alii postquam nonnihil crevere decidunt. Nonnulli pene iustam magnitudinem adepti a vermibus aut quopiam alio casu corrupti pereunt, quosdam et tempestatum violentia decutit. Sed provida natura ut his omnibus[3] occurreret tantam genuit principio florum copiam. Ut etiam si plurima pars pereat, tantum tamen ad extremum supersit, ut saepe ipsa sui fructus pondere arbor laboret. Tantum abest ut mala arbor dici debeat. Quod idem in[4] iusto homine fieri dico. Tantum recte factorum semen gignit in eo spiritus *sanctus*, ut etiam si non omnia perfecta evadant aut vitio careant, tantum tamen supersit ut recte factorum plenus dici debeat. Sicuti de Tabitha memoriae prodidit Lucas in actis: "Ea", inquit, "recte et benigne factorum plena erat".[5] Atque hic obiter animadvertendum est non idem a nobis vocari fructum vitiosum quod malum. Malus enim fructus est qui ex arboris natura sylvestris est ut sunt mala sylvestria, etiam si nihil in eis sit vitii, hoc est non putria sint, non flaccida, non a vermibus vitiata. At vitiosum eum dicimus qui casu aliquo non ex arboris natura laesus est, ut frigore, ut ardore, ut uredine, ut vermibus. Tales si quos fert arbor non iccirco malos, sed laesos fructus ferre dicitur. Idem igitur de homine iusto censendum est, non esse mala opera, quae manca aut[6] imperfecta reddidit casus aliquis; non enim ex iusti hominis natura talia sunt, neque continuo sylvestre est quicquid imperfectum est. Et de arbore ex eo iudicat agricola quod in ea bonum est et excellit, quod idem et de homine facit deus, hoc est hominem eum bonum iudicat qui iusticiae spiritu praeditus iusta facit.

## XXIX ff. 147b-148

Ex eadem similitudine perspicere licet quid sibi velit Iohannes in illo dicto: "Quisquis ex deo natus est, peccatum non committit, quod dei semen in eo manet; ideoque peccare nequit, quod ex deo natus est".[2]

---

[3] G: *malis*.

[4] G: *de*.

[5] Acts 9:36. Tabitha (Dorcas), a woman from Ioppe whom Peter raised from the dead.

[6] G: *et*.

[1] G: *hac*.

[2] I Jn 3:9.

Idem enim est quod dicit Christus: "Bona arbor malum fructum ferre non potest".[3] Exempli gratia: Castus homo luxuriae opera facere non potest. Nam semen dei hoc est natura castitatis ei divinitus data in eo manet eumque a luxuria tuetur; sicuti bonam arborem a malis fructibus ferendis natura cicur defendit. Quod autem idem dicit: "Si quis peccaverit, patronum habemus ad[4] patrem",[5] id non pugnat cum hac sententia, si de inferiore parte hoc est de hominis natura in quibusdam insitis illis quidem sed nondum adultis, nondum perdomita [carne dictum accipias].[6] In illis enim certamen est sylvestris et circuris natura,[7] quod Paulus certamen appellat carnis et spiritus; in quo certamine tanquam in bello, nondum parta victoria modo hic modo ille superior est. Sed si hominis voluntas carnem odit atque adversans spiritum sequitur, non dubium est quin spiritus sit tandem triumphaturus; sicut in insita[8] recens arbore si agricola stolones continenter extirpat nec corroborari patitur non dubium est quin pars superior tandem sit victrix evasura.

Ex eadem similitudine patet et quid sit, quod idem Iohannes "lethale peccatum"[9] vocat, videlicet cum ita invalescit hominis pars inferior, ut superior, tanquam in arbore insita, emoriatur. Hoc est cum homo Christianus sui culturam negligit et in pristinum iniusticiae statum atque naturam relabitur. *Et haec de iusticia dicta sunto*.

## XXX ff. 148-

### De Christi beneficio

Sequitur ut de Christi beneficio, hoc est quid Christus credentibus conferat, dicendum sit. Video enim hac de re esse controversiam duabus sententiis in diversa trahentibus. Quidam[1] enim Christum volunt reliquis iusticiae magistris fuisse similem, qui videlicet doctrina tantum et exemplo prosit discipulis et sit ille quidem omnium magistrorum summus maximarumque et antea ignoratarum rerum doctor, videlicet in primis resurrectionis, quam primus docuerit et doctrinam suam suo sanguine constanter testatus consignaverit. Hac eius docendi vi et constantia

---

[3] Mt 12:33.
[4] G: *apud.*
[5] I Jn 2:5.
[6] words in brackets possibly put in MS. by the other hand.
[7] G: *naturae.*
[8] G: *ipsa.*
[9] I Jn 5:16.

[1] Has Castellio perhaps some Unitarians in mind? See next note.

invitari discipulos ad imitationem et obedientiam atque ita salutem adipisci. Quod autem servator et vindex[2] appellatur, id ei cum Mose, cum Gedeone et caeteris esse commune, qui populi servatores et vindices propterea vocati fuerint, quod populo persuaserint, ut iugum servitutis excuteret ipsosque sequeretur. Quod autem pro populo immolatus dicatur, eodem spectare dicunt, videlicet quod doctrinae suae veritatem morte sua testatus discipulos ad eam doctrinam sequendam atque ita salutem consequendam allexerit. Hoc vocari sacrificium pacatorium, videlicet quod Christi doctrinae credentes ad frugem redeant atque ita peccatorum veniam a deo (qui ad frugem redeuntibus propitium se fore promiserit) obtineant.

Alii contra (sicut ante demonstravimus)[3] Christo tantum tribuunt, ut eum patri pro peccatis nostris satisfecisse tradant et ab eo tantum consecutum fuisse, ut nos pater, quamvis re vera iniustos, tamen pro iustis habeat Christi videlicet iusticiam nobis imputans eaque pro nostra contentus iniusticiae nostrae nullam rationem habens.[4]

Haec quoque controversia de earum genere est, quae sub animi sensus cadunt possuntque ratione dirimi, et quidem ex iis, quae modo de iusticia disputavimus, perspici res potest. Faciamus enim hic, quod in corporis morbis. Si quaeritur, quid praestet medicus aegroto, id nemo melius iudicaverit quam sanatus. Sic apud Iohannem caecus ille natus, cum esset a Iesu sanatus, dicebat "Unum scio, me, qui caecus fui, nunc videre".[5] Transferamus hoc ad animum et patebit negocium. Esto aliquis fide Iesu habenda factus ex ebrioso sobrius, is dicet: Hoc scio, me, qui ebriosus fui, nunc esse sobrium. Haec experientia, hic sensus omnibus est firmior argumentis nec ullo disputandi acumine refelli potest. Itaque hoc sensu iudice sic statuamus, Christum animarum medicum afferre aegrotantibus animis sanitatem, atque hoc esse Christi beneficium pronunciemus.

Iam et illud ratio docet, ebriosis sicut et caeteris vitiosis irasci deum, sobriis autem propitium esse. Cum sit enim deus iustus, fieri non potest, ut non et vitiis irascatur et virtutibus faveat. Nam similia similibus gaudent aversanturque contraria. Fuit ergo deus huic homini ebrioso iratus eidemque sobrio facto propitius est veniamque dedit ebriositatis praeteritae. Alioquin nunquam eum in suam domum atque familiam cooptasset, quemadmodum homines eos, quibus irascuntur, in suam

---

[2] See Ochino, *XXX Dialogi*, Basel, 1563, Dialogue XI, p. 288 (Jacobus).
[3] See above ch. VII, *De Justicia*.
[4] See Calvin, *Institutes*, 1536, Corp. Ref. XXIX, cols. 49 and 96.
[5] Jn 9:25.

familiam haudquaquam cooptaverint. Est autem dei domus et familia iusticiae domus sicuti contra Satanae domus est iniusticiae domus, ut, qui ex iniusto iustus factus est, is vere dicatur ex Satanae in dei familiam translatus et deum ex irato habere propitium. Quaeritur nunc, quis ei deum reddiderit propitium. Ad quam quaestionem respondet ratio, si Christus ei veniam oravit praeteritorum peccatorum (ut certe oravit, sicuti postea ostendemus), non dubium esse quin impetraverit. Quare de Christi beneficio[6] hoc iam rationis iudicio statuamus, Christum homini veniam impetrare praeteritorum peccatorum iusticiamque conferre.

## XXX, 2

ff. 149-

Iam ex sacris literis idem planum facere facile est ac de iusticia quidem satis iam probavimus. De peccatorum autem venia illud passim testantur, deum irasci peccantibus. Adducam unum aut alterum locum. Scribit Paulus ad Romanos: "Exeritur ira dei de coelo in omnem impietatem et iniusticiam hominum veritatem iniuste supprimentium".[1] Et paulo post: "Scimus autem severum dei iudicium in eos futurum, qui talia faciunt".[2] Item ad Ephesios: "Fuimus natura filii irae"[3] (sic enim ad verbum legitur) hoc est digni supplicio aut supplicio destinati. Nec ego hic de voce Natura disputo, quam ibi pro reipsa poni puto, sicut et alibi ponitur et ibi poni ostendit argumentum Pauli, qui de commissis re vera peccatis verba faciat. Sed de verbis illis loquor: Eramus "filii irae", quibus ostenditur deum peccantibus iratum fuisse. Iram autem illam Christi sacrificio et precibus placatam fuisse eaedem docent literae. Primum enim Christum fuisse agnum Paschalem[4] indicat Iohannes, dum Mosis locum de non frangendis illius agni ossibus allegat de Iesu in cruce pendente, cuius crura non fregerunt milites. "Acciderunt haec", inquit, "ut scriptum illud comprobaretur "nullum eius os frangetis"".[5] Item Paulus in prima ad Corinthios: "Pascha nostrum", inquit, "pro nobis immolatus est Christus".[6] Iam agni Paschalis eum usum fuisse tradit Moses, ut deus animadverso sanguine eius agni, quo sanguine notatae

---

[6] See below ch. XXXI.

[1] Rom 1:18.
[2] Rom 2:2.
[3] Eph 2:3 Castellio quotes here the Vulgate. His own formulation follows immediately: *digni supplicio*.
[4] Ex 12:46 and Num 9:12.
[5] Jn 19:36.
[6] I Cor 5:7.

essent domus Israelitarum, praeteriret eos, ita ut a clade, qua afficerentur Aegyptii, essent immunes.[7] Itaque in Christo, qui fuit verus ille Paschalis agnus, idem fieri censendum est, videlicet ut deus eius respectu non saeviat in eos, qui sunt Christi sanguine notati. Atque hoc confirmat ipse Christus, dum iamiam immolandus dicit suis discipulis: "Hic est sanguis meus pro multis effundendus ad veniam peccatorum".[8] Conveniunt haec cum loco illo Esaiae: "Ipse ob peccata vitiaque nostra peremptus poenas nobis salutares dedit eiusque vibicibus sanati sumus".[9] Et ad finem eiusdem capitis: "Quoniam obiecerit animam suam morti et sontibus annumeratus multorum peccatum tulerit proque sontibus interpellaverit".[10] Item cum loco illo Pauli ad Romanos: "Quem (videlicet Christum Iesum) proposuit deus placamentum per fidem in eius sanguine collocandum".[11] Item cum illo Iohannis in prima epistola: "Si quis peccaverit, patronum habemus ad patrem Iesum Christum iustum, qui idem piaculum est peccatorum nostrorum nec solum nostrorum, sed etiam totius mundi".[12] Item in eadem epistola: "In eo amor est," inquit "quod deus, non quod nos eum amaverimus, sed quod ipse nos amaverit, misit filium suum pro peccatis nostris piaculum".[13] Idem et in epistola ad Hebraeos in cap. 10 copiose demonstratur. Ex his et huius generis aliis locis patet Christi sacrificio et precibus patrem nobis fuisse placatum

## XXXI ff. 150, 150b

Sed sunt, ut ante recensui, qui Christi sacrificium et preces aliter interpretantur putantque non deum homini a Christo fuisse pacatum aut reconciliatum, sed contra hominem, qui deum sibi iratum esse falso putaret ideoque ab eo aversus esset, ad deum fuisse Christi doctrina conversum eique reconciliatum. Atque hanc suam sententiam tum ratione tum authoritate stabilire conantur. Rationem afferunt hanc: Deum nunquam irasci dicunt quippe immutabilem, cum ira sit quaedam animi perturbatio atque mutatio ideoque in deum non cadat. Praeterea negant credibile esse deum alicui veniam dare propter quicquam, quod sit extra ipsum hominem. Auctoritates autem allegant has. Primum Malachiae locum, ubi dicit deus: "Nec ego Iova mutabilis sum nec vos

---

[7] Ex 12:13.

[8] Mt 26:28.

[9] Js 53:5. In MS *vicibus* for *vibicibus* (Error?).

[10] Js 53:12.

[11] Rom 3:25.

[12] I Jn 2:1.

[13] I Jn 4:10.

Iacobidae finiendi".[1] Item illud Esaiae: "Ego, ego, tua delicta propter memetipsum deleo tuorum peccatorum immemor".[2] Item illud ad Romanos: "Deus suum erga nos amorem in eo commendat, quod, cum adhuc nocentes essemus, Christus pro nobis mortuus est. Ergo multo magis nunc eius sanguine iustificati defendemur per eum a supplicio. Si enim, hostes cum essemus, reconciliati sumus deo per eius filii mortem, multo magis reconciliati servabimur per eius vitam".[3] Ex his et similibus locis contendunt deum non fuisse nobis iratum aut a nobis alienum, ut esset reconciliandus. Amorem enim, quo nos adhuc sontes prosecutus est, non posse cum aversatione consistere. Nam si amabat, inquiunt, non irascebatur; sin irascebatur, non amabat. Non ergo deus homini, sed homo deo reconciliatus est. Allegant praeterea locos de poenitentia, cuius ope homines veniam consequantur peccatorum. Et in primis locum illum Ezechielis: "Cum impius omissa, quam exercuit, impietate ius aequumque facit, is vitam suam conservat".[4] Item illum Marci: "Iohannes poenitentiae baptisma publicabat ad peccatorum veniam".[5] Item illud dictum Petri: "Redite ad frugem et baptizamini cuncti in Iesu Christi nomine ad peccatorum veniam et donum sancti spiritus assequemini".[6] Ex his et huius generis aliis locis contendunt homines non Christi sacrificio aut precibus, sed vitae suae correctione consequi peccatorum veniam. Hinc surgent quaestiones duae, quarum prior haec est: Utrum deus sontibus irascatur. Altera haec: Utrum deus homini veniam det propter Christum aut omnino propter quicquam, quod sit extra ipsum hominem.

## XXXII ff.150b

Ad primam quaestionem, utrum in deum cadat ira aut omnino ullus animi affectus, nec disputare hic libet nec necesse est. Nostra enim nihil refert, utrum re vera irascatur sontibus deus an irae alioquin expers eos sic puniat, quasi irascatur. Fieri enim potest, ut nulla alioquin motus ira puniat, quippe cum etiam homines id facere videamus. Nam saepe magistratus sine ulla ira in maleficos animadvertit sola ratione et legibus

---

[1] Mal 3:6. See ch. XXXII, n. 1.
[2] Js 43:25.
[3] Rom 5:8.
[4] Ezek 18:27.
[5] Mk 1:4.
[6] Acts 2:38.

motus.[1] Sed cum talis animadversio in sacris literis ira vocetur et eius, qui punitur, nihil referat, utrum ab irato an a non irato puniatur, utpote qui aeque puniatur a non irato ac si ab irato puniretur, nos hoc ipsum, quicquid est, more sacrorum authorum iram et, cum fieri desinit, irae sedationem sive placationem sine ulla dubitatione appellemus. Quaeritur igitur, utrum sic sive iratus sive saeviens in sontes deus saevire desierit aut desinat placatus a Christo an potius placatus ab ipsis sontibus ad frugem redeuntibus.[2] Ad quod ego sic respondeo, eum utrumque fieri aperte, sicuti superius allegavimus,[3] tradant sacrae literae, utrumque verum est, videlicet deus homini interdum ob Christum, interdum ob ipsius hominis vitae correctionem ignoscit. Atque hoc tum ratione tum authoritate tum exemplis demonstrari potest. Ratio est haec, quod nos (qui hac in re, sicut et in caeteris non vitiosis rebus, dei similes sumus) idem facere solemus. Ignoscimus enim iis, qui nos offenderunt, interdum ab ipsis, interdum ab amicis nostris pro illis orantibus exorati. Itaque deum idem facere nec mirum nec absurdum est. Habet enim et deus amicos, qui apud ipsum gratia valent. Authoritas inprimis illa est, quod deus in Levitico[4] statuit, ut sacerdos sacrificio et supplicatione sontibus veniam exoret. Quod si exorabat sacerdos, multo magis de Christo idem dicendum est. Exempla sunt plurima. Abrahamus[5] precibus suis Abimelecho eiusque familiae sanitatem impetravit. Moses[6] precibus deum exoravit, ut ab Aegyptiis ranas propulsaret. Idem et sorori suae Mariae[7] et mox populo,[8] qui aureum illum vitulum fecerat, veniam exoravit.[9] Quod si quis dicet illos non precibus alienis, sed sua poenitentia impetrasse veniam, primum quaeram, cur ergo faciat historia mentionem alienarum precum. Si enim sola illis poenitentia satis erat, non video, cur alienae preces adhiberi debuerint et quidem interdum submovente deo. Abimelechum[10] enim monuit, ut Abrahamum reddita uxore sibi reconciliaret, ut

---

[1] Similar B. Ochino, *XXX Dialogi*, Basel, 1563, Dialogue IX p. 206: "Non ita irascitur, ut commutetur aut perturbetur cum sit simplicissimus: neque item ut commoveatur, sicuti solent irati, utpote cum sit immutabilis. Neque item irascendo dolet, cum sit Deus, continenter semperque felicissimus. Irascitur igitur non re vera, sed tantum factis, videlicet quod in sontes animadvertit. "Also p. 207.

[2] This seems to be a reference to Calvin's dispute with Osiander. Castellio comes close to the latter. See his favorable remark on Osiander above I, ch. XXVI, n. 22.

[3] See II, ch. VII.

[4] Lev 5:6ff.

[5] Gen 20.

[6] Ex 8:12.

[7] Num 12:13.

[8] Num 14:19.

[9] In margin reference to suppl. 15.

[10] Gen 20:7.

deinde eo deprecante vitam et sanitatem obtineret. Quod idem et de Iobi[11] amicis dico, quos monuit, ut Iobum adirent, quo eius precibus dei iram averruncarent veniamque impetrarent. Deinde exempla allegabo, in quibus venia alicui sine ipsius vel poenitentia vel precibus impetrata fuerit ab altero rursumque alia, in quibus veniam non obtinuerit poenitentia. Narratur in libro Numerorum,[12] quemadmodum Aharon seditioso et Mosem Aharonemque ad necem invadenti populo deum suffitu pacaverit. Hic certe nulla erat populi poenitentia. Quid de Loto[13] dicam, in cuius gratiam voluit deus eius generorum saluti consulere? Nan ne in his quidem ullam fuisse poenitentiam patet ex historia, quin ne quidem de excidio quicquam suspicabantur, cum Lotum monuerint Angeli, ut illos adiret ad servandum. Quod si illis suis amicis tantum tribuit deus, ut in illorum gratiam aliis veniam det et bene faciat, nemini debet absurdum videri, si filio suo idem tribuit. Rursum irritae poenitentiae exempla sunt haec: Saulus[4] deum invocans non est ex....[5]

## XXXIII ff. 151b

Sed illud quidam percipere non possunt, qui conveniat a deo missum fuisse aliquem ad ipsum deum placandum. Si enim placari se volebat deus, iam placatus fuisse videtur, quippe cum placari velle animi iam placati esse videatur. Atque huc pertinet ille locus ad Romanos[1] a nobis superius allegatus, in quo dicitur deus amore nos praevenisse. Verum si rem diligenter consideraverint, comperient nihil in eo absurdi esse. Potest enim idem simul et amare aliquem et tamen eidem irasci. Exemplo sunt parentes, qui saepe liberis suis ob ipsorum peccata irascuntur et tamen eosdem amare non desinunt. Quod idem a deo fieri aperte docet epistola ad Hebraeos his verbis: "Quem amat, Dominus castigat et verberat, quemcumque filium acceptum habet".[2] Neque non illud fit, ut, qui alicui, quem amat, irascitur, eidem placari se cupiat et modum ei placandi sui vel optet vel etiam suggerat et ostendat. Apparet hoc ex placatoriis sacrificiis, quae deus (ut supra demonstravimus)[3] ad se,

---

[11] Job 42:8.
[12] Num 16:47.
[13] Gen 19:14.
*[14] I Sam 15:24ff.
[15] The text is unfinished. In margin reference to suppl. 21.

[1] Rom 5:8. See II, ch. XXXI n. 3
[2] Heb 12:6.
[3] See above II, ch. XXXI.

quandocumque irasceretur, placandum instituit. Quod si quis hic excipiet deum tum, cum illa institueret, non fuisse iratum, sed in illud tempus instituisse, in quo futurus esset iratus, respondebo eundem interdum etiam tum, cum irascitur, eandem habere erga eos, quibus irascitur, benevolentiam, quam habuit, cum illa sacrificia pacatus institueret. Apparet hoc ex eo, quem paulo ante ex Iobo allegavi, loco, in quo disertis verbis Iobi amicos sic alloquitur deus:[4] "Irascor tibi tuisque duobus amicis, quoniam de me non recte locuti estis sicut meus Iobus. Quamobrem sumite septem tauros et totidem arietes et Iobum meum adite ac sacrificium pro vobis facite et Iobus meus pro vobis orabit et ego in eius gratiam non agam vobiscum, ut vestra meretur insania".[5] Hic certe irascens illis modum praescribit sui placandi. Idem facit et in Ioëlis[6] capite secundo copiosissime. Neque non in fine Malachiae idem se facturum promittit his verbis: "Ego vobis missurus sum Eliam vatem, antequam veniat Iovae dies magna ac terribilis, qui et parentum animos ad natos et natorum animos ad parentes convertat, ne ego veniam et afficiam orbem exitio".[7] Haec cum ita sint, nihil absurdi est, si dicatur deum succensuisse mundo ob ipsius peccata et eundem tamen amasse. Nunc respondendum est ad quosdam locos, qui superius[8] sunt allegati. Malachiae locus est: "Nec ego Iova mutabilis sum nec vos Iacobidae finiendi".[9] Verum is locus nihil ad iram pertinet. Iudicat enim deum non esse mutabilem hoc est non esse inconstantem. Irasci autem non est inconstantiae. Quod ad Esaiae locum[10] attinet, ubi se dicit deus delicta populi propter seipsum delere, is locus gratiae Christi non adversatur. Docet enim deum non ob Israelitarum merita, sed suo beneficio id facere. Potest autem et propter seipsum, hoc est ad sui nominis gloriam, et propter Christum, hoc est amore Christi, facere, quippe qui et seipsum amet et Christum. Neque enim absurdum est unius rei plures esse causas. Sic certe loquitur deus in Esaia his verbis: "Qua venit via" (scilicet Senachoribus), "eadem regredietur neque in urbem istam veniet, inquit Iova, me eam meo praesidio defendente propter me propterque meum Davidem".[11] Quod si quis sic interpretabitur: propter Davidem, hoc est

---

[4] See above II, ch. XXXII n. 11.
[5] Job 42:7. See previous chapter.
[6] Joel 2:12ff.
[7] Mal 3:23ff.
[8] Castellio refers to bk. II ch. XXXI.
[9] Mal 3:6.
[10] Is 43:25.
[11] Is 37:34ff.

quia promisit Davidi, non refutaverit dictum nostrum. Promisit enim Davidi, quia Davidem amavit, et quia eum amavit, ideo in eius gratiam ad laudem suam hoc facit.

## XXXIV

ff. 152b-

Sed in eo praecipua est difficultas, qui possint haec conciliari, videlicet quod deus et Christi sacrificio placatus sit hominibus et tamen ab iisdem ad se placandum exigat vitae correctionem. Si enim a Christo placatus est ante hominum vitae correctionem, quid deinde ea opus est ad ipsum placandum, hoc est ad id faciendum, quod iam factum est? aut si vitae correctione placatur homini,cur ante placatus dicitur? Atqui utrumque fieri testantur sacrae literae. Nam et Christi sacrificium fuisse placatorium supra ex eis demonstravimus[1] et deum vitae hominum correctione placari tum ratione tum multis authoritatibus ostendi potest. Ratio est haec, quod deus, cum sit misericors (id quod nemo negabit), placabilis est in eos, qui ad frugem redeunt. Est enim hoc misericordiae. Authoritates sunt plurimae. Primum Moses in Deuteronomio sic alloquitur Israelitas: "Cum autem haec omnia tum fausta tum infausta a me proposita vobis evenerint et vos ubicumque gentium a Iova deo vestro dispersi ad sanitatem redibitis ad eumque reversi eius dictis, quemadmodum ego vobis hodie praecipio, una cum vestris natis toto corde atque animo parebitis, tum Iova deus vester vicissim vos ex captivitate revocabit vestrique misertus ac vobis reconciliatus vos ex omnibus, in quas disperserit, nationibus colliget".[2] Item in Ieremia[3] et Ezechiele[4] promittit deus sese ad frugem redeuntibus fore propitium et a malo, quod ipsis propter ipsorum peccata minatus fuerit, sibi temperaturum sententiamque mutaturum. Marcus[5] quoque et Lucas[6] scribunt Iohannem Baptistam publicasse "baptisma emendationis vitae ad peccatorum veniam". Item Petrus in Actis: "Redite ad frugem", inquit, "et baptizamini cuncti in Iesu Christi nomine ad peccatorum veniam et donum sancti spiritus assequemini".[7] Idemque in eodem libro: "Hunc deus ductorem sanatoremque sua dextera extulit ad conciliandum Israelitis vitae correctio-

---

[1] In margin Castellio refers to bk. II, ch. XXX.
[2] Deut 30:1ff.
[3] Jer 18:8.
[4] Ezek 18:14ff.
[5] Mk 1:4.
[6] Lk 3:3.
[7] Acts 2:38.

nem peccatorumque veniam".[8] Ex his et huius generis aliis locis (quales passim inveniuntur) perspicuum est hominibus pacari deum ipsorum correctione vitae. Quinetiam, si cui sit placatus et is in pristina vitia relabatur, iterum ei irascitur deus neque quicquam ei prodest Christi sacrificium. Apparet hoc ex Christi verbis apud Iohannem, ubi sic loquitur: "Ego sum vera vitis et pater meus est agricola, qui omnem palmitem in me non ferentem fructum amputat".[9] Cum qua similitudine quadrat et illa Pauli ad Romanos,[10] qua docet eos, qui sunt in oleam insiti, amputatum iri, nisi in fide perseveraverint.[11] Amputatio certe non nisi irato fit deo. Hinc nascitur (ut iam diximus)[12] quaestio, quinam possint haec, quae pugnantia videntur, conciliari, videlicet quod deus et Christi sacrificio placatus sit hominibus et tamen ab iisdem ad se placandum exigat vitae correctionem.

## XXXV ff. 153b-154b

Ad hanc difficultatem explicandam considerandum est, quod docet Paulus ad Romanos, videlicet exeri iram dei in maleficos. "Hanc ob rem", inquit, "permisit eos deus in turpes libidines ac, quemadmodum dei cognitione non probe usi sunt, ita permisit eos deus in improbam mentem, ita ut nefaria faciant".[1] Laxaverat igitur habenas gentibus easque ruere sinebat in omnia flagitia eo videlicet offensus, quod, cum deum cognovissent, tamen non eum, ut par erat, honoraverant. Haec gentium desertio erat irae dei, qua fiebat, ut aversus deus eis doctrinam non mitteret, qua doctrina possent ab illis flagitiis avocari iusticiaeque spiritum a deo consequi atque ita "severum dei iudicium in tales, quales erant ipsi, futurum"[2] evitare. Eadem ira digni erant etiam Iudaei, qui, cum non solum naturae (ut caeterae gentes), sed etiam Mosis et vatum doctrinam haberent, tamen eadem flagitia perpetrabant. Sed deus, qui illi nationi propter foedus, quod ipsi cum Abrahamo et eius posteris, hoc est cum Hebraeis, intercedebat, potissimum favebat, eos nondum sicuti caeteras gentes deseruerat nec eis salutares doctores subtraxerat. Verum

---

[8] Acts 5:31.

[9] Jn 15:1ff.

[10] Rom 11:22ff.

[11] Similar B. Ochino, *XXX Dialogi*, Dialogue IX, p. 208: "Fatendum igitur est Messiae placaturum esse iram Dei, non quia sit eum mutaturus, et ex irato placatum redditurus: sed quia sit nos mutaturus, ita ut improbos deique inimicos bonos sit et eius amicos effecturus".

[12] See above II, ch. XXXII.

[1] Rom 1:26ff.

[2] Rom 2:2f.

id iamiam futurum erat, nisi alicuius opera intervenisset, imminebatque illis securis illa irae dei, de qua eos praemonens Iohannes Baptista dixit: "securim iam admotam esse radici arboris",[3] nimirum iamiam excidendae, nisi bonum fructum ferret. Igitur hanc dei tum in Iudaeos tum in gentiles iram, qua videlicet hi iam deserti, illi iamiam deserendi erant, Christus averruncavit fecitque, ut doctrina salutis et ad gentes (qui ea et carebant et carere digni erant) perveniret et in Iudaeis (qui eam indigni habebant) adhuc maneret. Ac de gentilibus quidem sunt illa in Actis Apostolorum verba Pauli ad Athenienses: "Igitur praetermissis ignorantiae temporibus deus nunc omnibus ubique hominibus denunciat, ut ad frugem redeant",[4] quasi hoc dicat: Esset deo ob commissa hactenus a vobis scelera iusta causa in perpetuum vobis irascendi evangeliique doctrinam nunquam mittendi, sed nunc ignoscit praeterita ea conditione, ut ad frugem redeatur atque ita futura ira iudicii (de quo mox loquitur ibi Paulus) effugiatur.[5] De Iudaeis autem est illa de ficu apud Lucam parabola,[6] quam ficum in vinea sua satam, quia sterilis esset, abscindere volens vineae dominus exoratus est a vinitore, ut adhuc annum illum differret excisionem eius; sese eam ablaqueaturum et stercoraturum, si forte hac via fertilis reddi posset, alioquin postea excidenda. Hunc enim vinitorem ego non video, quem alium possimus interpretari quam Christum, qui a vineae domino patre suo impetraverit, ut in docendis Iudaeis, quamvis a recte factorum fructu sterilibus, tamen adhuc pergeretur postea tandem deserendis, nisi illa Christi cultura ad sanitatem rediissent, id quod etiam factum videmus. Tandem enim repudiato pertinaciter evangelio deserti sunt, ut Paulus vocat, "amputati".[7] *Quod igitur a Christo placatus pater dicitur in eiusque gratiam hominibus veniam dedisse praeteritorum peccatorum, id non absque conditione accipiendum est, sed ita demum (sicuti iam docui)*,[8] *si ad frugem redierint*,[9] quemadmodum, quod illi ficui orante vinitore venia data est praeteritae sterilita-

---

[3] Mt 3:10.

[4] Acts 17:30 Castellio writes *frugem redire* for *poenitentiam agere*.

[5] In margin reference to suppl. 20.

[6] Lk 13:6ff.

* [7] II Cor 11:12.

[8] See above II, chpts. XXXI and XXXII.

[9] See Caspar Schwenckfeld, *Von der heiligen Schrift, ihrem Inhalt, Amt, rechten Nutz, Brauch und Missbrauch*..., Strassburg, 1594, ch. 16, fol 33b: "Darum suchen sie die Justification oder Gerechtigkeit also durch den Glauben an Christus, dass sie ihnen nicht allein zugerechnet und auswendig ihnen bleibe, sondern dass sie wahrhaftig, wesentlich und wirklich der Gerechtigkeit Christi in ihrer Seele, Herz und Gewissen, ja empfindend teilhaftig werden...". However, there are differences in their respective religious persuasions.

tis, id ita demum accipiendum est, si adhibita cultura fertilis evasisset. Alioquin illa venia fuerit paenarum dilatio. Ita tollitur illa, quae esse videbatur, discrepantia, quod peccatorum venia a Christo impetrata diceretur et tamen eadem ab hominis vitae correctione impetrari videretur. Utrumque enim verum est. Nam et Christus homini veniam impetravit et tamen, quia cum conditione impetravit, erit irrita venia, nisi homo ad frugem redierit.

## XXXVI

ff. 154b-156

Dicam parabolam, qua hoc fiat apertius. Civitas quaedam fuit, quae rebellavit in regem suum, qua rebellione iratus rex illam civitatem eversurus erat. Sed extitit in ea civitate quidam civis innocens et qui in rebellionem non consenserat; is, cum apud regem gratia plurimum valeret, oravit eum, ut veniam daret civibus suis. Rex, qui alioquin clemens esset et insuper illi civi propter ipsius singularem probitatem et innocentiam plurimum faveret, concessit, sed ea conditione, ut cives poenitentiam agerent et deinceps a rebellando abstinerent. Respondit civis ille id aequum esse neque se veniam illis alia conditione orare. Itaque aditurum illos et ad poenitentiam et correctionem hortaturum. Quod si se correxissent, bene esse, sin minus, non recusare, quo minus, qui in rebellione perseverarent, perirent. Hoc impetrato cives adit, demonstrat regis iram, se eis veniam impetrasse, si se correxerint, hortaturque, ut id faciant, alioquin perituri. Haec est parabola, cuius interpretationem hanc afferam. Civitas illa mundus est, qui in deum, regem suum, peccando rebellavit. Nam peccatum rebellio est in deum. Civis innocens Christus est, qui civis pro civibus suis, hoc est homo pro hominibus deum oravit et eis veniam praeteritae rebellionis impetravit, sed ea conditione, si se correxerint; quod ut faciant, demonstrat eis sua doctrina dei iram monetque, ut a peccando desistant, alioquin perituri. Est igitur hac conditione impetrata a Christo toti mundo venia nullo mortalium excepto. Quod si quis perit, is ideo perit, quia in rebellione perseverando aut etiam post sui correctionem et poenitentiam denuo rebellando irritam reddit illam veniam. Quod si quis locum ex Iohanne allegabit, in quo se Christus pro mundo orare neget, respondebo ibi non agi de venia peccatorum. Verba sunt Christi: "Ego pro eis (videlicet discipulis) oro; non pro mundo oro, sed pro eis, quos tu mihi dedisti".[1] Ibi certe non veniam peccatorum orat suis discipulis,[2] utpote quam

[1] Jn 17:9.

[2] In margin a reference to Jn 13 and from Castellio's hand the following sentence in

iampridem obtinuissent, quippe cum eos iam mundos esse (quod plus est quam veniam obtinuisse) Christus pronunciasset, sed orat pro eis, ut conserventur, sicut mox ostendunt haec verba: "Pater sancte, conserva per tuum nomen eos, quos mihi dedisti",[3] et paulo post: "Non oro, ut eos ex mundo tollas, sed ut a malo tueare".[4] Quod si quis porro allegabit illa mox sequentia verba: "Sanctifica eos veritate tua"[5] et hinc contendet ergo non fuisse sanctos, quippe qui essent sanctificandi, respondebo primum sanctificare non esse idem quod ignoscere. Deinde non valere hoc argumentum: Sanctificandi erant, ergo non erant sancti. Alioquin ne Christus quidem tunc sanctus fuisset, quippe qui ibidem continuo dicat: Eorum causa ego meipsum sanctifico. Sed sanctificari non solum is dicitur, qui ex non sancto fit sanctus, sed etiam qui ex sancto fit sanctior, sicuti calefieri, qui ex calido fit calidior. Sic positum est in fine Apocalypseos: "Qui sanctus est, sanctificetur adhuc".[6] Quod autem ad veniam attinet peccatorum, eam Christum orasse etiam non suis ostendunt eius verba in cruce patrem orantis, ut ignosceret iis, a quibus in crucem sublatus erat, qui certe non erant eius discipuli.[7] Atque haec de dei in genus humanum ira a Christo semel pacata.

Neque vero solum in universum semel oravit pro humano genere, verum etiam nunc orat pro suis, sicut docet ad Romanos Paulus his verbis: "Christus est, qui mortuus est vel potius resurrexit, qui etiam est ad dei dexteram et pro nobis supplicat: quis nos divellat ab amore dei"?[8] Item author ad Hebraeos: "Hic quia durat in sempiternum, nunquam transiturum habet sacerdotium et iccirco plane servare potest eos, qui per ipsum deum adeant, quippe qui semper vivat ad supplicandum pro eis".[9] Item in eadem epistola: "Non in manufactum sacrarium ingressus est Iesus, quod veri sacrarii exemplar foret, sed in ipsum coelum, ut nunc deo coram appareat pro nobis".[10] Et ante eum locum dixerat: "Non enim eum habemus pontificem, qui nostris infirmitatibus affici non possit, sed qui sit in omnibus similiter tentatus citra peccatum".[11] Et Iohannes in prima epistola: "Si quis peccaverit, patronum habemus ad

---

French: "Et que dirons-nous qu'il dit que son sang sera épandu pour le pardon de leurs pêches? Répond".

[3] Jn 17:12.
[4] Jn 17:15.
[5] Jn 17:17.
[6] Rev. 22:11.
[7] Lk 23:34.
[8] Rom 8:34f.
[9] Heb 7:24f.
[10] Heb 9:24f.
[11] Heb 4:15.

patrem Iesum Christum".[12] Ex his locis apparet Iesum nunc quoque in coelis pro nobis orare et veniam nobis impetrare, si quid infirmitate peccamus. Quid sint autem huiusmodi peccata, quae etiam in renatos cadunt, cum tamen dei natos peccare negent sacrae literae, superius disseruimus.[13] Atque haec de peccatorum venia, quam Christi beneficio consequantur homines, id quod primum Christi beneficium est.

## XXXVII

ff. 156-157

Alterum Christi beneficium est, sicuti supra demonstravimus,[1] iusticia. Eam autem homini confert, dum credentibus mittit sanctum spiritum, qui in eis iusticiam operetur; est enim Christo[2] omnis data potestas tum in coelo tum in terra, qua potestate largitur et alia et in primis illum, de quo loquimur, iustificum spiritum, sine quo iustus esse homo non potest. Eum autem a Christo mitti patet ex ipsius verbis apud Iohannem,[3] ubi sic loquitur:[4] "[E re vestra est],[5] ut ego discedam. Nisi enim discessero, confirmator ad vos non veniet. Sin abiero, eum ad vos mittam atque ille, ubi venerit, mundum arguet de peccato et de iusticia et de iudicio. De peccato, quoniam mihi fidem non habent, de iusticia, quoniam ad patrem discedo nec me videbitis amplius, de iudicio, quoniam huius mundi princeps iudicatus est. Adhuc multa vobis habeo dicenda, sed quae nunc ferre nequeatis. Verum cum venerit ille, videlicet veritatis spiritus, praehibit vobis ad omnem veritatem. Non enim sua sponte loquetur, sed quaecumque audiverit, eloquetur et futura vobis praenunciabit. Ille me illustrabit, siquidem de meo sumet, quae vobis exponat. Omnia, quaecumque pater habet, mea sunt; propterea dixi illum de meo sumpturum esse, quae vobis exponat". Esse autem illum spiritum non solum miraculorum aut doctrinae, sed etiam iusticiae effectorem docet Paulus et alibi et in primis in prima ad Corint.,[6] ubi negat quenquam posse dicere Iesum esse dominum nisi per spiritum sanctum. Item ad Galatas,[7] ubi recenset fructus spiritus. Hunc spiritum,

---

[12] I Jn 2:1.

[13] Castellio refers in margin to bk. II, ch. XVII.

[1] Castellio refers in margin to II, ch. XI.

[2] Castellio cancelled the words "Est enim Christo" in view of an addition that is lost. We left them in since otherwise the sentence would be incomprehensible.

[3] Jn 16:7ff.

[4] A reference in margin indicates a suppl. beginning with "Samaritanam". We have not reproduced the original text which Castellio has cancelled.

[5] The words in brackets have been cancelled by Castellio.

[6] I Cor 12:3.

[7] Gal 3:2ff.

sicuti modo ex Iohanne allegavimus, mittit Christus credentibus, eodem discipulos suos afflavit, sicut ostendit idem Iohannes, apud quem Iesus eos afflans dicit: "Accipite spiritum sanctum".[8] Hic est Christi spiritus iustificus, quem qui non habet, eum Christi esse negat Paulus ad Romanos.[9] Qui possint autem haec inter sese consona esse, ut eundem spiritum et pater mittere dicatur et filius (nam a filio mitti modo ex Iohanne ostendimus, a patre autem ipse Christus docet, dum apud Iohannem dicit: "Confirmator spiritus sanctus, quem mittet pater meo nomine",[10] sic accipiendum est. Pater est primus author omnis boni, sed is filio domus suae procuratori, sicuti vocatur in epistola ad Hebraeos,[11] omnia tradidit, sicut dicit ipsemet apud Lucam: "Omnia mihi tradita sunt a patre meo".[12] Itaque pater spiritum mittere dicitur, quippe qui sit eius author, eundemque filius, quippe qui sit tum illius tum caeterorum dei donorum arbiter et dispensator eaque, cui velit, largiatur arbitrio suo, sicut olim Iosephus,[13] alter Pharao, bona Pharaonis, quae ab ipso acceperat. Et hoc ipsum est, quod dicit Iesus: "Mihi data est omnis postestas tum in caelo tum in terra".[14]

Quaeretur nunc, an non esset idem spiritus ante adventum Christi: respondeo fuisse, nam et ipse Iesus conceptus est ex sancto spiritu, et eiusdem vi obedivere sancti deo, ante quam Christus venisset, et de hoc iustifico spiritu loquebatur David in quodam psalmo dicens: "Ne me a tuo conspectu reiice neve mihi tuum sanctum spiritum aufer".[15] Sed quemadmodum olim Mosi[16] eum spiritum deus ita dederat, ut ex eo deinde tanquam ex fonte quodam septuaginta senatoribus impertiretur, sic fit et in Christo. In eum enim ita contulit hunc spiritum sanctum, ut inde ad nos quoque dimanet. Hoc interest, quod Moses non sic habuit ipse spiritum, ut eum impertiretur aliis arbitrio suo, sed deus eum de ipso Mose sumeret et aliis impertiretur. Sic enim narrat ipse Moses in libro Numerorum.[17] Iova detraxit de spiritu, quo erat ipse Moses praeditus, et septuaginta senatoribus viris immisit, qui spiritus ubi in illis insedit, tum sine intermissione vaticinabantur. At Christus ipsemet eum suo arbitrio

---

[8] Jn 20:22.
[9] Rom 8:9.
[10] Jn 14:26.
[11] Heb 3:5f.
[12] Lk 10:22.
*[13] Gen 41:37ff.
[14] Mt 28:18.
[15] Ps 51:13.
*[16] Num 11:24.
[17] Num 11:16f.

impertitur, sicut ex eo patet, quod supra ex Iohanne allegavimus,[18], ubi dicitur Iesus discipulis afflasse spiritum sanctum. Neque vero latet spiritum illum, quo Moses praeditus erat, fuisse spiritum vaticinationis. Sed dico unum eundemque esse spiritum, qui efficiat omnia in omnibus, sicuti docet Paulus in priore ad Corinthios,[19] qui ita sit in Christo, ut de eius plenitudine (sicuti docet Iohannes Baptista)[20] omnes accipiamus. Atque hic simile quiddam accidit, ut in luce,[21] quae cum esset ante solem (quippe creata die primo, cum sol quarto demum die creatus fuerit), ita deinde in solem collata est, ut iam non aliunde nos affulgeat. Ita dei spiritus, cum esset ante adventum Christi, ita in Christum effusus est, ut deinceps non nisi ab eo in nos dimanet. Quod si quis quaerat, quid igitur sub Christo plus habeant pii quam habuerunt ante eius adventum, si quidem eundem spiritum habent, respondebo habere eundem equidem, sed longe copiosius. Quod idem et de iusticia caeterisque donis dico. Et haec de Christi in credentes beneficio, videlicet venia peccatorum et dono sancti spiritus, in quo dono ea omnia bona comprehendi volo, quae a spiritu illo in credentibus effici docent sacrae literae, quae deinde bonaqatur aeterna salus.

## XXXVIII

ff. 157-158

### De Coena Domini

Quoniam de Christi beneficio disserimus et de Coena Domini (quae est ipsa quoque Christi beneficium) graves sunt controversiae, dicendum aliquid de ea est. Igitur quoniam coena nomen est epularum et in ea agitur de cibo vitali, quem Christum esse constat, ante omnia cognoscendum est, quo pacto sit Christus cibus homini eique vitam conferat. Hoc enim cognito erit tota quaestio expeditu facilis. Ut autem hoc cognoscatur, considerandum est, quinam fuerit cibus mortifer, hoc est venenum, quod homini mortem attulerit. Venenum fuisse mendacem serpentis sermonem, qui sermo in homine genuerit inobedientiam, docet Moses[1] in narratione delicti hominis, ubi deus hominem ad mortem damnat, quia fuerit inobediens. Huic veneno contrariam oportere esse medicinam sive cibum vitalem et ratio docet et a ratione dictata confirmat illa medi-

---

[18] Jn 20:22.
[19] I Cor 12:6.
[20] Jn 1:16.
[21] Gen 1.

[1] Gen 3.

corum sententia, qua tradunt contrariorum contraria esse remedia. Erit ergo hic cibus vitalis sermo verax Christi gignens in homine obedientiam. Affert igitur Christus homini vitam verace illo sermone suo, dum eo sermone persuadet homini, ut veritati obediat, cui obediendo vitam consequatur, sicut Adamus contra mendacio obediendo mortem sibi conflavit. Atque haec est ratio. Hanc rationem licet plurimus authoritatibus confirmare, sed paucas afferam. Dicit Petrus Christo: "Domine, ad quem abeamus? tu aeternae vitae verba habes".[2] Dicit et ipse Christus: "Hoc vobis etiam atque etiam confirmo: si quis meae orationi paruerit, eum nunquam visurum esse mortem".[3] Haec Christi promissio contraria est dei minis illis, quibus, ut in Genesi habetur, homini mortem minatus est, nisi dicto audiens esset.[4] Ut enim hic inobedientia mortem, ita illic obedientia vitam affert. Simile est et quod Moses dicit alicubi Israelitis: "En propono vobis hodie tum vitam et bonum, tum mortem et malum. Me hodie praeceptore Iovam deum vestrum amando, eius viis gradiendo et praecepta, decreta, iura conservando vivetis. Sin autem non obtemperabitis, peribitis".[5] Ex his et huius generis aliis locis, quos, ne sim prolixior, recensere omitto, perspicuum est vitalem cibum Christi esse veracem sermonem, quo sermone gignat in credentibus obedientiam. Iam hoc idem in sacris literis, ut sunt foecundae, dicitur multis variisque modis, quorum partim sunt figurati, partim non figurati. Ac qui sunt figurati, ii per eos, qui non sunt figurati, sunt intelligendi atque explanandi, id quod neminem negaturum esse puto. Non figurati sunt hi: Christi esse. Iustum esse. Sanctum esse. Christi spiritum habere. Spiritualem esse. Fidentem esse, obedientem esse et si qui sunt eiusdem generis. Talibus enim vitam passim promittunt sacrae literae. Figurati autem modi sunt hi: Christum induisse. Vestem nuptialem habere. Christi sponsam esse. In Christo esse. Christum in aliquo esse. Novam creaturam esse. Renatum esse. Novum hominem esse. Ex spiritu natum esse. Cum Christo resurrexisse. Sibi renunciasse. Membra sua terrestria necasse. Veterem hominem interfecisse. Carnem suam crucifixisse cum suis perturbationibus. In coelestibus sive in coelis esse. Christi membra et carnem de carne et ossa de ossibus eius esse et si quae sunt eiusdem generis locutiones. Nam et talibus vita passim promittitur. Tales modos esse per superiores interpretandos quivis confitebitur. Exempli gratia: Christum induisse non sic accipiendum est, ut Christum indueris sicuti

[2] Jn 6:68.
[3] Jn 8:51ff.
[4] Gen 2:17 and Gen 3:3.
[5] Deut 30:15ff.

vestem. Id enim fieri non potest. Sed est naturam induisse, hoc est adeptum esse, qualis fuit Christi, videlicet iustam. Item Christi sponsam esse est mundos et Christo quodam sanctitatis quasi coniugio coniunctos esse. Item cum Christo resurrexisse est ita vitam ex mala in bonam mutasse, ut quasi ex mortuo vivus factus esse videaris. Christi membra et carnem et ossa esse est Christi spiritualiter cognatos hoc est similes et conformes esse, videlicet iusticia et sanctitate, sicut etiam alii aliorum membra esse dicimur, hoc est spirituali iusticiae cognatione coniuncti. Ac, ne sim prolixior, simili ratione explicandae sunt reliquae figuratae locutiones.

## XXXIX ff. 158-159b

Iam de quo agitur, videlicet de Christi carne comedenda et sanguine bibendo, utrum propria an figurata sit locutio, considerandum est. Figuratam esse evincit tum ratio tum authoritas. Ratio est prima, quod, quemadmodum, quod per os intrat, non coinquinat hominem, ita neque mundat aut sanctum reddit. Quod si non mundat, ne vivificat quidem, praesertim ea vita, de qua Christus loquitur, dum se dicit "panem esse vitalem".[1] Loquitur enim de ea vita, de qua et Paulus, cum dicit: "Crucifixus sum cum Christo. Vivo autem non iam ego, sed vivit in me Christus. Quod vero nunc in carne vivo, fide vivo filii dei, qui me adeo amavit, ut seipsum pro me dederet".[2] Ergo si Christi corpus per os intrat, hoc est comeditur, non vivificat hominem. Quod si quis quaeret de Adamo, an non esu coinquinatus fuerit, respondebo non esu, sed inobedientia (sicuti ex Pauli quinto capite ad Romanos apparet)[3] fuisse coinquinatum, quod idem accidisset, si quid aliud contra dei praeceptum fecisset. Nam et Saulus[4] inobedientia pollutus est non comedendo, sed dei praeceptum violando.

Quare ut illum inobedientia polluit et porro interfecit, ita nos necesse est ut obedientia mundet et porro vita donet, postquam, ut superius ostendimus, contrariorum contraria sunt remedia.[5] Altera ratio est, quod, si nobis vitam daret esus corporis Christi, Christus omnibus ad vitam consequendam praecepisset, ut corpus suum comederent. Itaque

---

* [1] Jn 6:48.
[2] Gal 2:19f.
* [3] Rom 5:19.
[4] I Kings 15:22ff.
[5] See end of first paragraph of previous chapter.

dicta illa: "Si vis in vitam ingredi, serva mandata"[6] item: "Si quis vult meus esse, renunciet sibi tollatque crucem suam et me sequatur",[7] denique omnia eius praecepta, quorum executoribus vitam pollicitus est, supervacanea forent frustraque homini proposuisset arctam viam, cum in promptu esset dicere: Comedite corpus meum, quemadmodum illi caeco nato dixit: I lotum te in piscina Siloa,[8] aut quemadmodum Elisaeus[9] Naamani Syro mandavit, ut ad sanitatem consequendam septies se lavasset in Iordane.

Authoritates multae sunt, sed una omnium longe maximi ponderis. Ea est Christi, qui apud Iohannem, cum dixisset homini ad vitam consequendam comedendam esse carnem suam bibendumque sanguinem et eo dicto multi eius discipulorum offensi fuissent, sic eos affatus est: "Hoc vos offendit? Quid si videritis filium hominis eo ascendere, ubi erat antea? Spiritus est, qui vivificat.[10] Caro nihil prodest. Verba, quae ego vobis loquor, spiritus sunt et vita sunt".[11] Haec Christi verba sunt diligenter consideranda, inest enim in eis totius nodus quaestionis.[12] Christus, ut solebat, figurate loquens dixerat suam carnem esse comedendam sanguinemque bibendum. Hoc dictum auditores sic accipiebant, quasi non figurate locutus esset, sed re vera suam carnem comedi sanguinemque bibi vellet eisque accidebat, quod illi Samaritanae, quae verba illa Iesu: "Si dei donum intelligeres et qui sit, qui a te potum postulet, tu peteres ab eo tibique ipse daret aquam vivam",[13] de aqua dicta putabat, cum Iesus de spiritu locutus esset, quam aquam propter similitudinem appellabat. Itemque quod Iudaeis illis, qui, cum Christus dixisset "Solvite templum hoc",[14] videlicet corpus suum, putabant de templo dictum. Item quod discipulis, qui eius verba monentis, ut fermentum caverent Sadducaeorum,[15] putabant de fermento esse dicta, cum ipse de doctrina dixisset, eam propter similitudinem nomine fermenti indicans. Similiter et hic, quae de comedenda carne sua dixerat,[16] ea de ipsa carne dicta putabant discipuli ideoque offendebantur. Iesus igitur ut

---

* [6] Mt 19:17.
* [7] Mk 8:34.
* [8] Jn 9:7.
* [9] II Kings 5:9.

[10] See Zwingli, *De vera et falsa religione commentarius*, Corp. Ref. XC p. 801.

[11] Jn 6:54ff.

[12] This part of the chapter is not very original. Castellio follows Zwingli and Oecolampad.

[13] Jn 4:10.

*[14] Jn 2:19.

*[15] Mt 16:6.

*[16] Jn 6:54.

offensionem illam tollat, verba sua explanat in hanc sententiam: Hoc vos offendit nec mirum, cum me de carne mea re vera comedenda loqui putetis, id quod est absurdum. Sed tamen nunc minus absurdum quam erit postea. Nam hoc meum corpus, quod vobis comedendum esse dixi, ascendet (videlicet postquam resurrexero) vobis spectantibus in coelum. Tunc vobis videri poterit longe absurdius meum corpus in terris comedi, quod in coelo erit. Nam praesentem comedi absurdum est non tamen ita, ut fieri non possit, quandoquidem et homines ab hominibus re vera comedi possunt, sicuti fit ab iis, qui humana carne vescuntur. Sed absentem comedi non solum absurdum, verum etiam impossibile est. Quare sic rem accipite. Locutus sum de cibo, qui vitam det. Vitam autem accipi volo spiritualem, videlicet animae, nam et regnum meum spirituale est. Iam vero cum similia similibus comparanda sint, ut caro carnem, sic spiritus spiritum alit. Itaque ad alendam hominis animam, quae spiritus est, nihil prodest caro. Atqui meum corpus caro est, itaque ad hanc rem nihil prodest. Et sane non comedetur, sed in coelum ascendet. Quid igitur vobis vitam dabit? Spiritus. Nam spiritus is est, qui vitam dat et mea verba de vita consequenda spiritus sunt, hoc est de spiritu accipienda sunt, quem ego carnis nomine propter similitudinem appellavi, quoniam, ut caro carnem, sic spiritus spiritum alit ideoque animi panis sive cibus appellatur.

## XL

ff. 159b-160

Haec est vera Christi verborum explicatio, ex qua palam est eius corpus non comedi, sed ipsum ita propter similitudinem locutum fuisse. Et omnino per similitudines loqui solitum fuisse Christum patet ex omnibus Evangelistis. Solet autem similitudinum occasionem plerumque e re nata sumere, sicut in eo, quem paulo ante allegavi, loco, ubi Samaritanam alloquens spiritui nomen aquae tribuit,[1] nimirum ex eo sumpta occasione, quod a Samaritana aquam petierat ad bibendum. Et mox post illum locum cibum suum appellat obedientiam: "Mihi cibus est", inquit "eius voluntatem exequi, qui me misit",[2] nimirum sumpta sic loquendi occasione ex Apostolorum verbis, qui eum hortati fuerant ad capiendum cibum. Item apud Lucam iniustos appellat nomine mortuorum propter similitudinem: "Sine", inquit "mortuos sepelire mortuos suos", nimirum sumpta occasione ex verbis cuiusdam, qui ab eo

---

[1] Jn 4:7ff.
[2] Jn 4:34.

veniam petierat eundi ad sepeliendum patrem suum videlicet mortuum.[3] Item in Iohannis capite nono illum alloquens, quem caecum natum sanaverat. "Ad eiusmodi discrimen", inquit, "ego in hunc orbem veni, ut, qui non vident, videant et, qui vident, caeci fiant".[4] Ibi caecos appellat eos, qui veritatis ignari sunt sumpta videlicet occasione ex eo, quod caecum sanaverat. Similiter igitur et in sexto Iohannis capite[5] occasionem sumpsit de pane loquendi ex eo, quod ipsum quaerebant Iudaei, quia de panibus illis ad satietatem comederant. Hanc ob causam ibi se panem appellat propter similitudinem,[6] videlicet quod, quemadmodum pane comedendo corpus, sic Christo comedendo alatur anima. Est autem Christum comedere non equidem credere (sicuti quidam putant), sed Christi spiritum sive naturam (id quod fit credendo) comedere, hoc est ex iniusto iustum fieri, quae res animae est salutaris et vitalis. Ut enim iniusticia animam interficit, ita et iusticia eidem vitam dat. Christum autem appellare Christianitatem, hoc est Christi naturam sive spiritum sacris literis familiare est et nominatim Paulo, qui cum alibi tum in primis ad Romanos sic loquitur: "Si quis Christi spiritum non habet, is Christi non est. Si vero Christus in vobis est, corpus quidem mortuum est per peccatum, sed spiritus vivus est per iusticiam".[7] Hic quod priore loco Christi spiritum appellaverat, idem posteriore Christum appellat et mox iusticiam, per quam hominis spiritus vivat. Hinc manifestum est cibum homini vitalem esse Christianam iusticiam et Christum comedere esse aliud nihil quam Christianitatem comedere, hoc est Christianum sive iustum fieri.

Christum co quid sit.

## XLI

ff. 160-1

Huius rei ignoratio peperit in ecclesia opinionem de comedendo Christi corpore ab omni ratione alienissimam et dumtaxat in Christi verbis perperam acceptis fundatam. Quoniam enim dixit Christus comedendam esse carnem suam et bibendum sanguinem, isti hoc unum urgent: Dixit Christus; ergo ita est. Et interim non considerant, in quae absurditatum monstra se coniiciant, quas absurditates si vellem omnes

---

3 Lk 9:59ff.

4 Jn 9:39. The Vulgate has *judicium* instead of *discrimen*.

5 Jn 6.

6 Similar Calvin, *Petit traicté de la Sainte Cêne*, Geneva, 1541, in Barth, *Johannis Calvini opera selecta*, 1926, p. 526: "...mais doibvent persister en cela, que les signes visibles retiennent leur vraye substance, pour nous representer la verité spirituelle dont nous avons parlé".

7 Rom 8:9f.

recensere, opus esset toto libro et eo bene longo, sed paucis contentus ero, ex quibus caeteras coniicere licebit. Dixit Christus[1] se esse pastorem, suos autem oves, atqui idem dixit suam carnem esse suis comedendam sanguinemque bibendum; ergo oportet, ut oves comedant carnem sui pastoris sanguinemque bibant. Dixit idem se esse portam;[2] ergo oportet, ut portam comedamus. Idem vocatur lapis et via[3];[4] ergo lapidem et viam comedamus. Idem se vocat vitem, nos autem palmites;[5] ergo vitis a palmitibus est comedenda. Idem vocatur sponsus, ecclesia autem sponsa;[6] ergo sponsus a sponsa comedendus est. Idem vocatur caput,[7] nos autem membra;[8] ergo caput a membris comedendum est. Idem frater noster;[9] ergo fratrem fratres comedemus. Certe si verba urgere volumus, haec omnia et alia multo plura absurda admittenda sunt. Sin in his ad evitandam absurditatem admittunt interpretationem et Christum pastorem et portam et lapidem et viam et vitem et sponsum et caput appellari fatentur, non quia re vera sint illa omnia, sed quia sit ei cum illis omnibus similitudo: fateantur idem et in eius esu carnis et potione sanguinis. Neque enim in hoc minor est quam in illis absurditas, si verba urgeas, et, si Christum fatentur, quamvis se vitem esse dicat, tamen non esse vitem, nimirum quia et ratio et sensus repugnent, fateantur et, quamvis suam carnem comedendam esse dicat, tamen non comedi, nimirum quia et ratio et sensus repugnent. Et omnino generalem hanc regulam teneamus, si quod dictum vel in profanis vel in sacris authoribus eiusmodi est, ut, nisi figurate accipiatur, manifeste rationi aut sensibus repugnet, id esse figurate accipiendum. Itaque interpretandum, ut cum ratione aut sensibus concilietur. Erit huius regulae ad multos nodos solvendos incredibilis utilitas. Exempla afferam primum ex profanis authoribus. Scripsit Cicero translatum a se de Graeco versiculum hunc de Bellerophonte:

Regula de interpretendis figuratis dictis.

Ipse suum cor edens, hominum vestigia vitans.[10]

Hunc nos, quia ab homine suum ipsius cor edi posse negat ratio, sic

* [1] Jn 10,11 and passim.
* [2] Jn 10:9.
* [3] Acts 4:11.
[4] In 14:6.
* [5] Jn 15:5.
* [6] Mk 2:19ff.
* [7] Col 1:18.
* [8] I Cor 12:12ff.
* [9] passim.
*[10] Cic. Tusc. 3,63.

interpraetamur, ut sit suum cor edens: hoc est suum animum excrucians. Item Terentius:

Hunc comedendum vobis propino,[11]

hoc est huius facultates. Item Iulius Caesar: "Conspicatae naves triremes duae navem D. Bruti"[12] pro: Conspicati homines, qui erant in triremibus duabus. Eadem est et sacrorum authorum ratio. Scribit Matthaeus omnem Iudaeam ad Iohannem fuisse profectam.[13] Hic ratio, quia Iudaeam proficisci non potuisse videt, Iudaeos interpretatur. Invehitur Christus in eos, qui devorant domos viduarum.[14] Et hic, quia domos devorari ratio posse negat, domos interpraetamur facultates. Sed quid opus pluribus? Omnia sunt et apud authores et in omnium loquendi consuetudine plena huiusmodi figuris, quarum verba rationi sensibusque repugnent ideoque duce ratione et sensibus sic interpraetanda sint, ut cum ratione et sensibus conveniant. Quod si id in caeteris omnibus facere non dubitamus, in Christi comedenda carne cur dubitemus, nulla causa est. Atque hanc, quam dixi, regulam licet maxime ipsius Christi authoritate confirmare, qui (ut superiore libro demonstravimus)[15] rationis iudicio solitus est Iudaeos vincere, sed in primis loco illo ex Iohannis capite sexto superius a nobis explanato,[16] in quo quia verba dixerat, quae rationi et sensibus repugnarent, videlicet carnem suam esse comedendam, et illi verba illa, sicuti dicta erant, sic accipiebant ideoque eis offendebantur, Christus ea mox sic interpraetatus est, ut nihil rationi sensibusque repugnarent. Nam Christi praesertim absentis carnem comedi sanguinemque bibi negat ratio, negant sensus, sed spiritum esse, qui animam sic alat, ut caro aut panis corpus alit, nec ratio nec sensus repugnant.

## XLII ff. 161b

Iam postquam Christi corpus non comedi demonstravimus, facile est cognoscere, utrum in ea ceremonia, quae Coena Domini vocatur, comedatur. Si enim non comeditur, profecto in Coena non comeditur. Superest, ut, cur tamen comedi dicatur et cur in Coena panis et vinum

[11] Terence, *Eunuchus*, 1087.
[12] *Bellum Civile*, 2, 4, 6.
[13] Mt 3:5.
*[14] Mt 23:14.
[15] See above I, ch. XXV.
[16] Comp. above bk. I, chapt. XXIII.

carnis et sanguinis Christi nomen habeant, explanemus. Comedi res in sacris literis saepe dicitur, cuius fructus comeditur aut a qua utilitas percipitur. Sic Adamus de arbore comedisse dicitur,[1] hoc est de fructu arboris. Sic apud Esaiam Rabsaces Iudaeis iubet, ut suam quisque vineam et ficum comedant,[2] hoc est fructus inde percipiant. Sic in quodam Psalmo comedere laborem manuum suarum dicitur,[3] qui labore parta comedit. Sic Rachel et Lia dicunt Labanem comedisse argentum ipsarum,[4] hoc est argenti fructum et utilitatem percepisse.[5] Hac igitur forma loquendi comedere Christi carnem et bibere sanguinem est eam utilitatem percipere, quam ipse suae carnis et sanguinis precio (hoc est sua obedientia, quae tanta fuit, ut vitam pro nobis profuderit) nobis peperit. Est autem ea utilitas venia peccatorum et spiritus iustificus, sicuti supra de Christo beneficio disserentes demonstravimus.[6] Huius autem beneficii memoriam nobis commendare Christus volens ceremoniam illam instituit, quam Paulus Coenam Domini[7] nuncupat, qua ceremonia ipsius mors perenni religione usque ad ipsius adventum recoleretur.[8] Est autem sciendum non esse idem Christi corpus comedere, hoc est Christianum sive iustum fieri, et eius mortis memoriam hac ceremonia celebrare. Hoc enim saepe, illud non nisi semel fit, et sine hoc servari homo potest; eius rei exemplum est vel latro ille, qui in cruce credidit in Christum,[9] at sine illo non item. Itaque in hac ceremonia non fit homo iustus, sed iam iustus factus hac ceremonia fungitur. Sed ceremoniae datur nomen, non cuius ipsa est ceremonia, sicuti nimirum fieri solet et in aliis ritibus. Nam et Pascha quotannis celebratur[10] a Iudaeis, non quod re vera esset quotannis Pascha, hoc est transitus Domini perdentis Aegyptiorum primogenitos, Israelitas autem transeuntis[11] (id enim semel fecerat), sed illa res solemni ceremonia quotannis recolebatur eique ceremoniae rei nomen tribuebatur. Sic apud Matthaeum vocatur dies natalis Herodis is dies, quo Iohannem Baptistam decollavit,[12] non quod eo die natus esset Herodes (nam multis ante annis natus erat semel), sed

---

[1] Gen 2:16.
[2] Js 36:16.
[3] Ps 127:2 (Vulg. 128:2).
[4] Gen 31:15.
[5] In margin reference to suppl. 31.
[6] See bk. II, ch. XXXIVff.
* [7] I Cor 11:20.
[8] One is reminded here of Zwingli.
* [9] Lk 23:40ff.
[10] MS *celebrabatur*. Zwingli too relates the sacrament of Communion to the Passover.
*[11] Ex 12:29ff.
*[12] Mt 14:6ff.

quod eius nativitatis memoria eo die celebraretur. Sic igitur et Coena Domini et communicatio corporis et sanguinis Domini vocatur haec ceremonia, non quia toties coenet Dominus cum suis totiesque corpus suum tradat ad necem (id enim semel fecit in perpetuum), sed quia sit illius rei (sicut ipsemet vocat) commemoratio. Tria sunt igitur in hoc negocio diligenter distinguenda. Primum quod Christus corpus suum in crucem semel pro nobis tradidit eoque facto seipsum hostiam pacis libavit. Deinde quod eius sacrificii beneficium tum percipimus, cum per fidem Christiani sive iusti fiamus, ac tunc eius corpus comedere dicimur. Tertio quod eius sacrificii semel facti memoriam toties recolimus, quoties hac Coenae ceremonia fungimur. His ita distinctis facilis deinceps erit totius argumenti explicatio.

## XLIII ff. 162r

Veniemus nunc ad verba Coenae, quibus explanatis nihil iam supererit scrupuli. Verba Coenae ex tribus Evangelistis sunt haec. Epulantibus eis Iesus panem coepit actisque laudibus fregit deditque discipulis et dixit: "Accipite, comedite. Hoc est corpus meum, quod pro vobis traditur. Hoc facite in mei commemorationem"[1].[2] Similiter poculum quoque sumpsit, postquam coenavit actisque laudibus dedit eis dicens: "Bibite ex eo omnes. Hic est enim sanguis meus novi foederis pro vobis et pro multis effundendus ad veniam peccatorum. Sic autem habetote, non me dehinc bibiturum esse de hoc fructu viteo usque ad illam diem, qua eum bibam vobiscum novum in regno patris mei".[3] Haec Christi verba sunt. Controversia autem in eo est, utrum verba illa "Hoc est corpus meum et hic est sanguis meus" proprie an figurate dicta fuerint.[4] Ad hanc controversiam tollendam meminisse oportet illius, quam paulo supra[5] hunc locum posui, regulae de figuratis dictis, quae si rationi aut sensibus repugnent, sint interpraetatione cum ratione et sensibus concilianda. Rationi autem et sensibus repugnare haec verba, nisi figurate dicta accipias, quid opus est probare, cum nihil sit manifestius? Cumque id vel clarissime ostendant tot theologorum tot et tam acres de hisce verbis disputationes? Nisi enim ratio sensusque reclamassent, non magis de

---

* [1] Mt 26:26.
* [2] Lk 22:19.
* [3] Mt 26:28ff.
[4] See Calvin, *Defensio sanae et orthodoxae doctrinae de Sacramentis*, Corp. Ref., XXXVII passim.
[5] See above II, ch. XXXIX p. 173.

pane coenae, utrum is vere corpus esset Christi quam de asino, in quo Christus equitavit, utrum is vere esset asinus, disputassent. Sed quia et ratio et sensus panem esse panem vel invitos docebat et tamen panem esse carnem invita ratione invitisque sensibus volebant, verterunt sese in omnem formam, ut panem esse carnem probarent et, quod est omnium absurdissimum, in eo probando argumentis et rationibus uti conati sunt, videlicet ut rationem rationibus opprimerent, cum deberent potius (postquam absurda credi volebant) auditoribus remota omni disputatione iubere, ut sepulta omni ratione et clausis oculis crederent. Ita enim tot et tam absurdarum disputationum dispendia unius absurditatis compendio lucrati fuissent. Sed ut ad rem veniamus, est tum profanarum tum sacrarum literarum tum quotidiani sermonis ea consuetudo, ut vel rerum imagines iisdem, quibus res ipsas, vel res ipsas iisdem, quibus imagines, vocabulis appellent. Exempla de plurimus pauca offeram duntaxat ex sacris literis. Dicit Iosephus Pharaonis praegustatori eius de vite somnium interpretans: "Tres palmites tres dies sunt".[6] Et mox pistori: "Tria canistra tres dies sunt".[7] Hoc est: sunt imago trium dierum sive tres dies quasi imagine quadam indicant. Item paulo post Pharaoni: "Septem vaccae generosae septem anni sunt"[8] eadem nimirum ratione. Similiter et Daniel Nabuchodonosori somnium interpretans dicit eum esse illius, quam in somnis vidisset, statuae "caput aureum".[9] Itemque in altero eiusdem somnio dicit eum esse illam, quam in somnis vidisset, arborem.[10] Neque vero est, quod hic quisquam causetur haec esse somnia. Nam, quod ad locutionem attinet, utrum somnia sint necne, nihil refert. Esset enim eadem, si haec extra somnia narrarentur, extra somnia quoque loquendi ratio. Itaque et extra somnia tales inveniuntur locutiones. Dicit Paulus: "Tu oleaster in eos insitus es et particeps factus radicis ac pinguedinis oleae".[11] Hic certe oleastrum vocat hominem, quia similitudinem habeat cum oleastro, sicut et ipse Christus se vitem, suos autem palmites appellat.[12] Sic et Ezechielem iubet deus obsidere Ierosolymam,[13] cum tantum gestus esset, quo gestu laterem insculpta in eo Ierosolyma quasi obsidebat. Itemque eodem in loco iubetur in latus suum cubans ferre culpam generis Israelitarum, videlicet similitudine,

[6] Gen 40:12.
[7] Gen 40:18.
[8] Gen 41:26.
[9] Deut 2:38.
[10] Deut 4:17.
[11] Rom 11:17.
[12] Jn 15:5.
[13] Ezek 4:1-4.

neque enim re vera tulit Ezechiel culpam illorum, sed eam rem illa expressit imagine. Simile est, quod mox facit in detonsis sui capitis mentique pilis,[17] qui pili ibi vocantur Israelitae. Idem dico de eo, quod petram illam, quae Israelitas in illa solitudine sequebatur, Christum fuisse Paulus dicit: "Petra" inquit "erat Christus",[15] hoc est simile quiddam. Ut enim illi de petrae aqua bibebant, sic nos de Christi spiritu quasi bibimus.[16] Huc pertinent et illae, quas supra[17] attigimus, locutiones, quod Christus vocatur sponsus et lapis et vitis et porta et agnus et pastor et caput et huius generis alia, videlicet propter similitudinem. Denique, ne sim prolixior, huius modi similitudinibus scatent omnia.[18]

## XLII, 2

ff. 164-

Igitur cum passim tales occurrant similitudines et eas, ubicumque ratio sensusque iubent, omnes sine ulla dubitatione admittant, idem in Coena (postquam idem in ea ratio sensusque iubent) faciendum esse dico, iamque verba illa Coenae: "Accipite, comedite, hoc est corpus meum", sine ulla dubitatione sic interpretor. Quemadmodum hunc panem fractum vobis ad pastum porrigo, ita et corpus meum in crucem frangendum[1] trado, quae res vobis sit pastui, hoc est salutaris. Morior enim ad impetrandam vobis peccatorum veniam, sine qua salvi esse et vivere non potestis, quemadmodum corporaliter sine cibo vivi non potest. Quod idem et de vino dico, quae imago est mei sanguinis effundendi. Esto igitur vobis hic panis imago mei corporis et vinum sanguinis, et deinceps huius rei memoriam perenni ritu usque ad adventum meum celebratote. Haec est brevis, simplex, vera, dilucida, explicata Coenae Domini explanatio; hac cognita, admissa tolluntur omnes offensiones, omnia disputationum dispendia, omnia absurditatum monstra, quibus ecclesia per tot secula vexata lacerataque est. In hac nihil absurdi, nihil incredibilis, nihil obscuri, nihil quod vel a sacrorum aut profanorum authorum vel ab omnium gentium consuetudine loquendi vel ab hominis ratione sensibusve discrepet. Quin omnia apta, credibilia, aperta, plana et caeterorum, quae citra ullam controversiam ab omnibus admittuntur similima. Itaque, ut aliae huius argumenti explanationes, quia absurdae

---

[14] Ezek 5:1.
[15] I Cor 10:4.
[16] In margin reference to suppl. 32.
[17] See above II, ch. XLI p. 175.
[18] In margin reference to suppl. 33.

[1] MS: *frangedum.*

falsaeque sunt, nulla verborum prolixitate satis aperiri queunt, ita haec contra, quia apta veraque est, paucissimis verbis expediri potest. Si enim dicas verbum "est" in his verbis: "Hic est corpus meum" similitudinis esse, explicaveris omnia. Atque equidem videntur quidam sive rationis ductu sive casu hoc vel vidisse vel aliquantum saltem olfecisse. Nam Hieronymus Vida Italus poeta, cum hunc locum in sua *Christiade* tractaret, haec verba verissime explanavit his verbis:

Corporis haec nostri, haec vera cruoris imago,
Unus pro cunctis quem fundam sacra parenti
Hostia......[2]

Imaginem enim, quod appellat, hoc ipsum explicat quod nos volumus. Quanquam idem paulo post, sive quia, quod dixerat, parum perspiciebat sive quia perspiciebat ille quidem, sed errorem tam inveteratum convellere non audebat, evertit totum negotium et, quod ipsemet bene dixerat, id non bono dicto foedat. Scribit enim haec verba:

Ipse sacerdotum verbis eductus ab astris
Frugibus insinuat sese regnator Olympi
Libaturque dei sacrum cum sanguine corpus.[3]

Usque adeo nondum potuit illo tempore quamvis gestiens in lucem erumpere veritas, sed erroris quasi nube tecta lucem suam distulit in futurum. Hic ego me continere nequeo, quin seculorum et superiorum et nostri infelicitatem deplorem, quod tantae et fuerint et etiamnum hodie sint tenebrae, ut ea res vulgo etiam a doctissimis hominum tot seculis ignorata fuerit, quam ab ullo mortalium unquam ignorari potuisse vix credet orta luce posteritas. Sed ita est: nulla est tanta caecitas, quae non cadat in hominem, si et duce usus est caeco et de duce dubitare religioni habuit. Inest causa: fuit maiorum nostrorum iniquitas dicam an imprudentia? Qui dum suas interpretationes oraculorum loco haberi volunt, posteros suos religione constrictos ab inquirendo, ne dicam a dubitando, deterruerunt, qua re factum est, ut multa praeclara ingenia, quae si vel tantulum dubitare ausa fuissent, haec facile vidissent, in iisdem tenebris mortua fuerint. Et utinam hodie non eadem violentia vigeat. Video enim quosdam illorum in hoc similes, in caeteris deteriores idem et moliri et apud nonnullos iam efficere, videlicet ut suas interpretationes plerumque

---

[2] *Christiados*, ed. Lyon, 1606 (first ed. 1550) vol. II, verses 12ff.
[3] *ibid.* verses 23ff.

falsas suis discipulis pro oraculis obtrudentes et nova fidei capita cudentes eosdem quasi laqueos tendant posteritatis conscientiis idemque persecutionum seminarium faciant. Neque enim dubium est, quin eorum discipuli, si et potentes erunt (ut plerumque esse solent, qui male sentiunt,) et persequendos esse censebunt haereticos (ut plerumque censent, qui ipsi sunt haeretici), eos persecuturi sint, quos pro haereticis habebunt, hoc est qui ab ipsorum interpretationibus discrepabunt. O lucis pater deus, averte casum hunc et nostris maiorumque nostrorum iustis poenis contentus posteritatem illumina. Et tu, posteritas, metuito casum hunc et exemplo nostro monita caveto, ne hominum interpretationibus sic adhaerescas, ut non eas tum rationis et sensuum, tum sacrarum literarum norma explores. Et vos, o doctores, declinate casum hunc et nolite vobis tantum tribuere, ut authoritatem vestram et corporis et animae multorum periculo sanciatis.

## XLIII, 2 ff. 165-

Iam demonstrata huius argumenti veritate falsas aliorum opiniones refellere non fuerit alienum, non quia non refutatae sint ipsa veritate demonstrata. Qui enim veritatem in lucem protulit, is omnia, quae contra dici possunt, satis refutavit, quemadmodum, qui ignem calidum aut nivem frigidam esse ostendit, nulli contradictioni locum reliquit. Sed quia hic error et in multorum animis supra quam dici potest alte radices egit et ecclesiae supra modum detrimentosus est, expedit eum quamvis iam iugulatum iterumque iterumque extirpare. Est autem geminus. Quidam enim volunt ipsum panem esse corpus Christi. Alii panem esse panem fatentur, sed tamen ibi Christi corpus esse comedique contendunt. Hos utrosque non ita refutabimus, ut absurda omnia, quae insunt in eorum sententia, recenseamus. Hoc enim et infinitum est et, quia iam ab aliis magna ex parte perfectum, minus necessarium. Tantum duobus quasi telis (quibus potissimum in toto hoc opere pugnamus), videlicet sensibus et authoris verbis, errorem in universum tollemus. Ac primum eos refellemus, qui panem esse corpus Christi, vinum autem sanguinem contendunt et hanc transsubstantiationem, hoc est rei in rem aliam mutationem appellant.[1] Quaero igitur, utrum hoc miraculo fiat an sine miraculo. Sine miraculo fieri non potuerunt dicere. Nam panem in carnem converti tam est miraculum quam aquam in vinum. Superest igitur, ut miraculum esse dicant et ego quaeram, quibusnam sensibus id

---

[1] A discussion of the "scholastic" concept of Communion follows.

iudicent. Nam de miraculis non nisi sensibus iudicari potest, id quod Iesus indicavit, dum Iohannis discipulis ita dixit: "Ite renunciatum Iohanni, quae videritis ac audiveritis. Caeci cernunt, claudi gradiuntur, leprosi purgantur, surdi audiunt, mortui resurgunt, pauperes evangelium docentur".[2] Atqui in Coena Domini nullus sensus miraculum esse iudicat contraque omnes sensus ullum ibi miraculum esse negant. Nam et oculi album esse vident et aures strepitum fracti panis audiunt et nares odorem olfaciunt et manus panem tangunt et palatum saporem sentit et venter ipse panem concoquit, denique nulla res usquam esse potest, de qua magis omnes sensus iudicent. Itaque necesse est, si velis homini persuadere ibi esse carnem, ut homini et oculos et aures et nares et manus et palatum et ventrem adimas, hoc est ut hominem ex homine exuas eumque in stipitem convertas. Et vere, qui hoc hominibus persuaserunt, eos quodammodo in stipites converterunt. Quod si se dicent non sensibus iudicare, sed simpliciter Christi verbis omnipotentibus, qui id corpus suum appellet, credere, quaeram, cur et alibi eisdem non credant. Nam quamvis se vitem esse dicat,[3] non credunt tamen eum esse vitem et caetera, quae supra commemoravimus. Cur? Nimirum quia sensus negant Christum esse vitem. Atqui iidem sensus negant panem esse carnem, cur hic eis non item, ut illic creditur? Et haec de sensibus. Quod vero ad Christi verba attinet, ne ea quidem istorum sententiae patrocinantur. Volunt enim fieri mutationem, at Christi verba sunt non imperantis, sed indicantis. Non enim dicit: Hoc fiat corpus meum aut convertatur in corpus meum, sed: " Hoc est corpus meum".[4] Iam quicquid ita enunciatur, id non a verbis accipit ullam mutationem, sed verbis idipsum esse indicatur, quod ante verba fuit. Ut quod dicit Moses: "Hic est sanguis foederis",[5] iam sanguis erat, antequam verba illa diceret. Item quod Christus dicit: "Ego sum pastor bonus",[6] iam id erat ante verba. Sic igitur, quod dicit: "Hoc est corpus meum", indicat, non imperat illum panem esse corpus. Itaque necesse est, ut ante verba illa panis iam corpus fuerit. Atqui non vere fuit corpus Christi, sed panis, sicut et sensus iudicant et Evangelistae appellant. Necesse est igitur, ut figurate corporis nomine propter similitudinem vocatus fuerit. Quid, quod et post Christi verba manere eandem rem nec ullam esse factam conversionem ex ipsius Christi verbis patet? Dicit enim[7] de vino,

---

[2] Lk 7:22.
[3] See previous ch. n. 17.
* [4] Mt 26:26.
* [5] Ex 24:8.
* [6] Jn 10:11,14.
[7] In margin reference to suppl. 28.

postquam id sanguinem esse pronunciaverat: "Sic habetote, non me dehinc bibiturum esse de hoc fructu viteo usque ad illam diem, qua eum bibam vobiscum novum in regno patris mei".[8] En panem vocat etiam post illa verba: "Hoc est corpus meum". Item vinum vocat "fructum vitis",[9] etiam post illa verba: "Hic est sanguis meus".[10] Atqui si caro et sanguis erat, falso vocat panem et fructum vitis, ne quid interim dicam de monstrosa illa absurditate, quae in eo est, quod se fructum illum bibiturum esse dicit. Si enim sanguis eius erat, indicat se suum ipsius sanguinem esse bibiturum, quo quid absurdius? Itaque et ex sensibus nostris et ex Christi verbis sic statuamus, nullam ibi factam esse panis et vini mutationem.

Quod si dicent transsubstantiationem[11] non fieri conversionem unius substantiae, hoc est rei in alteram, videlicet panis in carnem, sed panem evanescere inque eius locum Christi corpus subire, primum repugnabit id ipsorum transsubstantiationis[12] verbo, quod non rei fugam, sed conversionem notat. Deinde incident in absurditatem aliam superioribus non minorem, videlicet quod remanebunt panis ut vocant accidentia sine substantia, quam deinde sequentur aliae absurditates innumerae. Adde, quod non poterunt, quin Christi dicta figurata esse confiteantur. De pane enim dixit: "Hoc est corpus meum". Quod si panis non erat eius corpus, figurate locutus est. Atqui si figuram admittunt, debent potius eam admittere, quae et usitata est et nihil vel incommodi vel absurdi habet, videlicet metonymiam, ut, quemadmodum supra docuimus,[14] corporis similitudo corpus appelletur, quam ut eam comminiscantur, quae nec usquam est ac ne quidem nomen ullum habet et innumera secum monstra trahit absurditatum. Ut interim taceam, quod hac ratione falsum erit, quod isti dictitant, videlicet se ideo credere, quia Christus dixerit, qui sit omnipotens. Neque enim Christus dixit panem evanescere, sed de pane dixit: "Hoc est corpus meum". Ut, si eius verbis sine ulla interpretatione credunt, necesse sit, ut panem esse corpus credant. Sed hactenus contra transsubstantiatores.[15]

---

* [8] Mt 26:29.
* [9] *ibidem.*
*[10] Mt 26:28.
[11] MS: *transsubstatiationem.*
[12] MS: *transsubstantionis.*
[13] MS: *frangedum.*
[14] See previous page.
[15] MS: *Transsubstatiatores.*

## XLIV

ff. 167-167b

Nunc veniemus ad alteros, quorum est sententia, ut ingenue dicam, non minus absurda nec minus tum rationi et sensibus tum sacris literis contraria quam superiorum. Fatentur Christi corpus in coelum ascendisse ibique et esse et fore ad usque diem iudicii et tamen idem in terris comedi contendunt.[3] Hic quid opus est multis verbis? Nullum genus est falsa refellendi fortius aut invictius quam si ostendas id, quod dicitur, esse impossibile. Atqui, ut idem corpus eodem tempore et in coelo sit et in terra, est impossibile. Ergo Christi corpus, si in coelo est, in terra non est. Quod si in terra non est, in terra non comeditur. Neque enim absens profecto comeditur. Haec una ratio, hoc unum argumentum satis est ad refellendam istorum sententiam, ac simili argumento maxime pugnant et invicti sunt patroni causarum. Si enim possunt probare reum, quo tempore facinus patrasse accusatur, fuisse alibi quam ubi facinus patratum est, vicerunt neque quicquam ab accusatoribus tam probabile dici potest, quod non hac una veritate, quae sole clarior est, refellatur. Sic nos, si Christi corpus probamus esse alibi quam ubi comedi dicitur, vicimus. Neque enim ibi comedi potest, ubi non est. Atqui id in coelo esse ipsi quoque fatentur, ergo in terris non comeditur. Hic iam licet finem facere et, quicquid argumentorum ab istis unquam adduci poterit, hoc uno refellere. Sed tamen, quoniam tenacissimus est in multorum animis hic error, adhuc unum aut alterum afferemus.

Si Christi corpus comeditur, necesse est, ut ab uno quoque vel totum comedatur vel pars. Si totum, nihil aliis restat. Sin pars, discerpitur.

Si Christi corpus comeditur, necesse est, ut per os intret atque ita per excrementa ciborum eiiciatur. Quod si respondebunt, ut respondent, non ore, sed fide comedi, non diluent argumentum. Nam et Elias[2] fide panes illos comedit. Sed comedit videlicet ore, nam ore comedi necesse est, quicquid corporeum comeditur. Aut dicant, quid sit comedi. Et Rachaba[3] fide admisit exploratores, sed admisit. Et caecus ille natus[4] fide oculos suos lavit in piscina Siloa, sed lavit. Aut si dicent spiritualiter comedi, tantundem effecerunt; neque enim propterea non comedetur, si spiritualiter comedetur, aut declarent, quidnam sit eis spiritualiter comedere. Christi corpus spiritualiter comedere sic interpretabuntur, ut sit Christi spiritum aut naturam sive Christianitatem comedere, hoc est

---

[1] Now follows a discussion of Luther's concept of the Last Supper.

* [2] I Kings: 17:13.

* [3] Josh 2.

* [4] Jn 9:1-7.

Christianum fieri, hoc ipsum erit, quod nos volumus et quod supra demonstravimus.[5] Ita enim Christi spiritui propter similitudinem nomen tribuetur carnis et sanguinis, quomodo ipsi etiam deo oculi et manus et pedes tribuentur, cum tamen sit spiritus et omnium istorum membrorum expers. Atque ita remotis omnibus absurditatibus finita erit omnis disputatio et clare videbit religiosa mens, quo pacto Christum in spiritu et veritate, hoc est spiritualiter et vere comedat. Et hactenus ratione pugnatum esto.

---

[5] See above ch. XXXX.

# INDEX